William Cadenhead

The New Book of Bon-Accord

Guide to the City of Aberdeen

William Cadenhead

The New Book of Bon-Accord
Guide to the City of Aberdeen

ISBN/EAN: 9783337379797

Printed in Europe, USA, Canada, Australia, Japan

Cover: Foto ©Andreas Hilbeck / pixelio.de

More available books at **www.hansebooks.com**

THE NEW

BOOK OF BON-ACCORD;

OR

GUIDE

TO

THE CITY OF ABERDEEN

BY

WILLIAM CADENHEAD,

Author of "Flights of Fancy," &c.

SIXTH EDITION—THOROUGHLY REVISED AND ENLARGED.

Aberdeen:

LEWIS SMITH & SON, M'COMBIE'S COURT.

1886.

ACROSTIC.

.ˈˈ **B** UILD (to the Britons came the great decree)

O n yon brave isle amid the northern sea,

N ear where two twin-like streams steal placidly,

A gorgeous city.   Let her heaven-ward towers

C ome from Religion's shrines and Learning's bowers ;

C rowd tradeful navies in her busy haven :

O n her fair shield be 'Concord' deep engraven ;

R enown her sons ; her maids make good as fair."

D eem ye what city rose beneath their fostering care ?

PREFACE.

———:———

In issuing this Edition of the GUIDE TO BON-ACCORD, the Publishers have endeavoured to make it as complete and correct as possible, and hope it will be of much service to Tourists and the Public. They have to thank Alex. Walker, Esq., for the use of four woodcuts by George Reid, R.S.A., which originally appeared in Ramsay's Select Writings.

ABERDEEN, *June, 1886.*

INTRODUCTION.

—•◦•—

HE present publication is intended as an intelligent companion to the stranger in Aberdeen. I walk by his side, and instead of minutely describing the objects which are before his eyes—and which his own observation would enable him more rapidly and correctly to grasp, than would the repetition of any mere technical detail—I endeavour to give him the history of, and the associations connected with, such objects ; casting the antiquated allusions into as popular a form as possible, and yet retaining a smack of the old diction, on account of the charm which it possesses.

I shall not trouble the tourist with the enquiry, whether Aberdeen be the modern representative of the town known to the Romans as Devana, (this idea, I think is fairly negatived by Rev. Mr. Michie in his "Loch Kinnord"), nor endeavour to decide which of the many derivations offered by etymologists for the name of our good city is the correct one. With authentic documents, giving it an antiquity sufficient to satisfy any moderate desires, it would be useless to venture upon the tender ground of tradition or fable.

In 1179, William the Lion granted a charter, conferring on the burgesses of Aberdeen the right of trading when and where they pleased, as freely as their ancestors did in the times of his grandfather, David I., and this appears to be the first charter of which we have any due certification. William also seems to have had a palace and garden here ; and, some half century after the granting of this first charter, we have evidence of Alexander II. paying the town a visit, founding a Monastery of Black Friars, and conferring on the inhabitants the right of holding a weekly market. Some time after this the town is said

to have been consumed by an accidental fire—to have suffered
under the iron grasp of Edward I., during his usurpation as
Lord Paramount and Umpire, when he set up John Baliol as his
vassal-king, after the death of Margaret of Norway—to have
been the scene of one of Wallace's exploits against a party of
his mortal enemies, the English, then garrisoned in the castle—
to have been a place of refuge for Robert the Bruce after the
battle of Methven, and his residence for a considerable time at
an after period—to have turned out and routed with great
bravery, in 1411, at Harlaw, a barbarian Celtic pretender,
Donald of the Isles (a feat of which the Aberdonians yet speak
with some pride)—to have suffered considerable spoliation, in
common with the other towns of Scotland, under the hands of
the zealous Reformers in the sixteenth century, and to
have been fleeced by both parties in the Covenanting era
which followed—to have been for some time in the possession of
the rebels, when the standard of the Chevalier de St. George
was unfurled at Braemar in 1715, and the residence for a few
weeks of the Duke of Cumberland, when on his march to
Culloden in 1746. In short, it suffered all the vicissitudes
incident to a place of note in troublous times ; for, of its early
importance, we have the following testimony of an eminent
antiquary :—" Long before Edinburgh had acquired the pre-
cedency of a capital, or even the first place among the four
burghs of Scotland, while Glasgow was yet an insignificant
dependency on its Bishop, Aberdeen had taken its place as a
great and independent Royal Burgh, and a port of extensive
foreign trade."* Aberdeen as included in the recently extended
boundary, contains an area of about 9½ square miles. The population within this boundary according to the census of 1881,
was 105,003, and the number of inhabited houses 16,745.

---

* Cosmo Innes.

NEW BOOK OF BON-ACCORD.

AVING given this summary of the History of the "good town," we will suppose that the stranger has arrived at the Joint Station, where the South, North, and Deeside trains all arrive and depart ; and as he may have had a long morning ride, and nothing being a better preparative for a day's enjoyment than a good breakfast, we should advise him to avail himself of the proximity of the excellent hotels or coffee houses in the vicinity, where he may depend upon getting this meal in all the abundance for which Scotch breakfasts are celebrated.

As all the world knows that Aberdeen is the only place where "Finnan haddocks" are to be had in all their freshness of make and deliciousness of flavour, the tourist should stipulate that some of these should form a component part of his morning meal ; and there can be no doubt, if he does so, that he will agree with Sir Walter Scott in thinking that "a Finnan haddock has a relish of a very peculiar and delicate flavour, inimitable on any other coast than that of Aberdeenshire." It may be remarked, however, that the fishing village of Finnan, where this delicious viand is cured, is not on the Aberdeenshire coast, but about six miles south of Aberdeen, ·on the coast of Kincardineshire, not far from Portlethen, the second station from the city southward.

Being thus fortified against the cravings of hunger for the next few hours, we shall commence our peregrinations through the city.

The first public building which would have attracted your attention as you left the Railway Station—an erection in which the combination of various coloured stones is introduced—is Her Majesty's Theatre and Opera House. Whatever may be thought of its exterior appearance, it is allowed on all hands that its interior beauty and arrangements are not to be surpassed by those of any theatre in the kingdom. It is constructed to accommodate 1744 persons. The gallery has room for 700; upper circle and promenade, 400; pit and promenade, 480; orchestra stalls, 120; and the private boxes, 44.

MARKET STREET,

on which we are standing (the principal access from the Railway Station to the heart of the city), is one of our handsomest, as it is one of our busiest thoroughfares. It was opened in 1842, being part of a great improvement carried out by the company to which we are indebted for our splendid Market Buildings, converting a space formerly called *Puttachie Side*, covered by mean houses and a dilapidated manufactory, into the most direct access we have to the Docks, and the site of several public buildings. This building at the foot of the street is the Post Office. Previously to the erection of this building, the Aberdeen Post Office had rather a migratory sort of character, being now in one part of the town, and then in another. Not a great many years ago, the whole business was capable of being carried on within the present Market Cross, then an enclosed building. As the business expanded, the office was removed from one set of premises to another, until in 1841 a building was specially erected for the purpose. This building (which stands a little farther up the street) had for some years been still found inadequate, and the present more spacious office was built.

Opposite the Post Office, an old church was some years ago turned into a music saloon ; but there was an ecclesiastical reprisal, the old theatre in Marischal Street was purchased, and converted into a church. Farther up, on the same side, is the Thurburn Cooking Depôt ; and beyond, on the opposite side—an elegant building—is the branch office of the late City of Glasgow Bank, now that of the British Linen Co.

On the same side, a little farther up, is the old Mechanics' Institution. This building is at present used in a temporary way as the Reading Room adjunct of the Free Library, that Act being adopted in Aberdeen. The library of the Mechanics' Institution has been purchased by the Free Library Committee, and, with large additions, is now arranged, and open to the public provisionally, until a special building is erected for its reception.

THE NEW MARKET.

The foundation stone of this place was laid on the 8th October, 1840, and the Markets were formally opened in April, 1842. It consists, as you will notice, of the great hall, a basement floor, and the galleries ; and, for vastness, elegance, and compactness, · it is allowed on all hands to outrival every other market in the kingdom. The great hall is 315 feet long and 106 feet broad, with a height of 45 feet ; and besides the numerous stalls and benches which it contains, it is ornamented with a beautiful fountain, consisting of three basins of polished Peterhead granite. You are fortunate in coming to see it on a Friday, which is our market day : for I am sure you will be delighted to observe the good-looking country girls who occupy the stalls along the sides of upper end of the great hall, each with her baskets covered with snow-white napery, from which the rich butter, or fresh translucent eggs peep out in tempting plenty. Aberdeen has been as much celebrated for its butter as Cheshire for its cheese. Sir Walter Scott, who speaks so flatteringly of Finnan haddocks, also alludes to the Laird of Culrossie, who fought a duel for the honour of Aberdeen butter, and who, although worsted in the encounter, after thanking his adversary for his life, added, "But I'll say yet, that better butter than Aberdeen butter ne'er gaed down a southern thrapple." The plentiful supply of vegetables, too, with flowers in all their summer beauty, and strawberries in unmatched abundance and excellence, which are piled upon the gardeners' benches ; the great sirloins, and huge highly-fed carcases that hang on the butchers' stalls ; the stores of fish, in the basement floor, both fresh from the sea, and cured in all the different styles of golden Finnan or silver spelding—lucken, piper, or pin-the-widdie ; the noise of axe, saw, or cleaver ; the fresh sparkle of the fountain as it plays up, purifying and cooling the air ; and the hum of bargaining, rising up in a pleasant murmur—all contribute to compose a scene of business and plenty which it is delightful to contemplate, and pleasant to recall.

The Corn Exchange is situated in Hadden Street, close by. It is used as a News-room, open every lawful day from eight in the morning till ten at night (except during an hour or so in the forenoons of Fridays, when the Exchange is held). It is a spacious hall, 70 feet long by 40 broad, and is well fitted for both the purposes for which it is used. It is well supplied with newspapers, periodicals, and ample and frequent telegrams. The yearly subscription is five shillings, and single visits one penny each. Near by, in the Green, an ancient ornamental well, which once stood in Castle Street, is worthy of a visit.

Opposite the top of Market Street, that rather ornate building is the Town and County Bank—Mr. James Matthews, architect—and close by is a statue of the Queen, in Sicilian Marble, by the late Mr. Alexander Brodie. Opposite the Town and County Bank is a branch office of the National Bank of Scotland.

UNION STREET.

Walking now along Union Street eastward, you will be struck by the towering proportions of the Municipal Buildings. These buildings, in all their ramifications, contain the Town and Town and County Halls; the Sheriff and the Burgh Court-houses, with Chambers for various officials; the Police and Corporation Gas Offices; and, in close connection, the Prison. Indeed the whole apparatus of municipal and local government is concentrated in this great pile.

It having been found that many of the officials connected with both the City and County were but indifferently, or meanly accommodated; that the Town Hall, although a fine old place, was becoming frail; that the Court-house accommodation was both defective and limited; and that there was an acknowledged want of suitable public buildings in the town for Municipal and County purposes, it was resolved that a building should be erected suitable for these combined necessities. Accordingly, in 1866, an Act of Parliament was obtained, and next year the work was begun, and was only finished in 1873. The Great Tower, the chief characteristic of the building, is 200 feet high. It contains a clock, regulated by electric communication with King's College, Old Aberdeen, which shows the time on four illuminated dials, and two bells which give the hours and quarters.

Entering by the great doorway in the tower, the first object which takes your attention in the vestibule which is lighted by a double window of stained glass, is a suit of iron armour, which tradition affirms to be that in which Provost Davidson fought and fell at the Battle of Harlaw. On a landing a few steps farther up, is a marble statue of Provost James Blaikie, by Sir John Steele, Edinburgh. A circular flight of steps leads to the Council Chamber, Town Hall, &c. The Town Hall is spacious and elegant. From the ceiling there hang three old crystal chandeliers, and at intervals round the walls stand "sconces" from the old Hall; while it is adorned by portraits of Prince Albert (in the Highland costume) and Provost James Blaikie, both by the celebrated John Philip, who was a native of Aberdeen; Sir Alexander Anderson, an Ex-Provost of Aberdeen, who did a great deal for the interests and improvements of the city; Mr. George Thomson of Pitmedden; Mr. Peter Esselmont, M.P., and Mr. John Angus, late town clerk—all by Mr. George Reid, R.S.A., also an Aberdonian; and Provost James Hadden by Pickersgill. The hall also contains a bust of Philip by his friend and townsman William Brodie, R.S.A.; and a small portrait of Dr. Dunn, the founder of the Grammar School, by Jameson, the Scottish Vandyke. This elegant hall was a few years ago greatly improved by raising the ceiling four feet, when it was re-decorated. You will observe that the roof is handsomely panelled with oak, divided into eighty-four panels, into which are introduced the arms of the brave, learned, eminent, and public-spirited men connected with the city either by birth, services, or education. In a fire-proof chamber, in the Great Tower, the Town Charters and Records are kept. It is said that, next to those of the city of London, the Records of Aberdeen are the most complete in the kingdom.

Among the many curious documents which this room contains is the demand of Montrose, then at the head of a band of royalists, consisting of some of the Highland clans and Irish auxiliaries, for the surrender of this town in 1644. The letter runs thus :—

Looving Freindes, Being heir for the maintenance of religion and liberty, and his Mas. [Majesty's] right authority and service, thes ar In his Mas. name to require you that immediately upon the sight heirof, ye rander and give up yr toune, In the behalf of his Mas., otherwise that all old persons, women, and children, doe come out and retire themselfs, and that those who stayes expect no quarter. I am as you deserve,

MONTROSE.

A scroll copy of the reply of the magistrates to this demand is also preserved. It is a rather spirited document. After acknowledging receipt of his lordship's letter, they tell him that, so far from rendering up their town, they are determined to "maintain the same," and that, in so doing, they "sall be most willing to spend the last drope of their blood," but yet, although they will not abandon their town so lightly, they notwithstanding consider themselves "to be most loyal and dutiful subjects to his majesty." I may just add that, as Montrose's emissaries were passing through the Green to their quarters with this reply, their drummer was unfortunately shot, and this, along with the defying answer of the magistrates, so exasperated the royalists, that they wreaked a most bloody vengeance upon the inhabitants in the sack which followed their victory—for they were victorious.

It is no easy task, but is worth the pains, to climb to the balcony of the Great Tower. From it a fine bird's eye view can be had of the city and its sur-

roundings ; and as a stranger, with little time to spare,
can from this point very shortly acquire a good,
although superficial knowledge of Aberdeen, it may be
well to give a short detail of what can be seen from
this point of view.

You emerge from the Tower on the west balcony.
Here you look along the entire extent of Union Street,
seeing, pretty far westward, the spires of the Free
West and Free Gilcomston Churches piercing the sky-
line—the former on the south, and the latter on the
north side of the street—and the Free Church College
closing in the extremity of the buildings. On the left
you observe the upper end of the Docks, the old and
new channels of the Dee, with a fine bridge recently
erected over the latter, leading to what may be called
the new village of Torry, a rapidly rising place of
dwelling houses and business establishments; the
Railway Station, and south line with its bridge across
the river. The beautiful suburb of Ferryhill, with its
new Free Church with white granite spire, occupies
the middle distance, and the wooded hills of Banchory-
Devenick, and more remote Deeside mountains rise
between you and the sky. On the right hand side
you have the Churchyard of St. Nicholas, with the
East and West Churches, and their fine new granite
spire ; the Infirmary and Gordon's College, and in
front of this last the new Art Gallery and School of
Art. In the extreme distance from this point of view
you have the wooded heights of Woodhill. From the
south platform you have a view of the Docks and
shipping ; the village and hills of Torry, terminating
in the Girdleness, with its lighthouse ; the Battery and
new Breakwater, and the blue sea beyond on the left ;
and on the right, the cairn-topped ridges of the
Grampians. From the eastern side of the Tower you
look down upon Castle Street, with the Cross and

Duke of Gordon's Monument. You see on the right, the Pier, the Links and bents, with the Beach Battery on the margin of the sea ; the Ship-building Yards, and Gas Works. On the left you almost look into the yards of the Jail ; you see King Street, and King Street Road, which you can trace until you lose it in the green banks of Don ; while away northward you can follow the line of coast sweeping in a beautiful curve as far as Buchanness. Looking westward from the Tower, the Marischal College rises fair and white from the crowd of houses ; and between you and the sky, the eye sweeps along the heights from Cairncry to Woodside.

The Jail, at the rear of these buildings, is of a rectangular form, the enclosed court being divided into six compartments, used as airing yards for the prisoners, and having a turnkey's lodge in the centre.

Before leaving the Municipal Buildings, let me direct your attention to a sun-dial on the wall not far from the Great Tower, removed from the front of the old Town Hall, over which is inscribed the emphatic text, UT UMBRA SIC FUGIT VITA. As far back as 1597, a David Anderson informs the magistrates that he had " devysit ane instrument, of his awin ingyne, to draw and mak dyellis or sune horolages," and that he was willing to make one for the "foirwall of the said burgh, quhilk suld shaw houris very justlie to the sone, with every moneth of the year, the langest, schortest, and equinoctiall dayis ; " and that when he had completed the same he would refer his recompense to the discretion of the Council. He was ordered to proceed in the business, and informed that he would be paid for his "pane and verk, according to the dignitie and sufficience thairoff." I will not insist that the present is the same " sone horolage " which Mr. David Anderson set up ; but the Latin inscription which I have quoted, and which may be translated, " As the shadow, so flies life," is undoubtedly the text of the following verses :—

The Silent Preacher.

'Mid our city's throng and bustle,
    Underneath the Town-house tower,
Ever stands a silent Preacher,
    Preaching on from hour to hour.
Silent but emphatic Preacher !
    With his finger in the sun,
Marking how across the dial
    Swift the fleeting shadows run ;
And while pointing to their passage,
    Thus he ever seems to say—
" As the shadow o'er the dial,
    So fleets human life away ! "

Farther up the mart, where traffic
    Doth the seething crowd engross,
Ornate with its ancient sculpture,
    Stands our antique Market Cross ;
And within its quaint compartments
    The admiring eye may trace,
Ranged in high-relief, the portaits
    Of a faded royal race !
These are topics for the Preacher—
    " Monarchs, dynasties decay ;
As the shadow o'er the dial,
    So fleets human life away ! "

Yonder, where the groaning roadway
    Leads the traffic to the quays,
Stood the Earl of Marischal's mansion,
    Garden'd round with orchard trees ; *

---

* " Marischal's Hall stood at the north end of the street, which, from this circumstance, was called Marischal Street. It consisted of several buildings surrounding a courtyard or close, and having a large garden attached."
"On the 2nd November, 1562, Huntly's second son, the gallant Sir John Gordon, was led forth to execution on a scaffold erected on the Castlegate ; and a family historian has recorded that Murray had the brutality to force the Queen Mary to a window in the house of the Earl Marischal, that she might see the untimely end of a man she once tenderly loved."—" The

There the beauteous luckless Mary,
  Wept her love's untimely fate ;
There preached Cant and his stern colleagues —
  The covenant's triumvirate ;
Round these names the mists of centuries
  Hang their clouds obscure and grey—
" As the shadow o'er the dial,
  So fleets human life away ! "

Ceaseless o'er the granite pavement
  Now the rattling chariots go,
Some bedeck'd with bridal splendour,
  Some with nodding plumes of woe ;
Blooming youths and blushing maidens
  Pass within the Preacher's ken,
And sweet bands of rosy children,
  Madly longing to be men !
" Joyous cherubs," saith the Preacher,
  " Cherish youth while yet you may—
As the shadow o'er the dial,
  So fleets human life away ! "

Silent but emphatic Preacher !
  I would heed thy tacit lay,
Drink with eager lips thy moral,
  Work while it is called to-day ;
Not with airy flights of fancy
  Ever rear an idle rhyme,
But with steadfast heart accomplish
  Something worthy of the time,
Join, my peers, the brave endeavour—
  Study, labour, suffer, pray—
" For like shadow o'er the dial,
  So fleets human life away ! "

Having descended from the Tower, we will take a step into the next main entrance of the building.

---

house of the Earl Marischal was at this time (1638) occupied by Lady Pitsligo, 'a rank Puritan,' and the 'Apostles,' as they termed themselves, determined to expound their tenets (in the intervals between public worship) from a gallery in the court of her domicile. At eight o'clock in the morning the Rev. David Dickson commenced a controversial discourse of two hours' duration. He was followed at noon by the celebrated Alexander Henderson; and at four o'clock, the fiery Andrew Cant delivered a harangue."—*Dr. Joseph Robertson.*

The entrance-hall, staircase, and corridor here, leading
to the Court Rooms and Great Hall, are very fine,
and being well lighted, have a pleasant and elegant air
about them.   At the first landing a staircase divides
into two return branches, which, meeting, form the
entrance to the Great Hall.   This staircase is lighted
on both sides by fine stained glass windows, containing
various coats-of-arms.   The roof over the staircase is
of pitch-pine, richly moulded and panelled.

The Great Hall is a large, lofty, and elegant apartment, with open roof of pitch-pine, rising in ribs from
carved corbels, the compartments filled with Gothic
tracery.   This Hall is seventy-four feet by thirty-five,
having a height of fifty feet.   It contains at one end
portraits of Queen Anne, by Kneller ; James, fifth
Earl of Findlater, and his Countess, Sophia, by Cosmo
Alexander ; George, fourth Earl of Aberdeen, by Sir
J. W. Gordon ; and of Queen Victoria, in her younger
days. by H. L. Smith.   The other end of the Hall
has a large full length portrait of the last Duke of
Gordon, by Sir T. Lawrence ; and of Admiral Gordon,
by Pickersgill ; and also of Messrs. Thomas and
Newal Burnett—two late county officials—the former
painted by Sir J. W. Gordon.   Branching away from
the corridor below are passages leading to the Court
House, with all the necessary appurtenances of judges'
and witnesses' rooms, &c.   Prisoners ascend to the
dock by a stone staircase from the ground floor, on
which there are waiting rooms for male and female
prisoners awaiting their trial.   This place is in direct
communication with the Prison.

Before leaving the Municipal Buildings, I would
direct your attention to an erection in the rear of
them, entering by Concert Court—the Advocates'
Library.   This neat building, which is nearly hid
away from public gaze, is well worthy of a visit.

Whenever you enter within its doors, you are impressed with the air of not only substantiality and elegance, but of comfort, which pervades it. The Library proper is a spacious room, and the books are not all devoted to the subjects peculiar to the profession of the proprietors, but embrace a goodly selection of general literature. There is a private entrance from this building to the corridor leading to the various courts, for the convenience of the legal practitioners.

CASTLE STREET.

You are now fairly in Castle Street, which has been described as "the glory, the pride, the apple of the eye of Aberdeen." It is, indeed, a very spacious place, and justifies, to a considerable extent, the encomiums which have been bestowed upon it, although these go the length of saying that it is larger than the market-place of any other town in the kingdom, "nor can Scotland showe such ane other!" Looking westward from this point, the whole extent of Union Street is opened up to the spectator, and, with its graceful bend, its long line of white and glittering buildings, so finely closed by the towers and turrets of the Free Church Divinity Hall, it is allowed on all hands that this sight fully entitles Aberdeen to the flattering apellation it has received of the "Granite City." Such is the daylight appearance of Union Street. Night gives it a charm of another kind. So well does the bright moonlight harmonise with the pure granite, that seeing such a building as the Music Hall under this effect, you might almost fancy yourself gazing on some of the marble temples of ancient Greece in her palmy days ; and on moonless nights, when the lamps are burning in two long, wavy rows, the street appears lengthened out to ten times its

B

actual extent—in fact, the lights seem to dwindle away into a dreamy infinity.

That building which bounds the square of Castle Street on the west side is the Athenæum Hall, once a News-room, now a Restaurant. The building on the south side, opposite the Tolbooth Tower, is the Aberdeen Bank (now incorporated with the Union), built in 1801, and one of the first of our public buildings upon which the elaboration of the granite began to be attempted. This large and handsome building on the opposite side is the North of Scotland Banking Company's Office, built in 1836, and it may be contrasted with the Aberdeen Bank in regard to the working of the granite referred to—being one of the most ornate granite buildings in the town. The Duke of Gordon's Monument here, in the centre of the street, is also a fine specimen of the power now obtained over the obdurate but beautiful white granite of Aberdeen ; this, and the statue of Priest Gordon, in Constitution Street, being, it is believed, the only statues of any pretensions which have yet been wrought in that stern material.

THE CROSS.

That beautiful hexagonal structure a little farther up the square is the Market Cross. The Aberdonians are not a little proud of it, as without question it surpasses every other building of the same nature extant in Scotland, and excelles that of Edinburgh (so much lamented by Sir Walter Scott in "Marmion") as is evident from the recent restoration of the latter, by the patriotic munificence of Mr. Gladstone.

This Cross stood originally opposite the front of the Tolbooth, on an elevated pavement, called the "Plain-stones." It was built in 1686, and superseded a more ancient one, neither the age nor description of which has been preserved. As noticed before, the Cross was then an enclosed building, at one time used as the Post-Office, and latterly as a Coach-Office. On its removal to its present site, in 1842, the arches were left open as they now appear. You will observe the balustrade which surmounts the arches is divided into twelve panels, within oval-shaped wreaths of ten of these are portraits in high relief of James I., II., III., IV., and V., and of Mary, James VI., Charles I., and II., and James VII. The other two panels contain the armorial bearings of the burgh and the royal arms. The graceful column which springs from the centre is wreathed with thistles, and on the Corinthian capital which crowns it is placed a white marble unicorn, bearing on its breast a shield charged with the Lion of Scotland. The armorial bearings of the burgh, I may here remark, are *gules*, three towers triple-towered, within a double tressure, flowered and counter-flowered, *argent*. The supporters are two leopards, and the motto is BON-ACCORD.

As a great deal of the domestic history of a town generally centres in its market-place, so Castle Street has been the scene of many a varied event. There stood originally two crosses in Castle Street, the High Cross, called also the Flesh Cross, "by reassone of the shambles and Flesh mercat beside it;" and the *Laich* or less Cross, called the Fish Cross, "at which there is a *daylie* fish mercat kept;" for we find the magistrates, in 1580, limiting the sale of fish and flesh on the "Sabbath day," only "fra the ringing of the first bell afoir nune and efter nune quhill the sermun be done." It was from the High Cross that public proclamations were made, and, "lykeways (says Gordon, parson of Rothiemay, writing in 1661), it is at this Crosse that the citizens doe perform all their solemnities upon the festivall dayes." To begin at the Church with reli-

gious services, and end at the Cross with wine and
wassail was a common way of celebrating any joyous
event. Thus, in 1593, it having "plesit God to grant
to his Majestie ane sone," the magistrates ordain that
on Sunday the 24th day of February, after the afternoon sermon, a table shall be covered at the Market
Cross "for the Magistrattis and bayth the Consallis,
with twa bunnis of Inglis ber, to be placed and run at
the said Mercat Croce," that wine be liberally
drunken, confections cast among the people, glasses
broken, and every kind of merriment kept up. Like
rejoicings were held on the reception of the news of
the death of Queen Elizabeth, and accession of James
VI. to the Crown of England ; with the addition that
bonfires were kindled through all the streets of the
town, that the bells were rung, that the youths
accompanied the magistrates through the streets firing
their "hagbuttis" till late at night ; that the town's
"haill monition and artailyerie" was charged and
shot, and all goodly merriment and pastime used.
On the news arriving of "our hopeful Prince Charles"
having returned from Spain in 1623, a similar de-
monstration was made. The Cross was hung with
tapestry, "twa piece of wyne, ane of quhyt and ane
uther of claret," were broached and mingled with
"succor and spyce in abundance ;" and many similar
merry-makings are on record. The Cross was also
often selected as the place of public punishment.
Persons guilty of incontinence were here branded with
a hot iron on the cheek, or scourged, then drawn
through the town in a cart, and banished from the
city. Spalding gives the following description of an
interesting story, of which the Cross was the scene in
1640, when the town was in possession of the Covenanters :—" A quarrel having occurred among some
gentlemen who were escorting the Earl Marischal,

governor of the city, towards Dunnottar, the young laird of Tolquhon was wounded in the head by George Lesly. His lordship instantly disarmed the culprit, and on the next day sent him in irons to Aberdeen, commanding the provost to strike off his right hand for his breach of military discipline. The chief magistrate seems to have declined the execution of this order, and the Marischal proceeded to enforce it on his own authority. A small scaffold was erected at the Cross, the axe and block were made ready, and a fire was kindled to heat the instrument for searing the maimed stump. Lesly was then conducted from the Tolbooth, and descending the stair, amidst the lamentation of the crowd, laid his arm upon the block. The executioner prepared to give the stroke, when the Master of Forbes stepped forward, and taking Lesly by the hand, freely pardoned him, to the great joy of the people."

The Cross was also the scene of a strange exhibition, which, however, enters more into the regions of imagination than of history. The latter end of the sixteenth century was distinguished in Scotland for a furious onslaught against those suspected of the crime of witchcraft ; and, among many other curious charges, one Thomas Leys is indicted for coming to the Market and Fish Cross of Aberdeen, at midnight of halloweven, in company with a great number of witches, under the conduct and guidance of the devil, who was present with them, playing before them "on his kind of instruments," and dancing about both the said Crosses for a long space of time. Isobel Cockie, in another of these trials, is accused of being the ringleader of the said dance next to Thomas Leys, and because the devil played not so melodiously as she craved, she "tuik his instrument out of his mouth, then tuik him on the chaftis therewith, and plaid herself thereon to the haill companie."

Coming down to a later period, Castle Street has witnessed many a sad sight, and many a joyous revel. Many a snug dinner has been discussed in "Archibald Campbell's house;" many a deep potation quaffed in "Skipper Anderson's"—both Castle Street hostelries of great repute in their day—although the "jolly dogs" of the past were as much hemmed in by magisterial restrictions as the "choice spirits" of the present day are by "Forbes Mackenzie," if the resolution of council of 1606 continued long in effect. By this resolution the provost and baillies, in consideration of the enormities committed in the burgh "be persones of all sortes," ordain that it shall not be "lesum" for any "hostiler, tavernar, or vinter of wyne," to sell such commodities after ten at night, at which hour the college bell was to be rung as a warning; and any persons, man or woman, found walking on the streets after that hour, except such as should be known to have lawful errands, were to be fined in the sum of five pounds. In 1763, Castle Street was the scene of a tragical event which attracted much attention in the town. At a convivial meeting in the New Inn (which stood where the North of Scotland Bank now stands), Abernethy of Mayen and Leith of Leith-hall, having quarrelled, retired to the Plainstones (on which, as before noticed, the Cross once stood) to settle their dispute by duel. Leith was shot through the head, and Abernethy, slightly wounded, escaped from justice by retiring to the Continent. In 1802, there was quartered in the town a party of the Ross and Cromarty Rangers, an ill-behaved corps, whose temper had not been improved by their residence in Ireland during the time of the rebellion, and where they had no doubt been accustomed to fire on the people whenever any disturbance took place. On 4th of June, the king's birthday, the usual rejoicings were held—Castle Street, as usual, being the chief scene. Some of the officers of this regiment returning from the town hall, where along with some of the principal inhabitants they had partaken pretty freely of wine, were rather roughly handled by the squib-firers, and the final result was that they ordered the drum to beat to arms, marched the regiment down to Castle Street, and fired upon the people. Four persons were killed and several severely wounded. The inhabitants were exceedingly exasperated at this wanton outrage, and the regiment had to escape under cloud of night and by bye-ways from the town. The officers and some of the soldiers were arrested by the magistrates, but no punishment of any of the offenders followed : for although, after the lord advocate refused to prosecute, they were brought to trial at the instance of the relatives of some of the sufferers, yet a verdict of " not guilty " was brought in for the officers, and " not proven " for the soldiers.

Recollections of public executions also cling around Castle Street. Up to 1842, there lay imbedded in the causeway, near the spot where the Duke of Gordon's Monument now stands, a large millstone, which marked the spot where the gallows was wont for a long period to be planted on these occasions. The last person who expiated his crime on this spot was William Webster, who was hanged in 1787 for theft and house-breaking. From that time, any exe-' cutions that have taken place have been upon a scaffold erected in front of the Tolbooth. There has been no execution in Aberdeen since these expiations were confined to the precincts of the jail. In the minds of elder Aberdonians a feeling of sympathy yet hangs around the execution of James Ritchie, a young

lad of seventeen years of age, who suffered death in
1818 for sheep-stealing. There were no aggravating
circumstances connected with his crime, and, as has
been remarked, the sorrow which was felt for his untimely fate made people forget that he had ever been
a criminal. "A man who had been instrumental in
his apprehension afterwards came to ruin, and suffered
deep domestic affliction ; and the popular superstition
was, that the blood of this unfortunate boy had cried
to heaven against him."

On the modern Cross have been proclaimed
William and Mary, Anne, George I., George II.,
George III., George IV., William IV., and Queen
Victoria. It is said the Chevalier de St. George was
also *twice* proclaimed here in 1715, and Prince
Charles in 1745.

THE CASTLE HILL.

We will now take this turning at the south-east
corner of Castle Street, and thus reach the Castle Hill.
Here stood one of the six ports, or bars of the city—
the Fittie or Footdee Port. Each of the chief entrances to the town had one of these guarded ports,
and this, along with the building up of the ends of the
vennels, or smaller communications with the surrounding country, in troublous times, seems to have been
the only really tangible means of defence the town
ever had. This building opposite, as you will observe,
is the Sick Children's Hospital. It has beds for sixty
children, and the care and comfort bestowed upon
the suffering little ones is something to be admired
and imitated. The Institution is supported by
voluntary contributions. The Castle Hill is so named
from a fortress which was raised upon this eminence
so early as 1264, and, after having been destroyed and
rebuilt several times, was finally (along with a chapel

dedicated to St. Ninian, which was an adjunct of the castle, and in 1566, on being repaired, had its east end converted into a lighthouse) entirely demolished about 1794, to make room for the present Barracks. The Barracks, which are capable of accommodating 600 men, were built at an expense of £16,000. They are in an elevated and healthy situation, with a spacious parade-ground in front of them, enclosed by a high wall with iron railing, part of which formed the walls of the ancient fort. This new building in rear of the old barracks is for the accommodation of married soldiers. As an excellent view of the sea, the harbour, and the surrounding country is to be obtained from the Castle Hill, it has long been a favourite resort of the inhabitants. Sir Samuel Forbes of Foveran, writing about 1715, says that "the custom of going every Sunday to the Castle Hill has continued for a tract of upwards of four hundred years;" and although he assigns a rather apocryphal reason for this custom, there can be little doubt as to the fact of its existence. It is so refreshing to observe how this writer speaks of the built-up space between Virginia Street and Regent Quay, then a fine meadow, and of the Links, where he "had his harmless youthful pastimes," that I shall quote the entire passage relating to these places :—

The hill having given us a sight of the harbour, let us walk to it, which we will find of great breadth and length, at full sea ; and which affords a most safe station to ships from all winds and tempests ; and is so capacious that, about sixty years ago, a fair meadow of ground, formerly within the flood mark, was gained by making a long and broad terras, flanked in both sides with large and square stones ; and the harbour thereby nothing entrenched upon, but bettered. And this terras gives the citizens the warmest and driest walk in winter, and the coolest and most beautiful in summer ; having the water and ships on one hand, and a very flowery meadow, planted with willows, on the other ;

and likewise leads to another agreeable, more solitary walk, called the Carpet Walk, from the softness and thickness of the wreathed green moss with which it is overspread.

It might be reckoned a piece of ingratitude in one to have had his harmless youthful pastimes here, yet to forgett, or not to mention, what is adjoyning to this Carpet Walk. It is a smooth dry field, stretching in length almost betwixt the mouths of the two rivers Dee and Don ; and sheltered on the sea side by a mighty number of downs, covered with a strong greenish plant called *bent ;* and beautified, on the city side, with a well-cultivated ground, surrounded with a plantation of willows. The one end of which field affords a healthful summer recreation of short bowls ; and the other end the like healthful winter recreation of the gowlf ball ; and, all the year round, a pasture for fattening of mutton, and bringing forth early lambs ; so careful hath nature been that the inhabitants of this city should have a convenient intermixture of profit and pleasure.

The "smooth dry field" he refers to, is that tract of green common stretching along betwixt you and the sea, called the Links, and still used as a place of recreation by the inhabitants, old and young. That large manufactory to the north, on the verge of the Links, is a cotton-spinning mill, known by the name of the Banner Mill, belonging to Robinson, Crum, & Co., a most complete and well regulated establishment, which occupies the boggy ground that nourished the "plantation of willows" alluded to before, and thence derives the popular name of the "Bog Mill." Farther south are the Gas-works, and the Chemical Works of Messrs. John Miller & Co., and between us and the sea may be observed a Battery with its cannons and earthen mounds. Still farther south you will observe the steeple of St. Clement's Church, the stalks of iron-works, and large sheds under which were built those clipper ships for which Aberdeen had a world-wide fame; but, as we will pass these more closely when we take a walk to the New Pier, we shall say nothing more about them at present. That small hill on the other side of the ravine through which the roadway runs, is called the Heading-hill, as being the ancient place of death punishment by decapitation. It was here also that the incremation of witches, whose trials we alluded to in speaking of the Cross, took place. The entry in the Dean of Guild's accounts regarding the Thomas Leys then mentioned, ran thus—

Thomas Leis,
Item, the 23rd of Februar, 1597, for peattis, tar barrellis, fir, and collis, to burn the said Thomas, and to John Justice for his fie in executing him, iii*l*. iiis*h*. iiii*d*.

Such was the horrid fate of the victims of a cruel and silly superstition, two hundred and eighty-nine years ago. The Heading-hill was connected with the Castle Hill, in 1839, by that handsome iron bridge, for the greater convenience of all, but especially of the regiments which may occupy the barracks—the building, enclosed by the high wall on the other hill, being the barracks Hospital, erected in 1799, at an expense of £2000.

KING STREET.

We will descend by this flight of steps beside the iron bridge to Commerce Street, and thence by East North Street reach King Street. In our progress by this route to King Street, we pass nothing worthy of notice, if we except a neat little church, intended as a kind of Ragged Kirk, or place of worship for the more destitute of the community. It may also be mentioned that, in our way, we cross another of those streets which had a defensive port upon it—Justice or Thief's Port—so called from its being the *via dolorosa* by which culprits were conducted to the place of execution on the Gallowhill. This port was also used as the place where, according to the brutal custom of the "good old times," the mangled limbs of great malefactors were exposed. The narrow street leading past the ragged kirk to the links, now called Albion Street, is still well known as the Bowl Road, being the way the citizens used to take when going to the links to follow the healthful and exciting game of bowls. This game is now nearly extinct about the town—the more is the pity—but at one time it was pursued so eagerly, and so little were the inhabitants carried away by the engrossing trade competition which now prevails, that it was no uncommon thing, when calling at a professional man's office, or even at a merchant's shop, to find the door shut, and an intimation wafered on it—"Gone to the links; will be back at" such and such a time. On reaching King Street, the first object of interest is the North Church, that handsome building in the Grecian style of architecture, which fills the angle made by the junction of King and Queen Streets. The North Church was built in the years 1829-31, after a design by Mr. John Smith, and at a cost of £10,500. The plan of the church is a parallelogram, 120 feet 8 inches, by 64 feet 2 inches, over walls. The tower is 150 feet high, and the church is capable of containing 1600 people comfortably seated. Proceeding up King Street, the next building we see on the same side as the North Church, is the Surgeons' Hall. Only the centre part of the building, that with the portico of four Ionic columns, is used for this purpose; but, in accordance with the original plan, the houses on each side are built so as to appear wings to the main building. The building contains a handsome hall, a library, museum, laboratory, &c., and is adorned with several portraits of the founders and benefactors of the society. This building was erected in 1818, at the expense of

£2000. Opposite the Surgeons' Hall is St. Andrew's Chapel—that rather ornate freestone building. The interior is as elegant as the exterior ; the congregation belongs to the Scotch Episcopal body. An apse has recently been added to the east end of this church, having a large window of stained glass, divided into five compartments, the subjects being, the Crucifixion in the centre, and on one side the Nativity and Baptism, and on the other the Resurrection and Ascension. There is also a fine reredos, cut in caen stone, divided into three ornamental niches, having in the middle one a figure of the Good Shepherd, and on one side a group representing the Blessing of the Children, and on the other the Sermon on the Mount. This chapel also contains a statue, by Flaxman, of the late Right Rev. John Skinner, a descendant of the celebrated author of "The Ewie wi' the Crooked Horn," and "Tullochgorum." Adjoining the Surgeons' Hall—part of it, in fact, forming one of the wings mentioned—are the offices of the Board of Inland Revenue, Excise, Stamps and Taxes, while behind, entering from Lodge Walk, are the offices of the County Police. Passing the office of the Commercial Bank of Scotland, on the same side as the Excise Office, you again reach Castle Street.

MARISCHAL COLLEGE.

We will now proceed up Broad Street—noting, at No. 64, the house in which Lord Byron lived with his mother in his boyhood—and see Marischal College, the entrance to which, you will perceive, is by a small archway, giving little promise of the spacious quadrangle and splendid pile of buildings within, which almost stun you by their contrast with the commonplace street from which you have entered. Marischal

College stands upon the site of a Franciscan Convent, which was founded about the year 1471. The friars, however, were not many years allowed to remain in peaceable possession of their humble residence, for, fearful of the outrages which report told them the Reformers were committing upon similar establishments in the south, early in the sixteenth century, they resigned their sanctuary into the hands of the magistrates, who, in 1593, "voitit thocht guid and expedient, that the Greyfriars place thereof, sal be resignit in favouris of ane nobill and potent Lord, George Erll Merchell, Lord Keith and Altri, to be giffen to the said Erll, to be ane College according to his institution and erectioun thairof." The Earl Marischal accordingly executed the foundation charter of the College on the 2nd April, 1593, and granted in mortmain certain properties for its support. The buildings of the monastery, however, continued to be those of the College for nearly a century after this time. In the years 1684-9 a new edifice was erected, which continued until 1837, when the present beautiful structure began to be built. It was finished in 1841, at a cost of from £21,000 to £22,000, £15,000 of which was granted by Government, and the balance raised by public subscription.

This obelisk of polished Peterhead granite, rising to the height of seventy-two feet, has been erected to the memory of Sir James M'Gregor, who presided over the medical department of the army for thirty-six years, and was several times chosen Lord Rector by the votes of the students of this College.

The College has commodious class-rooms for students of Law and Medicine. The vestibule and the stair which leads to the Hall, Library, and Museum, are considered very fine. Immediately in front of you, as you enter the principal doorway, is inserted a stone from the former building, having the pertinent and fearless motto

THEY HAVE SAID | WHAT SAY THEY | LET THEM SAY.

The motto probably referred to the odium incurred by the Keith family in getting the Abbey lands of Deer erected into a temporal lordship. Not a few eminent names have been connected with Marischal College, both as professors and students. The Hall contains a collection of pictures, portraits of patrons, early students, &c., many of them of great merit. The Library is a compact apartment, with a pleasing, undisturbed air of tranquility about it which would woo the most careless to become a

Haunter of old tomes,
Sitting the silent term of stars to watch
His own thoughts passing into beauty.

The Museum is also a neat and interesting place. Here again an excellent panoramic view of Aberdeen and surrounding country may be obtained from the central tower or observatory. After a severe contest on the part of the inhabitants of Aberdeen and the neighbouring counties, Marischal College was incorporated by Government with King's College, under the name of the University of Aberdeen, in 1859, so that Marischal College and University has ceased to exist as a monument of the liberality of its founder.

This church, which stands in the College Court, is Greyfriars Church, one of the six sub-parish churches of the City Parish of St. Nicholas. It is proposed to remove it and the other buildings in front of the College, and to open a street opposite, from Broad Street to St. Nicholas Street, so as to throw the College building more open. The present Greyfriars Church is a modification of the old church of the Greyfriars, whose convent, as already noticed, occupied the place where the College now stands. For a considerable time, in the beginning of the seventeenth century, this church seems to have been unused, and to have gone into decay; for, in 1633, Dr. William Guild, "ane of the ministeris of this burt," undertakes to "glass all the wyndoes" of it; and that this work may not be bestowed in vain, the town council appoint that morning and evening prayers be read therein daily, both summer and winter, by the town's reader, as it is a "magnifick edifice, lyand in the hart of the toune, verie commodious and easeful for the whole inhabitants." It was finally altered and repaired, much as it now stands, in 1768. This quarter of the town (top of Broad Street) has just been very much improved by the erection of business premises, &c., of considerable architectural beauty.

As I have a wish to lead you as seldom as possible twice over the same ground, we will endeavour to reach Market Street, from which we started, by Netherkirkgate and St. Nicholas Street. This long lane off the Netherkirkgate, near its top, is called the Guestrow, whether, as Gordon says, "after strangers lodging there, or after spirits [*gaist* the Scotch word for *ghost*], cannot be easlie conjectured." In favour of the latter hypothesis, it has been observed that in some old charters it is called "*vicus lemurum*"—the street of goblins ; while, in accordance with, if not in corroboration of, the former view, it may be remarked that the Duke of Cumberland was lodged here, in the house of Mr. Alexander Thomson, advocate, in 1746. The Netherkirkgate is another of the streets which had a bar or port, being one of the chief entrances to the town from the south. The port stood a little above Wallace Nook, that old building before us, with the rude statue of the hero of Scotland in the niche of its ancient tower.

While the people in Scotland talked of erecting a monument to the immortal Knight of Ellerslie, the good folks of Aberdeen had long *possessed* the thing desiderated ; and lest you should feel a slight inclination to sneer at the comparison betwixt our statue and the monument erected on the Abbey Craig, near Stirling, I will let you hear a poetical pleading for the figure before you—

Wallace Nook.

Speak ! speakna o' intrinsic worth—an auld heir loom may be
O' unca sma' intrinsic worth, and yet be dear to me ;
The kin' *memento* that we gat frae some auld-farrant frien'
Is hoarded up wi' jealous care, though hardly worth a preen.
The rashen cap and buckie to the loon a joy can yield
That crown and sceptre ne'er gave him wha doth a sceptre wield ;
And Scotland's auld bleak heather hills to Scotsmen are as dear
As to the Indian is the vale, the rich vale o' Cashmere.
Then dinna smile wi' scornfu' smile, if I the truth declare,
That though I've gazed on sculptur'd forms baith classical and rare,
Yet nane wi' stirrring thoughts have e'er repaid my earnest look
Like the rude form o' Scotland's chief that graces Wallace Nook.

When we were laddies at the skweel, and simmer days were lang,
How many a joyous pilgrimage to spots o' fame we'd gang !
Out by Dee Village, where our thirst at its wee well we'd slake,
Aye mindin' still to leave a preen for ilka drink we'd take ;
Then roun' by auld Hugh Jolly's house beneath the trees we'd go,

c

Or clamber up by Ferryhill to visit the Roun' O ;
Or, if some other course we'd take, our hearts were in a lowe,
To see the bonnie gow'nie banks and braes o' Carden's Howe.
And, O! the marvellous tales we'd tell, the wonders we'd proclaim,
To shame the hincom-snevie loons wha aye holled on at hame.
Of trees a' loaded doun wi' fruit, that shook in ilka gale,
An' a' the glorious "images" o' fairy Cherryvale ;
Of angels on the kirkyard dyke, wi' a' their wings outspread,
And tooting on their trumpet horns, as if to wake the dead ;
Of houses a' clad o'er wi' shells, stars, diamonds, and the cross,
And a' kin-kin' o' shapes and hues within the "Shelly Close ;"*
But ae thing still o'er a' thing else our constant notice took—
Sir William's brave aul' statue in the niche at Wallace Nook.

Had we not seen the sword that hew'd the coordy English doon?
Beneath his helmet had we not beheld his haughty froun ?
Had we not seen his stalwart limbs encased in doughty mail ?
The very sight of which had made a thousand English quail,
When, only wi' the wee bit dog that by his foot is seen,
From an enormous host of foes he rescued Aberdeen,
Although his casque he never closed, nor yet his broadsword drew,
(For *we* had many a tale of him blind Harry never knew) ;
And if 'twas questioned what we said, why just come here and look,
Sir William, armour, dog, and a', are carved at Wallace Nook.

What tho' it canna boast "the lines o' beauty and o' grace,"
Tho' modish taste turns up its nose when passing by the place ;
Yet there is nane wha's patriot heart beats true to Scotland's richt,
But will revere the statue o' her dauntless champion Knicht.
Your granite Duke, exalted high, may frown on common rank,
And Commerce' fancied form o'erlook the entrance to the Bank,
And the guid Provost's monument may light wi' marble-smile,
What in our younger days was kent as Drum's auld haunted aisle;
But if you want a sample o' the stalwart men o' yore,
Wha, brac'd and girded *cap-a-pie*, their iron armour wore,
Just speil wi' me Carnegie's Brae, and wi' admirin' look,
Regard the brave auld form that fills the niche at Wallace Nook.

Then speakna o' intrinsic worth—an auld heir-loom may be
O' unco sma' intrinsic worth, and yet be dear to me ;
The kin' *memento* that we gat frae some auld-farrant frien'
Is hoarded up wi' jealous care, though hardly worth a preen.
Let virtuosos dote upon, let connoisseurs revere
Their Venuses de Medicis, Apollos Belvidere ;

---

* Stronach's Close.

Let testy politicians fight, wi' mony a wordy blow,
If Cromwell's statue get a place among the kings or no ;
Let Edinburgh's "Oldenbucks," frae time's destroying shocks,
For mony towmonds yet preserve the tenements o' Knox ;
But, Oh ! wi' deeper reverence still let Aberdonians look
On brave Sir William's statue in the niche at Wallace Nook ! *

The rapid march of extension and improvements
has rendered obsolete several of the allusions in the
above lines, but they have been retained as memor-
andums of old land-marks of the city. The provost's
monument mentioned as then gracing Drum's aisle, is
that of Provost James Blaikie, which was pointed out
to you on the stair-landing of the Town House.
Cherryvale has lost most of its pristine beauty ; and
Carden's Howe and the Round O are so encircled by
modern residences that their whereabouts are not
now much known to the present generation. In connection with Wallace Nook it may be mentioned that
a colossal statue of Wallace is now being cast for the
Duthie Park, as will afterwards be mentioned.

Rounding Netherkirkgate and St. Nicholas Street,
we again reach Union Street, proceeding westward
along which, the first object of attraction is the
beautiful façade which forms a gateway to St. Nicholas
Churchyard, in which stand the East and West
Churches. The former has recently been restored,
after a calamitous fire which occurred on the night of
9th October, 1874. This fire, which reduced the
East Church to the bare walls, destroyed also the old
steeple with a fine peal of bells. Two of the bells
destroyed, named "Lawrence" and "Maria," were of
great antiquity, having been gifted to the church in
1351 by William Leith, Provost of the town, as a sort

---

* It should be mentioned that Wallace Tower is considered a corruption of
Well-house Tower, and that the upright statue in the niche may have been a
recumbent figure from some old tomb.

of expiation for having killed "one Catanach, a bailiff here (whose cairn is near the barkmiln)."—*Gordon.*

The West Church was built in 1751-5. It is a massive edifice; and being the High Church of the City, contains a pew for the Magistrates, with a rich canopy in the centre, supported by fluted mahogany columns of the Corinthian order, and with the town's arms in *alto relievo* gilt on its pediment. The east gallery contains a fine organ, and the church is graced by four pieces of tapestry executed by Mary Jameson, daughter of the celebrated painter, representing Susanna and the Elders; the Finding of Moses; Jepthah's Vow; and Esther kneeling at the feet of King Ahasuerus. These have been renovated from the damage they received by water at the fire alluded to, and now appear in almost their pristine quaint beauty. Beside the west door there is a beautifully-conceived and finely-executed monument to the memory of Mrs. Allardyce of Dunnottar, by Bacon; and near by is the only monumental brass which our town possesses, being that of Dr. Duncan Liddel, who died in 1613.

The West Church narrowly escaped the fate of the East, but was fortunately preserved from fire, although a good deal damaged by water. The opportunity was taken advantage of, and the church underwent a renovation and embellishment, having the ceilings repainted and ornamented, and the windows filled with larger panes, and these of faintly stained glass. The great western window has recently been filled with Scripture subjects in stained glass, as a filial memorial of his parents, by a worthy citizen. The East Church, which you will observe is built of fine white granite, in a plain Gothic style, was erected in 1836. Two aisles run across between the two churches, the southward being called Drum's, and the northward one Collison's Aisle. Drum's Aisle was

converted into a spacious vestibule for the East
Church, and, restored after the fire, will continue to
give an imposing entrance to it.   Some of the
columns of the original bell tower have been laid bare
during the restorations consequent on the fire, and it
is believed that their forms, and the order of their
capitals, indicate a remote antiquity.   Collison's Aisle
has also been restored ; its windows filled with stained
glass, and the ancient character, as far as possible,
preserved of what was once known as the Aisle of
the Holy Blood.   Replacing a wooden spire, covered
with lead, which also was destroyed by the fire, the
great granite one you now see is raised upon the old
firm foundations, and will soon be made melodious by
a peal of thirty-six bells, now being cast at Louvain,
by Von Aershodt, at a cost of £2,500.

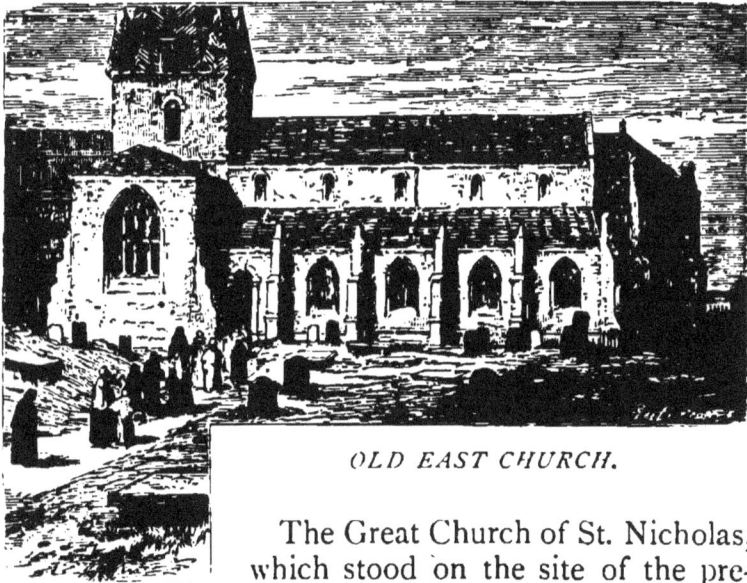

OLD EAST CHURCH.

The Great Church of St. Nicholas,
which stood on the site of the pre-
sent churches, was begun to be built, says Gordon,
about 1060, "the fabric augmented by little and little,
and enriched by gifts dedicated thereunto."   The choir

was built betwixt the years 1478 and 1493. The
present West Church superseded the oldest part of
the original church, and the present East Church is
built on the site of what was called the New Church,
under the east end of which was a small chapel called
the *cell* of our Lady of Pity, or "The Lady of Pity,
her Vault." This still exists in a renewed form,
adorned with carved wood-work from the East Church,
as St. Mary's Chapel; and having a stone roof, was
preserved intact from the fire in the East Church,
although temporarily damaged by water.

The wood-cut on page 37 shows the East Church
which preceded the present one.

Gordon, the parson of Rothiemay, writing in 1661,
and of course speaking of the appearance of the place
previous to the erection of any of the present buildings, says—"There is no church so neat and beautiful
to be seen in Scotland." And it must certainly have
been an imposing sight to have witnessed some religious spectacle in the old Cathedral of St. Nicholas,
with the light streaming through its great windows, or
sparkling from its "aucht chandlers of fyne silver,"
and its "fifty-twa brazen chandlers," upon its "great
latroun of massive brass, within the quire, in form of
the pelican with her birds, quharin the evangell was
red;" or upon its thirty-one altars, with their "furni-
tures, or hingers, before the altar, of fyne crommassie
veluot, crommassie satyn, reid dumass, quhyt, black,
and violat welvets and satynes, dropit with gold and
golden letters;" while its priests, clad in their "fine
mass cloathis of cloath of gold, crommassie grein,
black, and purpour velvet, stornit with gold," kept
some solemn festival, and displayed their "aucht siluer
chalices, with their patennes, tua siluer eucharists, ane
siluer steip, ane crosie siluer stock, six siluer altar
spunes, tua censures fyne siluer," and timed their

chants to the peals of the "pair of fyne organes, weill furnishit with their sang buird and all their tungis," and the fitful song of nature's organ—the wind—sighing through the "aught gryt aiken trees, growin' within said kirkyard," * all mingled up into a pageant of grandeur such

> As youthful poets dream
> On summer eves by haunted stream.

I may remark that there is nothing particularly original among the inscriptions on the gravestones in the Churchyard. There is, however, the brave exultation of the old mariner—

> Though Boreas' blasts and Neptune's waves
>   Have tossed me to and fro,
> In spite of both, by God's decree
>   I harbour here below ;
> Where at an anchor I do lie,
>   With many of our fleet,
> Till once again we do set sail,
>   Our admiral, Christ, to meet !

There is also, on a stone near the west wall of the churchyard, and now nearly overgrown with grass, and obliterated by footsteps, an inscription which I have thought worth while to preserve. There is neither date nor obituary upon this stone. It merely recounts that—

> ROBERT FORDYCE
> was one who
> even in these days
> of prevailing degeneracy
> and polite dissimulation,
> had the fortitude to approve himself
> an Israelite indeed in whom there was no guile.

---

* A summons against the magistrates of Aberdeen, dated 1591, for having "sauld, desponit, delapidat, and utherwayes usit and away put" the goods of the burgh, furnishes the catalogue of church property from which the above items are taken.

With a warm heart
he possessed a cool understanding.
To sufficient sensibility of temper
he joined an entire command of it.
His integrity
no temptation could corrupt.
His composure
no calamity could conquer.
While other men talked of philosophy,
he was satisfied to practise it.
Cheerful, but temperate ; active yet calm.
Candid to others, to himself severe.
In every relation conscientious.
Of so much excellence,
the foundation was laid in piety,
a piety steadfast because profound,
strict and amiable at the same time.
Having fixed his eye on another world,
he passed through this with innocence,
and, although young,
prosperous and happy in his family,
he left it with resignation.
In his life
he was blessed by the poor, beloved by his friends,
and honoured by all.
In his death
by all lamented :
by none more than by him who writes these lines,
who writes them,
not as a trial of skill,
but as the language of truth.
Not to excite the applause of his readers,
but to soothe the sadness of his soul.

Again reaching Union Street, passing the Conservative Club, and looking westward, that building of rather florid architecture on the other side of the street, a little farther up, is the Trades' Hall. It contains, besides apartments for the keeper, several committee-rooms and a charter-room, a large and splendid hall, hung round with portraits of the benefactors, patrons, and office-bearers of the various crafts. Its windows, seven in number, corresponding to the

number of crafts in the Incorporation, are filled with
stained glass emblems of the different fraternities.
The Incorporation consists of the followers of seven
different trades—the bakers, fleshers, weavers, shoe-
makers, tailors, hammermen, and the wrights and
coopers ; their dates of incorporation, ranging from
1398 to 1527. In the lower part of the building,
looking towards the Denburn, there is a large hall, the
entrance to which is by a curious gateway removed
from the old hall at Trinity corner, where once stood
the palace of William the Lion, which he in 1211
bestowed on the order of the Red Maturine, or
Trinity Friars, whose monastery, in 1632, Dr. William
Guild granted to the Trades, when he founded an
hospital for indigent brethren of the crafts. The
Trades have husbanded their funds well, and the extension of the town westward, taking up their lands as
feuing ground, has increased their store to an extent
they could never have originally calculated upon.
They are now able to keep the widows and orphans
of their deceased members in comfort, and to pay
handsome annuities to their decayed brethren. In
imitation of their masters—who, by the payment of
certain fees, the production of indentures, and the
display of a specimen of their workmanship, have
become participators in the honours, and have procured a prospective right to the bounties of their
craft—the junior members of the various trades had
also their elections of conveners, deacons, and box-
masters ; and on occasions of public rejoicings, these
had wont to turn out in grand procession, with bands
playing, mimic knights riding on prancing steeds,
banners flying, and all the insignia of their crafts displayed in the most holiday order. This practice had
its origin at a remote period. As far back as 1442,
we find the town council ordaining that—" Thir crafts

vnderwritten sall fynd yerly in the afferand of our
Lady at Candlemas, thir personnes vnderwritten : that
is to say—

"The littistares (dyers) sal fynd,
"The empriour* and twa doctoures,† and alsmony honest
squiares as thi may.
"The smythes and hammermen sall fynd,
"The three kingis of Culane,‡ and alsmony honest squiares
as thi may.
"The talzours sal fynd,
"Our Lady Sancte Bride, Sancte Helone, Joseph, and
alsmony squiares as thi may.
"The skynnares sal fynd,
"Two Bischopes, four angels, and alsmony honest squiares
as thi may.
"The webstares and walkers (veavers and waulkers) sal fynd,
"Symon and his disciples, and alsmony honest squiares, &c.
"The cordiners sal fynd,
"The messynger and moyses, and alsmony honest squiares, &c.
"The fleshowares sal fynd,
"Twa or four wodmen, and alsmony honest squiares, &c.
"The brither of the gilde sal fynd,
"The knightes in harnace, and squiares, honestly arrait, &c.
"The baxteiris sal fynd,
"The menstralis, and alsmony honest squiares as thi may."

Again, in 1505, we find the council confirming the
above, "and atour statut and ordanit that the said
craftsmen, and their successors, sall perpetualie, in
tyme to cum, observe and keip the said procession als
honorably as thai can." Then follows the order of
procession, much the same as the above ; "and giff
ony persone or personnes happinis to failye and brek
ony poynt befor written, and beis convict tharof [he]
sall pay xl. sh. to Sanct Nicholas werk, and the bayleis
unlaw unforgevin : Ande to the observing and keping

---

* This is supposed to have been the Emperor Agustus.
† The doctors whom the Saviour heard and questioned in the temple.
‡ The three wise men, who came from the East to worship the infant
Saviour.

of the samyn, all the said craftsmen was oblisit, be thair handis uphaldin."

A conspicuous character in ancient pastimes was the Abbot of Unreason, or Lord of Misrule. Under the title of the Abbot of Bon-Accord—a title borrowed from the motto of the town's arms—this character seems to have held a very prominent place among the festivities of the "braiff toune of Aberdeen;" and several minutes of council refer to his serio-comic reverence.

These processions, however, did not always go off without a brush, for we find on several occasions parties brought before the magistrates for "strublins of my lordis of Bonacordis." Neither did his reverence always deport himself with due decorum, for while his assailants went the length of "takin his horse and quhynggar" from him, he was charged with "casting of draff on them throw malyce." Those who thus "strublit the guid towne, in stoping of dansing, and plesure dewisit to the plesure of the samyn," however, were condemned to "cum the morn within the queyrs of Sanct Nicholace kyrke, in tyme of the hemes, bar-head, ilk ane of them with ane candill of vax of one pound in their hand, and syt doune on thair kneis and beseyk the prouest, in the tounis name, to forgyf them for the strublins don thairto be theme, in time of thair solace and play ; and in lyk-wyss to beseyk the said provost and guid men of the toune to make request to the lordis of Bonaccord to forgyf thame the falt and strublins done to them."

These were, perhaps, jovial, and there is no doubt they were ignorant times ; but, silently working its way at first, the Reformation at last came, and these revels ceased ; and the " Empriour and the three Kingis of Culane," "the zoung abil men in their grene cottis, and agit men in honest cottis, afferend to thame," the Abbot and Prior of Bon-Accord, with their horses, their "quhynggars, and cuttit out hoyss," must all give way before an increased improvement of public morals.

In 1565, the town crier appears before the magistrates, and gives evidence that he had executed their commands in proclaiming that it should be unlawful any longer to practise these revels, and that he had put the ban upon the public playing of the tabour, pipe, or fiddle, and upon the assignations for choosing Robin Hood, Little John, the Abbot of Unreason, or the Queen of May. The New-Year processions of the Trades, which we have alluded to, were the only relics of these forgotten festivals that remained ; and they, too, have now become amongst the things that were.

Union Bridge, which we have now reached, is a magnificent span of 150 feet, and is one of the finest parts of the great undertaking that gave us the splendid entrance to the town from the south which we now possess, in place of the narrow, up-hill-and-down-dale one which we formerly had. While we are looking at the bridge, I will endeavour to give you some idea of the change which the opening of Union Street produced upon the town.

Previous to the year 1800, the access to Aberdeen from the south was down the steep, and often dirty, Windmill Brae—the low road spanned by Bridge Street, the new approach to the railway station. This road crossed the Denburn, at a spot now tunnelled over, by the Bow-Brig, a stone bridge of a rather handsome kind, and descended, in a dangerous and inconvenient manner, over the *bow* of this bridge into the Green. At the upper end of the Green, you had the choice of descending again in a precarious way by the Maltmill Brig, and then ascending to Castle

Street by the narrow and sinuous track along Trinity Corner and Shiprow; or you could climb up by Wallace Nook and Netherkirkgate, and find your way to the Cross by the Round Table or Rotten-row. The opening up of Union Street, by levelling the hills and bridging the valleys that came in its way, at once gave a spacious, direct, and almost level road from the elevation of Castle Street to the high grounds west-ward of the town. The opening of St. Nicholas, George, and King Streets did a like service to the approaches from the north.

Long after the improvement of the accesses to the town, and when the tradesmen in the new streets had begun to assume a rather modish appearance, the dwellers in the old thoroughfares continued to cling to their antiquated fashions; to lounge about in their shirt-sleeves and aprons, and hang over their half-doors in their bonnets and paper caps. The Bow-brig, already mentioned, with its roadway deserted by its former traffic, and its broad, flat, seat-like parapet, was one of the favourite rendezvous of these old-world burghers. As might be supposed, the youths in these localities took their cue from their elders—spurned the new-fangled idea of the restraint sought to be imposed on them by police regulations, and played their games, and fought their stone battles, in the open streets. A graphic poem, by Mr. Wm. Anderson, who was himself a boy at this era, and who has done much by his writings to illustrate it, will give you a better idea of those now obsolete manners, and of the behaviour of the youths of the lower order at that time, than anything I could tell you on the subject :—

Jean Findlater's Loon.

The winter was lang, an' the seed-time was late,
An' the cauld month o' March sealed Tam Findlater's fate;
He dwined like a snaw-wreath till some time in June,
Then left Jean a widow, wi' ae raggit loon.
Jean scrapit a livin' wi' weavin' at shanks—
Jock got into scrapes—he was aye playin' pranks;
Frae the Dee to the Don he was fear'd roun the toun—
A reckless young scamp was Jean Findlater's loon.

Jock grew like a saugh on a saft boggy brae—
He dislikit the school, an' car'd mair for his play;
Ony mischief that happened, abroad or at hame,
Whaever was guilty, Jock aye got the blame.
Gin a lantern or lozen was crackit or broke,
Nae ane i' the toun got the wite o't but Jock;
If a dog was to hang, or a kitlin to droon,
They wad cry, gie the job to Jean Findlater's loon.

He rappit the knockers—he rang a' the bells—
Sent dogs down the causeway wi' pans at their tails;
The dykes o' the gardens and orchards he scaled—
The apples an' berries an' cherries he stealed.
Gin a claes rope was cuttit, or pole ta'en awa',
The neighbours declared it was Jock did it a';
Wi' his thum' at his nose, street or lane he ran doun—
The widdy was sure o' Jean Findlater's loon.

He pelted the peatmen, e'en wi' their ain peats—
Pu'd hair frae their horse tails, then leugh at their threats;
An' on Christmas nicht, frae the Shiprow to Shore,
He claikit wi' sowens ilka shutter and door.
We hae chairs in our college for law and theology;
If ane had been vacant for trick or prankology;
Without a dissent ye micht votit the goun,
To sic an adept as Jean Findlater's loon.

On the forenoons o' Friday he aften was seen
Coupin' country foulk's carts upside doun i' the Green;
An' where masons were workin' without ony fear,
He shoudit wi' scaffoldin' planks ower their meer.
To herrie birds' nests he wad travel for miles;
Ding ower dykes an' hedges, and brack doun the stiles,
Swing on gentlemen's yetts, or their palin's pu' doun;—
Tricks and mischief were meat to Jean Findlater's loon.

He vexed Betty Osley,* wha threat'ned the law—
Ritchie Marchant† wad chase him an' had him in awe ;
Frae the Hardgate to Fittie he aye was in scrapes,
An' a' body wondered how Jock made escapes.
Jean said he was royet, *that* she maun aloo,
But he wad grow wiser the aulder he grew ;
She aye took his pairt against a' body roun',
For she kent that her Jock was a kind-hearted loon.

At seventeen, Jock was a stout, strappin' chiel,
He had left aff his pranks, an' was now doin' weel ;
In his face there was health, in his arm there was pith,
An' he learnt at ance to be ferrier an' smith.
His character, noo, was unstain'd wi' a blot,
His early delinquencies a' were forgot,
Till the weel-keepit birthday of Geordie cam roun',
Which altered the fate o' Jean Findlater's loon.

The fire-warks were ower, and the bonfire brunt done,
An' the crowd to Meg Dickie's gaed seekin' mair fun ;
They attackt the White Ship,‡ in rear an' in front—
Took tables an' chairs, whilk they broke an' they brunt.
Jock couldna resist it—he brunt an' he broke—
Some sax were made prisoners—among them was Jock ;
Ten days in the jail, an' his miseries to croun,
Bread an' water the fare o' Jean Findlater's loon.

Jock entered the Life Guards—bade Scotland adieu—
Fought bravely for laurels at fam'd Waterloo ;
An' his conduct was such, that ere five years had past,
He was made by Lord Hill master-farrier at last.
Jean's rent was aye paid, an' she still was alive,
To see her brave son in the year twenty-five ;
An' nane wad hae kent that the whiskered dragoon
Was the same tricky nickum—Jean Findlater's loon.

Looking northward up the valley of the Denburn
from the Union Bridge, you had, until the north railway was laid up the valley, perhaps as fine a little
peep of fresh greenery in the gardens of Belmont
Street and the shrubbery of Union Terrace—whilom

---

* A dealer in sweet-meats in front of the jail.
† A town sergeant.
‡ An infamous public-house.

"the Corby Heugh"—as the centre of any manufacturing town could boast of; and it only wanted a
pure stream instead of the dirty open sewer, and
natural, instead of artificial, banks to the burn, to
make this view a perfect thing of the kind. The iron
roadway for the iron horse has now, however, greatly
changed this scene; but the view is still very pretty,
and the sloping bank and spare ground at the foot of
it have recently been finely laid out as a People's Park
on a small scale, and in a few summers, when the
shrubs and plants have had time to grow to greater
maturity, the Denburn Valley here, will be again
something to be proud of. The prospect is partly
intercepted by a very handsome church, belonging to
the Congregational body, and closed in by a group of
Free Churches—the East, High, and South—built in
the cruciform manner, and adorned by a spire of
graceful and elegant proportions. That building with
the dome in the extreme of the vista, is the Royal
Infirmary, a chaste and beautiful building which will
be more particularly noticed afterwards. Still proceeding out Union Street, you come, at the corner of
Union Terrace, upon a bronze statue of the late
Prince Albert, by Marochetti, the merits of which
you can judge for yourself. The fine building on the
opposite corner from the statue contains the offices of
the Northern Assurance Company, and is the most
ornate granite building in the city. A little beyond
you will be struck by the noble portico and colonnade
of the *quondam* County Buildings. This edifice,
which contained all the necessary apartments—ball-
room, banqueting-room, supper-room, card-room,
promenade, &c.—for holding of public assemblies,
was built by the gentlemen of the counties of
Aberdeen, Banff, and Kincardine, in the year 1820, at
a cost of £11,000. Such were the County Buildings;

but, having some years ago been purchased by a joint-stock company, a splendid hall was formed by greatly enlarging the former ball-room, and they are now called the Music Hall Buildings. The Hall, which is furnished with an admirable organ, was opened by His Royal Highness the late Prince Consort delivering, in presence of a brilliant audience, his thoughtful address as President of the British Association for the Advancement of Science, on 14th September, 1859. Silver Street, along which the Music Hall Buildings extend for 156 feet, opens into Golden Square, which presents a specimen of the plan on which it was proposed to lay out all the feuing-grounds west of Union Bridge, and a visit to which will cause you to regret that such an excellent plan was never carried out. Huntly Street is the first street beyond the Music Hall Buildings which opens off Union Street to the north. This building at the corner of Union and Huntly Streets, is the Royal Northern Club, having all the requisites and conveniences of this species of institution. A little up Huntly Street you come upon St. Mary's Roman Catholic Cathedral, with its handsome spire and sweet chime of bells. You cannot but admire the exterior, although a little hemmed in by its close surroundings, and the interior is finer still, and very well worthy of a visit. In this street, a little beyond, is the Blind Asylum, an elegant building, erected by funds left by Miss Cruickshank for the relief of the blind. Here, as in other blind asylums, the trades of rope-making, weaving, basket-making, &c., are carried on.

Proceeding out Union Street, you pass on the left hand the Free West Church, and on the right, Free Gilcomston Church, both elegant edifices, externally and internally. This building which you see in the Elizabethan style of architecture, with the small

D

octagonal tower appended to the square tower, is the
Free Church College, or Divinty Hall, where the
aspirants in this quarter to the ministry of the Free
Church receive their theological instruction. It was
built in 1850, at a cost of £2,000, and at the
expense of a few private gentlemen who were anxious
to prevent the necessity of the Free Church students
in the north proceeding to Edinburgh for their clerical
education. A fine view is to be obtained of the
western suburbs and of the surrounding country from
the tower of the College. To the south you have the
villages of Holburn and Hardgate—the latter lying
along the old south access to the town ; and beyond
these, in a south westerly direction, the village of
Ruthrieston, lying near the Old Bridge of Dee, while
the fast-rising beautiful suburb of Ferryhill is laid
against the background of the green hills of Torry.
To the west you have Rubislaw Bleachfield, and the
huge mounds of *debris* which indicate whence a great
part of our glittering granite is quarried, with the
Deeside hills rising up, peak above peak, to close in
the scene ; while, spread out like a carpet beneath
you, the recently laid-out grounds of Rubislaw present
their terraces, streets, and villas, to your admiring gaze.

A little beyond the Divinity Hall, on the same line
of road, is one of the most chaste of all our public
buildings—the Orphan Asylum. This edifice was
erected at the cost of Mrs. Emslie, and endowed by
her for the education of a limited number of orphan
girls, being one of the few instances of active be-
nevolence carried out to the extent of setting an
institution of this importance into full working order
during the life of the donor.

Proceeding along Albyn Place, with Rubislaw
Terrace on the right, and a varied succession of villas
on each side, you reach Queen's Cross, the termin-

ation of the tramway in this direction. The fine granite church here belongs to the Free Church connection, and that one of sandstone to the Established Church.

About a mile farther on, if you are inclined, you may visit the granite quarries of Rubislaw. We will retrace our way by Carden Place, passing on the right St. Mary's Episcopal Chapel; and on the left a fine church recently built by the adherents of the U.P. body. Proceeding along Carden Place, the attention is directed to a building retired from the road on the left. This fine building, in the baronial style of architecture, is our new Grammar School. It was opened in 1864, and supplied a long felt want, the old school, noticed a little farther on, having been for many years found far too small for the purpose it was intended to serve.

Going eastward along Skene Street, the suburb of Gilcomston lies on the left, along the hollow through which the Denburn runs, and up the height beyond. The access to this—the Rosemount—suburb was long felt to be very inconvenient, and its upper end was recently made easily accessible by Esselmont Avenue, the street passing the east end of the Grammar School; and the lower end can now be reached by this new viaduct, the stately arches of which levelly span the valley.

Having crossed the Denburn at the foot of Skene Street, it is worth while stepping aside a little to see the Well of Spa. This spring long had a great renown for the healing virtues of its waters. Dr. William Barclay, who flourished in the latter part of the sixteenth century (born 1541, died 1606), wrote a treatise called "Callirhoe, or the Nymph of Aberdeen Resuscitat," in its praise; and Jameson the painter, mentioned before, at his own expense built

over it a vault of hewn stone, which Baillie Alexander
Skene, in 1670, rebuilt also on his own charges, as an
inscription on the well—"Spada rediviva, 1670"—
indicates. Latterly, the Well of Spa became rather
neglected, until the poetical and patriotic influence
which afterwards had the effect of re-erecting the old
Castlegate well in the Green, was brought to bear
upon the more ancient fountain, and in 1851, the
Well of Spa underwent a thorough repair, and to its
old motto, "As Heaven gives me, so give I thee," and
to the "rediviva" of 1670, was added, "Renovatum
et opus, MDCCCLI." It is to be regretted that certain
works connected with the Denburn Junction tunnel
have almost entirely cut off the supply of water from
this fountain, and some means should be employed to
carry the fine springs from the Woolmanhill to the
Well of Spa, and thus continue its ancient celebrity.

The name "Garden-nook-close," which you see
given to that alley opposite the well, marks out the
"four-square field, which of old served for a theatre,
since made a gardyne for pleasure by the industrie
and expense of George Jameson, ane ingenious
paynter, quho did set up therein ane timber house,
paynted all over with his owne hand." You will
recognise in this vast and elegant building on the
elevated platform, the Royal Infirmary, which I
pointed out to you from Union Bridge. The present
building, which superseded a former factory-like
erection, was finished in 1840, at a cost of some
£17,000. Although it has a most efficient staff of
medical officers, and has accommodation for about
3co patients, owing to the increased demands upon it
for accommodation, and the better modes of treatment now given to the sick, it is found that more
room is required, and the managers are at present
devising plans for its enlargement. In connection

ART GALLERY AND MUSEUM, AND GRAY'S SCHOOL OF ART.

FROM A PHOTO. BY G. W. WILSON & CO.

with the Infirmary, may be mentioned the Lunatic
Asylum, which lies a little farther up the same line of
road, at the bottom of a beautiful, well-wooded
valley, thickly clustered with suburban villas. The
Lunatic Asylum is also an elegant dome-topped
building, and has received vast additions within the
last few years, the most important of which is Elmhill
House, a new establishment within the same grounds
of almost equal extent with the old house, and with
more extensive airing grounds. A little beyond this,
on the same (Low Stocket) road, is the Victoria Park,
which, at a considerable expense, was laid out by the
Corporation, for the benefit of the public. Coming
past the main front of the Infirmary you reach the
Free East, High, and South Churches, with their
graceful brick spire, which partially closed in the green
vista of the Denburn when we looked up the valley
from Union Bridge.

These two buildings, with the archway between
them, over which is a covered connecting corridor,
are the Art Gallery, and Gray's School of Art. The
former is the west-ward building, and is intended, and
has already been used, as an Exhibition of Works of
Art, and also as a Museum devoted to the display of
curiosities, and objects of natural history and antiquarian interest. It has been erected by subscriptions
from the inhabitants of the town. The School of Art,
the east-ward building, is the gift of Mr. John Gray,
engineer, who is still alive, and has long taken an
interest in this and kindred institutions. It has a fine
collection of casts for the benefit of the students, and
may be considered as a splendid revival of the Art
School of the defunct Mechanics' Institute.

Passing through the arch connecting these two
buildings, the erection at the bottom of the well laid-
out grounds, is Robert Gordon's Hospital, now

Robert Gordon's College.   The original founder of
this institution was the only son of Arthur Gordon,
advocate, who was the ninth son of Robert Gordon of
Straloch and Pitlurg, one of the oldest and most
distinguished branches of the noble house of Huntly.
Having acquired a fortune as a merchant in Dantzic,
Robert Gordon returned to his native country, and
settled in Aberdeen in the beginning of the eighteenth
century.   The well-authenticated stories told of Mr.
Gordon's sordid and penurious habits would scarcely
be believed of one who had obtained a liberal
education, and who had abundance of wealth.   His
station in life, and the respectable family from which
he sprang, led him frequently to be a guest at the
table of others, and on these occasions he is said to
have partaken of the good things before him with a
gusto, and to an extent which he used as a seasoning
for the spare fare of his own miserable home.   He
died in 1732, and, by a deed executed a few years
before, it was found that he conveyed all his property
to the provost, magistrates, and town council of
Aberdeen, for the erection of an hospital for the
education of boys who are sons and grandsons of
Burgesses of Guild, with certain preferences in favour
of his own relations, or those of the surnames of
Gordon and Menzies.   The Hospital was opened in
1750, when thirty boys were admitted to be boarded
and educated on the premises.   The number of
beneficiaries was increased from time to time, the
buildings being enlarged for that purpose, until in
1881 the Hospital was merged in the College.   There
are now over 600 day scholars in the College, and
the evening classes are proportionally large, technical
instruction being a prominent feature in the education
given.   The claims of the foundationers are preserved
by the free education of thirty presentation scholars,

who also receive £15 yearly for five years in lieu of
board, and other thirty by competition receive the
same benefits, in all there are ninety foundationers by
presentation, and thirty by competition. · A convent of
Black Friars stood on the spot occupied by the Hospital,
but it was demolished in 1560; and although, in 1661,
part of the high wall which enclosed it was still standing, Gordon says, "there is nothing of the building to
be seen;" and adds, "true it is that some private citizens
have raised up goodlie houses out of its robberies."

On a site in front of Gray's School of Art the old
Grammar School stood.

OLD GRAMMAR SCHOOL.

It was erected in 1757; and in it Beattie and
Byron, and many other celebrated individuals have
received the elements of their classical education.
The Grammar School figures pretty largely for a long
course of years both in the town council records and
those of the kirk-session—the boys seeming to have
evinced a certain amount of wilfulness, which has not
left them up to the present time   Jealous of their play-
day privileges, it was very difficult at the time of the
Reformation, to make them abstain from certain

observances which had become by that time obnoxious to their elders. In 1568, they present a supplication to the magistrates to restore their old privileges, which request is granted in a compromise kind of way, although again withdrawn in 1575. Not inclined to yield without a struggle, however, we find the "bairnis and scholaris" of the Grammar School rebelling against the master, and "takyn of the schuill" from him, insisting upon having their old holidays at the "tyme of yeir afoir Yuil, called Natiuite of our Lord." It became necessary, in consequence of this insubordination, to cause all youths wishful of entering the school to present themselves before the magistrates, and find caution for their obedience to the master and rulers. Notwithstanding this precaution, the boys still rebelled, and insisted on their old rights, and the magistrates had to compound with them by granting three vacation days at the end of each quarter. As if stilled by this concession, we next find them in 1603, sitting quietly in pews set apart for them behind the pulpit of the old church, and their masters complaining that, in consequence of the inconvenience of the place, "they can not heir the voice of the minister." This complaint caused them to be distributed in and under the lofts of the new church, where they were to "tak their nottis of the preechings." There seems to have been a grand *rumpus* in 1604, when they were again charged with taking the school from the masters, and holding it with swords, guns, and pistols, and also with taking the poor folk's gear, such as geese, fowls, peats, "and otheris vivaris." And, in 1612, along with some students and their associates of the Writing and Song School, they took possession of the latter, and kept it for three days against all authority, till the magistrates were compelled to apprehend and imprison a certain number of them—so difficult was it to put down the saturnalia indulged in by the boys at the time of Yule, or even to bring their license within reasonable limits. The old erection was long felt to be too small and inconvenient ; and a building better adapted to the business of teaching, and more in accordance with the taste and liberality of the age, has now, principally through the exertions of Sir Alexander Anderson, been erected on the west side of the city (as pointed out to you near Carden Place), at a cost of nearly £10,000. This was a very necessary improvement ; but when the old structure, the desks of which were completely covered with names cut by the errant pen-knives of several generations of pupils, was taken down, there was a dreadful demolition of those old associations which always cling around

The school-boy spot
We ne'er forget, tho' there we are forgot.

It is worth while to go a little farther down the Schoolhill to see a picturesque building, on the same side of the street as the School of Art, which is known as Jameson (the painter's) house. This fine specimen of ancient street architecture is now doomed to demolition, but the excellent engraving of it in Billing's Antiquities, and other memoranda, will keep its quaint features in loving remembrance. Retracing your steps a little and returning to Union Street by Belmont Street, you pass, on your right, a large old mansion-house now occupied as the Deaf and Dumb Institution. On the same side of the street is a fine church belonging to the Congregational body, and opposite it a U. P. church, while before you the South Parish Church lifts up its massive gables and tower to the sky ; and in the cross street, along which part of the South Church stands (Little Belmont Street), the Girls' High School hides its fair Grecian proportions from all except enquiring eyes.

After a considerable circuit, we have now again reached our starting place, Market Street. Our next walk will be by the Docks and Harbour. From the examination of old records and the discovery of ancient remains, there seems to be little doubt that all the plain which you see from the rising ground along the bases of St. Katherine and Castle Hills, to the hills that slope down to the river on the south side of Dee, had wont at high tide to be one vast sheet of water, through the sandy or muddy bottom of which, at low tide, the river on the one hand, and the Den and Trinity burns on the other, sought their devious ways to the sea. Near the Craiglug the flowing into this estuary of the Ferryhill burn opened up another inlet to the sea ; and there is reason to believe that, in the hollow westward of Dee Village, lay a sheet of water spoken of in an old charter as the Loch of Dee. The alluvial deposits of these waters in course of time formed large low mounds, and these again would have the effect of keeping the waters into more constant channels ; and thus the Inches sprung up, which, in the memory of those much less ancient than the "oldest inhabitant," were islands covered with a thick short grass, blooming with tufts of sea-daisies, and full of little pits or holes plentifully supplied with bansticles.

For hundreds of years after Aberdeen was of some note, the harbour was nothing but the huge basin we have endeavoured to describe, having a precarious communication with the sea by the narrow mouth of the river, which forced its way to its goal through hills of shifting sand. The first attempt to render the Harbour other than a mere creek was the building of what was called the Quay-head, near the Shore Brae. This was extended by little and little, until, as Gordon, so often quoted, writing in 1661, says—

After you have gone eastward a little thorrough a street, the Quay or wharfe is next to be seen. Builded it was anno 1526, Gilbert Menzies of Findone being provost. It was enlarged and repaired afterwards in the year 1562 ; Patrick Menzies, then thesaurer, with the citizens' consent, did bestow upon that work the price of the utensils of St. Nicholas Church.* Anno 1624, citizens Consil build a Weghhous or packhous upon the Keyhead, which serves lykewayes for a custom hous. From thence the Key runs downward toward the village of Futtie, no fewer than 500 walking passes, and it joins with Futtie ; a work of many yeires, oft times broken off. It is facit upon every side with drystone, and filled up in the middle with sande. It was finished at last in the yeir 1659 with much labour, by means quhairoff it has com to passe that a large quantitie of ground, which before was daylie at every tyde [over-flowed], and was in pairt of the firth, the sea being now keept quyt off, is become a fertile corn field.

The space thus reclaimed from the estuary is that on which Virginia, James, and Commerce Streets are built, and on which lay the carpet-walk, so enthusi-astically spoken of by Forbes of Foveran, as men-tioned when we were looking from the Castlehill. Gordon continues—

The entrie into the Harbour is somequhat dangerous by reasone of a sand bed, comonelie called the Barre, that croces the mouth of the harbour into the sea ; nor dar any venture but expert pillots quho can guyde the way, and hav the hilp of the wind and tyde. Once entered, the harborie will conteene many and great ships. Men of warre and merchant ships of greatest syze and burthen ly at Torrie in the verie channell of the river Dee. Lesser vessells goe up to Futtie, or by help of the tyde at high water goe up to the citie, and ly closse all along the peer, when they ather unlode ther goods or take in their fraught.

That such a catastrophe as that of "blocking up the Harbour" had actually taken place, we learn from Spalding, who notes that, on St. Stephen's Day, 26th December, 1637, such a bar was cast across the mouth

---

* See note page thirty-nine.

of the Dee, that ships could neither go out nor come in : and that, at low water, a man might have passed dry-footed from side to side. After fasting and prayer, the inhabitants, young and old, cast down this bar ; but to no effect. Then gloomy forebodings of the ruin of Aberdeen filled their minds, and they advertised along the coast that no ship should approach the harbour. Spalding continues, " But while they are at the pain of despair, the Lord of his great mercy removed clean away this bar, and the water did keep its own course as before, to the great joy of the people of Aberdeen, and comfort of the people round about. But this bar came not for nought, but was a token of great troubles to fall upon both Aberdeens ; and it is to be remarked, that, as there were fearful signs by water, so there was many monstrous high winds all this year—no good token more than the rest." Had the good chronicler told us from what point the winds blew, it would have been of more importance, as probably showing the cause of the accumulation of the bar at the mouth of the Harbour.

The bar here spoken of, which even yet sometimes accumulates, was long a great perplexity to the Harbour authorities. In 1770, the magistrates procured from Smeaton the celebrated engineer, a plan for its removal. He attributed the formation of the bar to the agency of the north-east winds on the flat and sandy shore extending northwards from the Dee to the Buchan-ness, whereby the sand and gravel are driven to the southward, till, meeting the promontory of the Girdleness, they are deposited at the angle of the coast which forms the mouth of the Harbour. But for the river forcing a way through this deposit, he adds, it would soon block up the Harbour altogether, and his plan was to build a bulwark on the north side of the Harbour, which, by confining, would increase the power of the river in its natural tendency to clear away this bar.

Following out this plan, the foundation-stone of the New Pier, as it is called, was laid in 1775, and completed in five years at a cost of £18,000. It extended eastward 1200 feet, and had the effect of greatly diminishing the bar, and of preventing future accumulations. Still a greater depth of water was sought, and greater accommodation in the inside of the Harbour, and a plan was obtained from Mr. Telford to effect these objects. His plan was a further extension of the North Pier, and the conversion of a portion of the inner Harbour into a Wet Dock. His project is now fully carried out, but it was long before anything more was done towards it beyond the extension of the Pier; and it was from a plan furnished by Mr. Abernethy, the resident engineer of the Harbour at the time, that the construction of the Docks was finally carried into effect. The Docks, you will observe, are divided into two parts by means of a draw-bridge, which forms a most commodious and much-used road-way to the now busy Inches. The Docks cover thirty-six acres of land, and perhaps contain as large a body of water as any docks in the kingdom. These rails laid along the quays connect the North, South, and Deeside Railway Goods Stations together, the carriages being drawn between them by horse-haulage, and by means of their various sidings, they enable the railway trucks to be loaded from, or delivered into, the vessels. This is the Shore Brae, near which the old Quayhead stood. There was a crane erected at the Quayhead, by means of which criminals were ducked by lowering the rope to which they were attached, until the culprit was immersed in the water. This was a punishment often inflicted on the frail sisterhood.

On the 5th December, 1602, the Kirk-Session
"ordanis Jonett Scherar, quha was baneshit obefoir
for harlatrie, and is cum in agane within this burt, but
licence, and sen hir incumming hes fallin of new
agane, to be apprehendit and put in the kirk wolt,
and thereaifter to be doukit at the cran, and publictlie
baneshit of new agane at the mercat croce; prouyding
gif she pay ten merkis of penaltie, to be fre of
hir douking, and no vtherwayes." Again in 1607, a
war ship of Dunkirk (then in possession of the
Spaniards) having been sheltered for some time in the
Harbour, and the Session, fearing that, while the
excitable Southerns were in the place, the interests of
morality might suffer, ordains that, in case of such a
result taking place, and a foreign paternity being
alleged, "the persone or persones being fund giltie,
are decernit to be incarcerat in the kirk wault for the
space of aucht dayes, vpon bread and water, and
thairefter takin out and doukit at the key-heid." And
again, in, 1638, an erring female is sentenced "to be
cartit from the mercat croce to the key-heid, thair to
be doukit at the cran."

This fine building before you, with the handsome
clock-tower, is the office for the officials of the
Harbour Commissioners. It stands on the site of
the old Weigh-House, or "Pack-hous," long a land-
mark of the town. A little farther on, you reach
Marischal Street which, you will see, leads direct from
Castle Street to the Quay, and which, before the
opening of Market Street, and an improvement that
was made upon Commerce Street a good few years
ago, was the chief means of communication betwixt
the town and the harbour. These new streets being
not nearly so steep, Marischal Street is now greatly
relieved of its rather overabundant traffic.

A few houses up Marischal Street from the Quay,

was the old Theatre, now converted into a church. Aberdeen seems to have been long famed for theatrical exhibitions; indeed the earliest of these on record in Scotland is the play of the "Haliblude," which was acted here in 1440, on the Windmillhill. These miracle plays, as they were called, continued to be performed in Aberdeen until the middle of the sixteenth century, on a piece of ground about the Woolmanhill, hence laid down in James Gordon's map as the "playe green." In 1479, the town council resolved to pay the expense of the "arayment and utheris necessaris of the play to be plait in the fest of Corpos Xti" (Corpus Christi) out of the common good. In 1601, the company of comedians playing at the Globe Theatre, London, having visited Edinburgh, came to Aberdeen, bearing a letter of recommendation from the king, and "played sum of their comedies in this brught," for which they were rewarded by the council, who paid "thair haill chargis" during their stay, and bestowed upon their manager, Laurence Fletcher, the freedom of the burgh to boot. It is well known that Fletcher was afterwards associated with Shakespeare, in the patent granted to them and others by James I. in 1603; and Charles Knight, in his biography of Shakespeare, does not hesitate to say that the immortal dramatist was one of the company who visited Aberdeen at this time. The building with the Royal Arms in front of it is the Custom-house. On the construction of the quay walls on the south side of the harbour, the green islands or inches lying betwixt them and the river Dee, were made up to their present level, principally with deposit dredged by a powerful machine from the bottom of the harbour—lime-sheds and bone-mills were erected—and, what with these and the wood, stone, and building yards which now cover

them, the Inches, as the place still continues to be
called, is now about as busy a spot as the town
contains. Not only so; but within the last few years,
in order to provide additional space for the growing
fishing and manufacturing requirements of the town,
the bed of the river Dee was, at a very great expense,
shifted much farther southward, reclaiming on the
town side an immense space of ground, which will no
doubt some day pay as well as the Inches has done.

Proceeding down the Quay, we cross the end of
Commerce Street, in which may be observed the
Mariner's Church, built in 1844, and then come to
the goods terminus of the Great North of Scotland
Railway. This railway, as far as Inverurie, goes much
on the track of the Aberdeenshire Canal, which was
opened in 1807—a useful, but not remunerating
undertaking—which it has superseded. It extends to
Keith, a distance of 53½ miles, where it is joined by
the Inverness and Aberdeen Junction Railway; and
has branches to Alford, Peterhead, Banff, .&c.
During the last few years, the whole face of this
quarter of the town has been entirely changed by the
removal of the Canal with its terminal basin, the
erection of the railway station, and the building of
the office, granaries, and works of the Northern
Agricultural Company.

About this quarter stood the old village of Fittie,
which was inhabited by a few white-fishers, apparently
not of an over-industrious kind, for, in 1591, we find
the baillies of the burgh obliged to ordain that they
must fine them, if they pass not to the sea in their
boats for taking of fish to serve the inhabitants and
the king's lieges, "wynd and wedder servand." And
not only were they themselves generally idle, but they
seem to have been opposed even to those of their
number who were industrious; for, but a year after-

wards, we find two of them making complaint to the magistrates against other four for cutting and destroying " ane labster nett," which they had set up at " the Grey Hoip within the Girdleness, quhairwith not only lapsteris, but also partins and padillis, with other sort of schell fish, was takin "—" a new ingyne (it is added) deuysit to that effect, quhilk had nocht bene wsit obefoir," and for that very reason perhaps, according to the superstitious notions which still prevail among the " fisher folk," destroyed, they not agreeing with counsel that " the samen was ane necessar ingyne," however much it might be " profitable for the commoun weill."

Passing along Church Street, we observe, when it reaches St. Clement Street, St. Clement's Established Church immediately before us. The present structure was built in 1828, at a cost of £2500. It replaced the former church, which was built in 1788, which in its turn superseded the original edifice, founded about the year 1498, for the worship of the white-fishers, who paid one shilling yearly for each line, for which the priest was bound to celebrate two masses weekly—one on Sunday and another on Friday. " The churchyard, not long since, was builded and enclosit with a goodlie wall of lyme and stone, by a citizen of Aberdeen," says Gordon, writing in 1661 ; and that black stone enclosed in the new wall bears testimony to the correctness of the parson of Rothiemay, for its inscription runs thus :—

George Davidson, elder burgess of Abd, bigit this dyke on his ovin expenses, 1650.

The large Iron Works of Messrs. Blaikie Brothers, lie at the back of the church ; and, indeed, the whole grounds round about are covered with the sheds, workshops, and yards of shipbuilders, rope and sail

makers, blockmakers, ironfounders, and all those
trades necessary for the construction and equipment
of our mercantile marine.

Retracing our steps to the Quay, we soon reach the
Dock Gates, which close in the thirty-six acres of
water in which the vessels lie afloat.   You will notice
that the locks are built of dressed granite, and in the
most complete order ; and I may observe that the
gates and swing bridge are worked by hydraulic
power, the steam engine necessary for this purpose
being also used for pumping out the graving-dock, a
little south of the dock gates, on part of the old
channel of the Dee, which is used as part of the
tidal harbour.

The huge sheer-poles which you observe are used
for lifting masts, boilers, machinery, &c., into vessels
which are in progress of being fitted up.   They are
wrought by steam power, and it is a treat to see how,
by their varied movements, they lift vast weights and
lower them to their appointed places.

Passing the shipbuilding yards, under huge sheds
in which the celebrated Aberdeen clippers have been,
and still continue to be built, we reach the New Pier.
Having already spoken of this magnificent bulwark, I
may only now remark that it is two thousand feet
long, and thirty feet broad ; that the elevation of the
parapet is about fifteen feet above the level of high
water ; and that some of the masses of stone, which
are bound together with iron to protect the foundation, exceed forty tons in weight.   The Harbour
Commissioners, intent in carrying out still further the
improvement of the harbour entrance, have recently
finished the great breakwater, which you see extending
a length of 1050 feet from the opposite shore.   The
break water is constructed of concrete, and the same
material is used in extending the pier, 500 feet being

added to its former length. After our long walk, it is refreshing to sit on the breezy bulwark that terminates the pier, and contemplate the scene which lies around. That promontory on the south is called the Girdleness, from a sunken rock—the *Girdle*—which lies immediately off it. You will observe there is a battery on this headland, as well as one on the beach, for the protection of the town and harbour. The Torry battery has six 68-pounders, and three shell guns; the beach one, four 68-pounders. At both these batteries the Volunteer Artillery frequently practise, and good practice they are said to make. The Lighthouse beyond has two lights in its tower —the one 115 and the other 185 feet above the medium sea level. The lower light is visible in clear weather at a distance of 13, the higher at that of 16 miles. A little northward from the lighthouse lies the small bay of Greyhope, the scene of many a shipwreck, the most fatal of which is still fresh in the recollection of many of the elders of Aberdeen, being that of the Oscar, a whale-fishing vessel, in 1813. Only two, out of a crew of forty-four men, were saved on this occasion; and, when the bodies, which were cast ashore, were carted away and laid out for recognition in the churchyard of Nigg near by, it is said that the scene was one of the most harrowing description. The sea is now rising and falling with the most gentle murmur, and all along the golden sands to the north the bathers are out in the cooling waters; while, rounding the iron Girdle to the south, sail after sail comes in sight, and the anchor is dropt to wait the tide in the quiet bay. The waves just ripple round the fatal Greyhope, and scarcely break against the pier, and all appears to be a scene of beauty and of calm; but when the rude east winds for some time prevail, it is grand to see the waters advancing in great billows, roaring like thunder, and churning themselves into yeasty foam, as they make the pier tremble to its foundations, and send their spray up in fierce jets to the sky. There is no small danger then in endeavouring to enter the harbour, which is increased by the current of the river, and not a few calamitous shipwrecks have taken place at the point of the pier. By the building of the New Breakwater, and the extension of the pier these dangers are very much reduced.

Did your time permit, a visit to the village of Torry on the other side there (which is reached by means of a ferryboat), with its two leading lights (these white towers, one beyond the other, which, kept in a straight line by vessels entering the harbour, mark out the true channel), would well repay your pains. And you would be still more gratified if you could extend your walk to the Breakwater, or go to the top of the Lighthouse tower, from which a most extensive view is to be had, and then take a saunter round the coast, which has some of the most sublime rock scenery, with the sea wailing up great lonely ravines, where the solitary heron sits watching its prey on some stone covered with brown sea-weed, or the sea-mew flies screaming from its rocky nest, or floats silently on the heaving wave.

There is a good, although I fear rather apocryphal story told in connection with the Aberdeen harbour. When the trade to the West Indies was first opened up, it is said that the Magistrates of Aberdeen were tempted to try their fortune in what promised to be such a lucrative business, and sent a vessel out there on speculation. The many anxious gazers from the Castlehill for the arrival of the *shippie* were at length rewarded, and when safely moored in the " harborie," the civic dignitaries paid it a visit. After having exhausted the occidental wonders which had been brought home, the Provost and Baillies retired to the cabin to partake of the skipper's good cheer. While thus engaged, a monkey, which was part of the importations, amused with the tie of the Provost's wig, honoured it with an occasional pull, much to the good old man's annoyance. " Odd, laddie ! " he would say aside, " ye'd better be quiet." " What's the matter with you, Provost?" said the Captain, over-hearing one of the Chief Magistrate's remonstrances. " It's that laddie o' yours," was the reply. " What laddie, Provost?" " That ane there, wi' the rough foul face, an' the sair e'en." " That's nae a laddie, Provost ; it's a monkey." " Is't, is't, " said the worthy dignitary, " Fat better kent I ? I thocht it was some o' your sugar-makers' sons come o'er to our University to get's education ! "

Before quitting the subject of the Harbour, I may briefly state that the number of vessels belonging to the port is (1886) sailing vessels, 113, tonnage 75,655; steamers, 78, tonnage 61,089 ; total vessels, 191, tonnage 136,744, exclusive of tugs and trawlers.

On our way from the New Pier to the Links, we pass the present fisher town of " Fittie," or Footdee. It consists of two large quadrangles of cottages, and other buildings, and is inhabited by a race of fisher-men and their families, who, as they seldom intermarry with any one of those who dwell beyond the precincts of their own " Squares," inherit manners and a dialect peculiar to themselves. We now pass on to the Marine Parade—an embankment, the produce of the dredgings from the harbour, which has already proceeded to a considerable distance, and may some-time be carried on to the downy heights which guard the mouth of the Don. You now see before you that recreation ground, the Links, which I pointed out to

you, and allowed Sir Samuel Forbes to expatiate upon,
when we were on the Castlehill.   Sir Samuel speaks
of the Links with a warmth of gratitude only
surpassed by that of a later writer, from whose
encomiums, however, I must omit their too bitter
rancour.   He speaks of them as—

> The wide green Links, where I have seen
>   In the brave days of old,
> The gallant Pikemen exercised,
>   And the Volunteers enrolled.
> The Locals, Towers, and Finlaysons,
>   And the rare old Battery Corps ;
> And witnessed many a grand sham fight
> From the green Broadhill's sloping height,
>   In the brave days of yore.
>
> On the days when the *five Counties* met
>   Around the grand race-stand,
> And lords and dames, the fairest
>   And noblest of the land,
> With rich and poor commingling,
>   Gay chariots, foot, and horse ;
> While the fleet racers winged their flight
>   Along the level course.
>
> And o'er the beach and waving bents,
>   Far as the golden sands,
> The City's joyous thousands thronged,
>   In merry laughing bands.
> The City's joyous thousands,
>   Clad in their best array,
> Thronged o'er the beach and sandy bents,
> And upwards where the swelling tents
>   O'erlooked the sunny bay.
>
> Where the brisk and hardy golfer still
>   Pursues the flying ball,
> And the merry cricketer's ringing shout
>   Proclaims the wicket's fall.
> Where still the bright and shining quoit
>   Flies flashing in the sun,
> And troops of children round " The Course,"
>   Their mimic races run :—

And the old men linger on the hill,
    To breathe the fresh sea gale,
And wives and mothers anxious look
    To catch the distant sail ;
Where still the honest craftsman,
    When his hard day's work he drops,
Comes to shun the tempting tap-room
    And the fatal tippling shops.
And bands of girls rejoicing,
    Come trooping o'er the hill,
As the last sound of the evening bell
    Is heard from the Banner Mill.

The Bannermill here spoken of, which I pointed out to you before, is that large manufactory beyond the gas house. It is solely devoted to the spinning of cotton yarns, and is a most excellently-conducted establishment, employing about 66 male and 579 female workers, who spin about 1,716,000 lbs. of cotton yearly. On the fine sandy beach opposite the Banner Mill there is an excellent bathing station, well patronized in the summer season, where you can from the bathing coaches enjoy a plunge in the pure salt water, or in the baths, close by, have a dip in the same element, either hot or cold. Rounding the corner of the Bannermill at Constitution Street, we come upon the Granite Polishing Works of M'Donald & Co., Limited. Here the Duke of Gordon's Monument in Castle Street was cut, after a model by Campbell of London, and here the most obdurate granite is polished to a glassy brightness and smoothness. A little farther up, on the opposite side of the street, after having crossed by a bridge the Great North of Scotland Railway, are the Roman Catholic Schools, with their motto on the front, " Religioni et Bonis Moribus." The statute in the niche is that of the late Rev. Charles Gordon, who, as the inscription intimates, was for sixty-two years priest of this community in Aberdeen, and died in 1855, at the age of eighty-three years. The statue is cut from a model by our townsman, the late Mr. Alexander Brodie. Passing up Park and Justice Streets, you again reach Castle Street.

GEORGE STREET.

It were a pity that any of our readers should ever be as far north as the city of Aberdeen, and let so good an opportunity slip without gratifying themselves by a visit to the Brig o' Balgownie. Not but that the "Granite City" would amply repay a visit, even although this *lion* should be missed ; but there are so many literary and other associations connected with it and the surrounding scenes, and they possess besides so many natural attractions, that, to use the common hyperbole, if the tourist has not seen these, he has seen nothing.

Starting again from Market Street, therefore, we will now proceed to Old Aberdeen. George Street, along which we are walking, is another of the improved entrances to the town—the former entrance in this direction from the North being along the narrow and tortuous Gallowgate. Turning off from George Street at the Loch-e'e, as it is called, we reach Loch Street, which derives its name from a large marsh that covered all the low grounds from the bottom of the hill on which the Gallowgate stands, as far as the back of Gordon's College and the base of Woolmanhill. The grounds reclaimed from the loch still retain the name of the Lochlands, and an old Church in George Street was known amongst the old folks in Aberdeen as the Loch Kirk. Long after the loch was reduced to less extensive dimensions, it used to flow, or rather stagnate, along this street which is now called Loch Street, being then only a narrow passage along the margin of the filthy stream, called the Loch-side. You may observe that the street has all the sinuosities of a stream, the latter having given shape to the former. St. Paul's Street, by which we reach the Gallowgate, is a recently opened street, and superseded the last of the old vennels, hence called emphatically *The* Vennel. It contains two Churches, Mr. Dickie's (U. P.), Mr. Brown's (E. U.), and one of the Board Schools. St. Paul's Episcopal Chapel, re-built a few years ago, is also close by; the old church was erected in 1721, for the administration of the ordinances of religion according to the forms of the Church of England, and it gave its name to the street. The Gallowgate, where we now are, was once the principal entrance to the town from the North. It has still a rather antiquated air about it, although the bulk of the houses are of recent origin—Mar's or the Auld Castle, as it has long been called, near the top of Innes Street, being the most ancient building it contains. Near this spot the Causey Port stood; and we are told that, as far back as 1518, it was considered ancient. No trace, however, of it now remains. Emerging from the Gallowgate at Causewayend, Nelson Street crosses over to King Street. In this street, the Poor-house for the City Parish of St. Nicholas stands. It is a very handsome building in the Elizabethan style, capable of accommodating 590 inmates, and is provided with every comfort and convenience.

Opposite the east end of the Poor-house, that low building on the eminence betwixt you and the sea, is the old Powder Magazine. The height on which it is built is called the Gallowhill, from its having been at one time the place where the gibbet stood; and this circumstance also gives its name to the Gallowgate, which we have just left, as one of the ways to said gallows. It is believed, also, that ancient courts of

justice were held on this hill, as the place where such
courts were held, and the place where their decrees
were carried into effect, were often identical. So late
as 1752, persons were hung in chains here, and later
still, it was the place of sepulture for those executed
in Castle Street. This hill overlooks Trinity Cemetery,
laid out a few years ago, the property of the Incorporated Trades.

This neat building in King Street Road, nearly
opposite Nelson Street, is the Boys' and Girls'
Hospital. Its objects are the maintenance and edu-
cation of poor children of the parish of St. Nicholas.
There are at present 100 inmates in the institution.
Close by here is also another of the Board Schools.

We can return from King Street Road to the
Spittal by Love Lane, along the side of this huge pile,
the Militia Barracks. Here of old stood the Leper
House of Aberdeen. The existence of this hospital
indicates, what history also bears out, that this loath-
some disease, now almost unknown in Europe, was
once common among us. " In the tenth and eleventh
centuries (says Brown), this terrible distemper was
common in Europe, introduced, I suppose, by the
Arabs and Moors ; and it is said there were about
15,000, or rather, according to Matthew Paris, 9000
hospitals for lepers." In Walter Cullen's " Bookes of
Baptisme, Marriage, and Buriall," we find the following
entry :—" Ane lipar boy, in the Lipar Howiss of
Aberdeen, departitt the xviii day July, 1589 years."
In 1592, James VI. granted to the house one *peat* from
every load exposed for sale either in Aberdeen or the
Old Town, because the inmates were constrained in
winter, "for halding in of their lyves, to retein themselfes
to the townis amangist clene persounes throw the
vehementis of the cauld, quherthrow they perrell the
health of money clene folkis." On the 13th May, 1604,

the kirk-session ordained "Helene Smyth, ane puir woman, infectit with leprosie, to be put in the Hospitall appoyntit for keeping and haulding of lipper folkis betwixt the townis ; and the keyis of the said hospital to be deliverit to hir." From this it would appear that she was then the only inmate ; and we know that, in 1661, both the Leper House and a Chapel connected with it, dedicated to St. Anne, " quhom (says Gordon) the papists account patroness of the lepers," were both gone into decay, " and now scarcelie (he adds) is the name known to many."

Proceeding onward, the Spittal Burying-ground is passed on the right, and the Snow Churchyard on the left. The former of these is now a handsome and extensive cemetery, the original part of it occupying the site of an hospital founded by Matthew Kyninmundie, Bishop of Aberdeen, in the reign of William the Lion. "It was dedicated (says Kennedy) to 'saint Peter, the chief of the apostles :' and designed for the reception and support of indigent and infirm persons, who might resort to it." Besides these charitable purposes, the institution was intended for the celebration of masses for the soul of King William, and of his ancestors and successors, as well as for the soul of the founder, according to the custom of the age. No vestiges of the ancient buildings now remain. The Snow Churchyard, now used as a place of sepulture by a few Roman Catholic families, once surrounded a church founded by Bishop Elphinstone, about the year 1497, and dedicated to *Maria ad nives*.

KING'S COLLEGE.

We are now in full view of the beautiful ancient structure of King's College, with its sequestered court, its buttressed walls, and great tower, rising in form of an imperial crown, venerable and hoary, to the quiet sky. King's College is now merged in the University of Aberdeen. This College was founded by William Elphinstone, Bishop of Aberdeen, in the year 1500, and dedicated to the Virgin Mary. Its most ancient portion now standing is the chapel which forms the north side of the quadrangle. In its pristine state this must have been a beautiful edifice.

KING'S COLLEGE.

The celebrated Hector Boece, the first Principal of the College, thus speaks of its Chapel :—" In it (the College) is a church of Polished hewn stone, with windows, ceilings, seats for the priests, and benches for the boys, in a most magnificent style ; marble alters and images of the saints ; pictures, statues, painting and gilding, brazen chairs, hangings and carpets. The furniture for sacred occasions is of gold tissue, fifteen crosses, and chasubles, twenty-eight mantles of coarse cloth, all embroidered at the sides with the figures of the saints, in gold and purple, and other colours ; seven of fine linen, adorned with palm branches, and the borders embroidered with stars of gold ; twenty of linen, with palm branches and waves, for the boys. Besides these, many others of linen and scarlet for daily use ; a crucifix, two candle-sticks, two censers, an incense box, six phials, eight chalices, a textuary, two pixes in which to expose the host, a third, two cubits high of most curious workmanship, a bason, a vessel for the font, a holy-water pot, with a sprinkler, all of gold and silver ; several altar cloths of the finest linen, embroidered with gold, and flowers of various colours. A chest of cypress wood elegantly set with pearls and jewels, in which the reliques of the saints are lodged in gold and silver. The steeple is of great height, surrounded by stone-work, arched in form of an imperial crown over the leaded roof, and containing thirteen bells of most melodious sound."

Bishop Elphinstone did not long survive the foundation of the College, having died at Edinburgh in 1514, at the age of seventy-seven. His remains were brought to Aberdeen and interred before the high altar of the chapel here. This chapel is considered one of the finest antique remains in the country, the interior yet exhibiting a great deal of its " ancient braverye," as Gordon calls it, having its prebends' stalls of black carved oak still standing entire. " Here," Gordon continues, " Wm. Elphingstoune lyes buryed, his tombestone of black towtch stone ; the upper pairt upheld of old by thretteine statues of brasse ; his statue of brass laying betuixt the two stons. All thes," he goes on, however, in a lamenting tone, "robbed and sold long agoe."

Part of the ancient Chapel was converted into a Library, which contained 25,000 volumes. A new Library, however, has recently been built, extending eastward ; the south side of the College has been re-built, and the Chapel restored as far as possible to its pristine condition.

As the College session ends in April, the courtyard here, lately swept by the sable robes of the Professors, and enlivened by the scarlet gowns of the students, is now silent and empty; and indeed the whole *Aulton* has rather a dejected and deserted-like air, compared with what it has when hundreds of students are passing to and fro in the old fashioned streets.

Proceeding along High Street, and passing the Free Church on our left, we come to the Town-house— that building with the small spire and clock, which fills the angle formed by the junction of the Chanonry and Don Street.   Above the entrance, you observe the Town's Arms—a pot with lilies, with three salmon crossing fretwise below.   The lilies ("which, by their whiteness, are an emblem of chastity") indicate that the town was under the patronage of the Virgin Mary, and the salmon cannot be considered out of place in the arms of a burgh which, no doubt, shared in the celebrity that gained for its neighbour, New Aberdeen, the expression of Buchanan, "*piscatu salmon um nobilis.*"   The motto, "Concordia res parvæ crescunt," may be considered as an amplification of our own more pithy *cri de guerre*, BON-ACCORD.   In the open space before the Town-house stood the ancient Market Cross, and a few paces in the Chanonry there is a garden enclosed by a high wall, and yet known as Cluny's Garden, which marks the spot where the residence of Sir Alexander Gordon of Cluny stood. Cluny's Port had the following incription :

> Hac ne vade via, nisi dixeris, Ave Maria ;
> Invenies veniam sic salutando Mariam ;

or,

> Do not enter by this way,
> Save you *Ave Mary* say ;
> But, saluting in this strain,
> You indulgence shall obtain !

The parson of Rothiemay says that this house ("Clunie's lodgings") was, in 1662, "enlarged by the additione of a brave gallerie, adorned with varietie of paynting, as also with a gairding, the goodlist and the greatest in Aberdeen." Close by Cluny's lodgings stood the Chanonry Port, which divided the ecclesiastical from the civic part of the town.

Gordon mentions, when speaking of the lodgings of "the Chanons who made up the Chapter of Aberdeen," which were all close by here, and which gave its name to the Chanonry, that "ane of this for many yeires past was infested by evill spirits;" and, before leaving the civic part of the town, I will repeat to you another legend of the Aulton which I have heard—

AH me! when we think on the follies and crime
That *have* been, and *will* be, committed in time,
We can't but confess, though perhaps 'gainst our will,
That there's no doubt but man has a proneness to ill—
A certain untameable, mad inclination,
Whether urged by desire or by potent temptation,
To leave all undone what he ought to pursue,
And what he ought not, that as madly to do;
In short, a desire (the expression's scarce civil,
But true to the letter) to go to the d——l!

But here I'd remark (and I beg leave to state
That it's pat to the story I mean to relate)
That if man, though aware of the sin and the woe,
Has a morbid desire to the d——l to go,
The d——l—(I hate any story to slim)—
Desires just as strongly to come unto him.
And he comes in all shapes, too—an angel of light,
With specious temptations the soul to invite—
Or a black burly fiend, with a sneer and a frown,
To goad him to evil, and laugh when he's gone.

If you've mosses to cross when out drinking and bantering,
He'll meet you in semblance of "Jock o' the Lantern;"

Or a river to ford when you're jolly—Heaven help you !
He'll drown you in shape of a huge water kelpie ;
And still worse and worse, 'tis by no means uncommon
To tempt you in shape of a beautiful woman—

As the clergyman said
Who had three times been wed

(His first wife had cash, and his second had beauty,
And the third, if she knew it, would not do her duty),
" I have three times been wed, nor mean aught that's uncivil,
But I've married the *world*, the *flesh*, and the *d——l !* "
But let's on to our tale.   When the great Reformation
Like fierce raging torrent had swept o'er the nation,
And Popery and Prelacy sung very small—
For Kirk and the Covenant crow'd over all—
There lived in the High Street of Old Aberdeen
(Which long has been famed for its *beets* and its *sheen*)
A tailor, who fitted his patrons so well,
That in his full pride he was oft heard to tell,
Although nowise profane, and as far from uncivil,
That he thought he'd make clothes that would fit e'en the d—l.
'Twas as good as a challenge—the fiend took it so,
As I mean, with your leave, in the sequel to show.

One sweet summer eve, as the gloaming was sinking,
And behind Cairncry the bright sunset was blinking,
A carle, whose demeanour no one could find fault in,
Came pacing deliberate through Spittal and Aulton.
Thus stepping along in a sauntering mood,
He had rounded Love Lane, where the Leper-house stood,
The Hospital passed with a step staid and slow,
And the shrine of our Lady the Saint of the Snow,
While bright in the sunset the College looked down,
With its tower and its turrets, its cross and its crown ;
Still onward he passed, then paused with a shrug
By a signboard emblazon'd with lilies and jug—
'Twas the shop of our tailor, whose success to aid,
The arms of the town on his signboard displayed.
In entered the stranger.   Quo' snip, "Sir, your pleasure ? "
" For a whole suit of black, sir, I want you to measure,
And as time is to me of the greatest avail,
I must have it on Saturday night without fail ;
With regard to the fit, you will see that I love
My garments to lie to my frame like a glove."

Said the tailor, in a manner complacent and civil,
" I have often made boast I could fit e'en the d——l,
So your worship I think I will suit to a T ; "
With significant look, said the stranger, " We'll see ! "

Down bustles the tailor with papers and scissors,
And the length and the girth of the gentleman measures ;
While the better to aid him his measures to handle,
His sister stood by kindly holding the candle,
Which do what she might would now flare and now flutter,
Burn blue as 'twere brimstone, spit sparkles, and splutter,
Nor marvel—for just as the stranger departed,
Red flames from his eyes unmistakably darted,
And neither the sister nor tailor could fail
To catch a short glimpse of the cloven feet and tail.
In fact 'twas the d——l, who wanted to test
The boast which the tailor so oft had expressed,
And, to cover his sins, thought he sometimes might lack,
Like a great many more—just a good suit of black.
What was now to be done?   The tailor was plighted,
And the orders were such as were not to be slighted ;
For the tailor well knew that he could not afford,
When pledged to the d——l, to not keep his word.

Many plans were discussed, but at length in the end,
The tailor resolved for his parson to send ;
The minister came—'twas the famed Andrew Cant,
Whose virtues from me no eulogium can want ;
And after the sin in strong language declaring
Of courting the d——l by boasting and swearing,
He counsell'd the tailor his bargain to keep,
Lest the fruit of his sin to his cost he might reap ;
" And see ye be prayerful, and humble, and steady—
To the hour and the minute the clothes have them ready,
And mind to abstain from the vice of your trade,
Nor *cabbage* one *clipping*, nor button nor thread ;
And when the fiend offers reward for your labour,
As you'd shrink from the stab of a sword or a sabre,
Avoid it, reject it, for mark what I tell—
'Twill be but the *arles* of service in hell ! "

As duly as Saturday evening came round,
In the shop of our tailor the stranger was found.
The clothes were put on, and they fitted him well—
In fact, it is said, the old gent was a swell—
So drawing his purse with a hearty good will,

F

He questioned the tailor how much was his bill ;
But, judge his surprise, when the tailor replied
That *gentles like him* he for nothing supplied !
He urged and he argued in manner quite able,
And he flung the gold temptingly down on the table ;
They were sound ringing coins—why this idle palaver ?
The tailor's resolves were beginning to waver—
When, just as he stretched out his hand for the pay,
In burst the fierce parson in wrath and dismay—
" Avoid thee, foul fiend ! would'st thou venture to lure
To perdition the souls of my own very cure,
With thy smooth specious words, and thy gold's tempting glow--
Avaunt to thy home of dark horror and woe ! "
The fiend turned him round with a frown and a sneer,
And exclaimed in cool bitterness, " Andrew ! you here ?
It is strange (and his voice grew malignant and hollow)
That wherever I go *you* are certain to follow !
It shall not be my blame (and he pointed below)
If it do not continue to always be so."
And darting a glance of infernal-like ire,
He vanished away in a great globe of fire !
Just then a blythe party was crossing the Don,
From sweet Kettock's Mills o'er to steep Tillydron,
When a black cloud stoop'd suddenly down on the river,
And the trees, without wind, 'gan to tremble and shiver,
And from the black cloud shot a hand arm'd with slaughter,
And sunk the frail bark in the midst of the water.
O, then the fierce thunder in terror broke out,
The wild flaring lightning danced madly about,
And 'mid the loud wind and the tempest's dark frown,
The great eastern tower of St. Machar's fell down,*
Spreading ruin and woe through the echoing pile ;
While fiends rode the tempest through transept and aisle,
And for one suffered hour wrought all ill and disaster,
For ire that a priest should have baffled their master !

Coming along the Chanonry, this neat little building, which you see forming three sides of a square, is Mitchell's Hospital. It was founded by David Mitchell, Esq., of Hollowaydown, in the county of Essex, a native of Old Aberdeen, for the maintenance

---

* See quotations from Gordon page 84.

of five widows and five unmarried daughters of merchant or trade burgesses, or of gentlemen connected with the town. You may see the old ladies plying their busy knitting wires, as they sit enjoying the fair sunshine.

OLD MACHAR CATHEDRAL.

This grey pile now before us, with the great western window, and the twin towers surmounting it, is the Cathedral of St. Machar. Here John Barbour, author of the well-known and valuable metrical history of "The Bruce," was Archdeacon. The Cathedral was begun to be built upon the site of the old church about the year 1378, by Bishop Alexander Kyninmundie, and not finished until about the year 1552, by Bishop Gavin Dunbar. "He also ceiled the nave of curious workmanship, which may vie with anything of the kind in Scotland. It consists of three compartments of square panels, joining at the opposite angular points. On these panels are painted the arms and titles of the princes, nobles, and prelates, who contributed towards the expense of the building. Along the top of the walls are also inscribed the

names of the successive sovereigns from Malcolm II.
to Queen Mary, on the south side ; also of the several
bishops from Nectanus to William Gordon, the last
Roman Catholic Prelate, on the north side., Gordon
says—

> Nor was the furnitur of the church less costlie than the
> church itselff, having crucifixes, chaleses, and uther utensils, all
> made of silver, some of thame of pure gold, set with many
> great and precious stones. The weight of all this was verie
> great ; and then for the apperrell usit by the popish bischops
> and churchmen, they wer all ather of silk or velvett, or
> broydered with gold or silver, and thes lykewayes in great
> varietie. It will hardlie be believed what the weght of the
> plaite amounted to, wer it not that ane old MS. yit extant,
> which conteens the particular accompt of all that belongit to
> that church, putts it out of all doubt.

One of these utensils is described as " one
eucharist of silver gilt, in the form of a castle, with a
peryl stone set in it, and, on the top, a jewel of gold,
with the image of devotion."   Gordon adds—

> To this church lykewayes belonged a bibliotheck ; bot about
> the year 1560 all wes taken away, or destroyed, or embaseled ;
> the bibliothec then burned, and no book spared, wher any reid
> letter wes to be seene. The spire of the great steeple wes then
> uncovered, as the church was, and not many yeers afterwards,
> was overthrowne by the violence of a great storme of wind.

Wandering about this ancient and massive pile,
observing its empty niches, and the other tokens of its
former grandeur, the admirer of art will be ready to
condemn the Reformers for sweeping the statuary
away, and sympathize with Clerk Spalding's account of
their spoliations, as if mortal pangs had been inflicted
by them in their zeal against statues or carvings, or
anything else that they thought " smacked of
Poperie."   " They came all (says he) riding up to
the gate of St. Machar's Kirk, ordained our blessed
Lord Jesus Christ his arms to be cut out of the fore

front of the pulpit thereof, and to take down the portraiture of the blessed Virgin Mary and our Saviour in her arms, that had stood since the up-putting thereof, in curious work, under the ceiling at the west end of the pend whereon the great steeple stands unmoved till now ; and besides, where there were any crucifixes set in glass windows, those they caused pull out in honest men's houses. They caused a mason strike out Christ's arms in hewn rock, on each end of Bishop Gavin Dunbar's tomb, and siclike chizel out the name of Jesus, drawn cypher ways, out of the timber wall on the foreside of Machar's aisle, anent the consistory door."

In the "View of the Diocese of Aberdeen" (1732), it is said that "this Cathedral had the privilege of a sanctuary, or girth, and had a girth-cross, on the Bishop's dovecot-green, which was a sure refuge for manslayers, or such as had committed slaughter by pure accident and misfortune, without any malice or design."

At the east end of the present church you can see the pillars and one of the arches which supported the great eastern tower, and the space covered by the Transept and Choir may yet be easily traced—the walls of the Transept, in fact, though only now of a few feet in height, are still almost entire.

I may just mention, in connection with the church in more modern times, that, in 1749, a boy of the name of William Martin was convicted of the crime of breaking into the poor's box and stealing its contents, and that he was detected from the circumstance that, when playing at cards with his comrades, during the Christmas holidays, he had nothing to lay down as stakes but "boddles, doits, farthings, and bad halfpence," which gives but a low estimate of our forefathers' liberality to the poor, although the meanness of casting "bad halfpence" into voluntary collections is not yet unknown. And that in 1753, Gideon Duncan, a weaver in Old Aberdeen, was fined for disturbing the congregation by singing out of time. About that period a great movement for the improvement of psalmody took place, and Gideon was one of the choir appointed in consequence of that movement. Having fallen out, however, with the Professor of Humanity—one of the patrons of the improved system—Gideon joined with some others and resolved to confound the scientific singers and mar the whole harmony, by singing so slow that the choir would be done with the verse before the others had got half over it. The result was, that a tumult was created in the Church, and Gideon Duncan was fined in the sum of fifty pounds Scots for his offence.

Gordon, to whom we are so much indebted for the description of the former aspect of this spot, goes on—

Upon the west end of Machar Church, in the street interjected, stands the hospitall, founded by B. Gavin Dunbar for the maintenance of 12 poore men ; the revenues thereoff much diminished in our dayes ; and the old men quho live ther are little better than beggars. The Bischope of Aberdeins pallace of old closit up a syde of the churchyarde. It was large and fair ; its buildings and gardings, and its quholl circuite, all enclosite with a strong wall divyding it from the neighbour buildings. B. Alexander Kininmonth builded it ; but presentlie, except the garding, ther scaircе remayns one stone of it untaken away. Anno 1639, B. Adame Ballandine, then bischope of Aberdeen, wes glade to abandone it, and leave it as a prey to the Covenantours soldiers, quho at that tyme rifled and spoyled it, leaving nothing but bare walls. Anno 1655, the Englishes took away the stones of the walls, having compelled all the neighbouring shyres for to transport them to the Castlehill of New Aberdeine. The rubbish or stones which they left behind theme wer caryed doune to the King's College, anno 1657, to ther new worke. Nixt to the Bischopes hous stood the chapplan's chambers, so called of old. Thes doe enclose a large squair court, now in pairt ruined. A pairt of that which remayne ther wes bought in our tyme by D. Johne Forbes of Corse ; and albeit he was thrust out of his place by the Covenanters in anno 1640, yet did he mortifie his hous ther to such as should be professors of divinity after him, who keep it as yit.

The Cathedral has recently been restored by the removal of the galleries, and the plaster which con-cealed the original stone work. The east end, which, since the falling of the middle tower, and the destruction of transept and choir, had until lately a very patched up appearance, has now been fittingly closed in by a wall and large, fine window, in keeping with the other parts of the building. The great western window with its seven long lights has been fitted with designs in stained glass ; and the others may continue to receive further decoration in this way if the good example of some private citizens be followed, there being already four memorial windows put up in the side aisles, one being in commemoration of three native artists of celebrity—Jameson, Dyce, and Philip.

The famous old Brig o' Balgownie, which we are now¹ approaching,· is a perfect Gothic arch over the river Don, about a mile from the sea ; it is strong both by art and nature, being founded on a rock on each side. There is some diversity of opinion with regard to the builder of this fine old structure. Some ascribe it to Henry Le Cheyne, Bishop of Aberdeen in the time of King Robert the Bruce, but others with greater probability, to that monarch himself, to whom, during his struggles for Scottish independence, the inhabitants of Aberdeen had given the most decided proofs of their loyalty and attachment. In 1605, Sir Alexander Hay mortified a small property for the repair and · preservation of this structure, which has accumulated to a vast sum, notwithstanding that

£14,000 of it was expended in building a new bridge
about half a mile nearer the sea.   In his deed of
mortification, he states, on the authority of certain
annals, that the bridge was erected by the order and
at the expense of The Bruce.

But see! here is the Brig o' Balgownie, and we are
sure you will confess that a sweeter scene you never
looked upon.   See how quietly the water glides
through the deep salmon pool, and how the trees on
the high precipitous northern bank pour down a very
cataract of leaves, as it were, upon the stream below;
while the rocks—here grey with lichen, there green
with ivy—seem ever to contemplate their fairy
reflection in the watery mirror,

> As if they slept beneath the wave,
> Secure from trouble, toil, and care,
> A world than earthly world more fair!

Here Byron says he used often to lean with such
delight when a boy, that the recollections of it in after
years was a source of infinite pleasure to him.   "My
heart flies to my head," he says,

> As "auld langsyne" brings Scotland, one and all,
>   Scotch plaids, Scotch snoods, the blue hills and clear streams,
> The Dee, the Don, Balgownie's brig's black wall,
>   All my boy feelings, all my gentler dreams
> Of what I then dreamt, clothed in their own pall,
>   Like Banquo's offspring; floating past me seems
> My childhood in this childishness of mine:
>   I care not—'tis a glimpse of "auld langsyne."

And he adds in a note, "The brig o' Don, near the
'auld toun' of Aberdeen, with its one arch and its
black salmon stream below, is in my memory as
yesterday.   I still remember, though perhaps I may
misquote the awful proverb which made me pause to
cross it, and yet lean over it with a childish delight,
being an only son, at least by the mother's side.   The

saying as recollected by me was this, but I have never heard or seen it since I was nine years of age :—

> Brig o' Balgownie, wight's your wa',
> Wi' a wife's ae son, and a mare's ae foal,
> Down ye shall fa' ! "

Although this prophecy is ascribed to Thomas the Rhymer, yet the strength of the "auld brig" bids fair to avert its doom for many a day ; so that it might say to its modern neighbour, as Burns makes the auld brig of Ayr say to the new—

> I'll be a brig when ye're a shapeless cairn.

To those whose memories can go a little while back there is, however, one drawback to the pleasure of visiting the Brig o' Balgownie, and that is the shutting up, by a neighbouring proprietor, of a pathway along the south bank of the river, a little above the bridge, from which a fine view was to be obtained of this romantic spot. We have mentioned Byron's partiality to this scene ; and there is nothing more likely than that the good Bishop William Elphinstone, the "man of Ross" of the "Aulton ;" the credulous but erudite Hector Bœce ; the amiable Henry Scougal, author of the "Life of God in the Soul of Man ;" and a host of other ecclesiastics of the olden time, whose memories throw a halo around this locality, issuing from the "watergate" of the bishop's palace, "leading to the Don and the Bow-butts," have often perambulated this path, which is now no longer patent to the public. Nay, who knows but that the splendid apostrophe to freedom, which occurs in Barbour's Bruce, after the description of the slavery to which Scotland had been reduced by Edward, was composed while the good archdeacon wandered or reclined on this very spot :—

A ! fredome is a nobill thing !
Fredome mayks man to haiff liking ;
Fredome all solace to man giffs ;
IIe levys at ease, that freely levys !
A noble hart may haiff nane ease.
Na ellys nocht that may him plese.
Gyff fredome failyhe ; for free liking
Is yarnyt our all othir thing.
Na he, that aye has levyt fre,
May nocht knaw weill the propyrte,
The angyr, na the wrechyt dome,
That is cowplyt to foule thyrldome,
Bot gyff he had assayit it,
Than all perquer he suld it wyt ;
And suld think fredome mair to pryse
Than all the gold in warld that is.

Truly we envy not the man who could lock up from
his fellow-men a scene which might suggest such a
host of fine remembrances ! We think that there has
been too much supineness on the part of the Aberdonians on this point ; for we should ever regard the
enjoyment of beautiful scenery, and the indulgence of
sweet reminiscences—like freedom—as

Mair to pryse
Than all the gold in warld that is.

The obstruction to the ancient pathway alluded to
compels us to retrace our steps by Seaton Dykes to
the Cathedral, taking the road leading from the north-
west corner of which we reach Tillydrone—that
conical hill with the trees planted on it. Tillydron
was long considered an artificially constructed hill, but
the theory of Dr. Davidson of Inverurie in regard to
a similar mound (the Bass) there, may be applicable
to this burrow, viz : that it is the deposit of water
currents when the land and waters were at other levels
than they are now. Such being its natural construction,
it was perhaps afterwards used as one of the moothills
where the courts and assemblies of the people were

held, and possibly also (as in the case of the Gallow-hill) where the decrees of justice were carried into effect. From the top of Tillydron an excellent view may be obtained of the windings of the Don, and of the manufactories which stud its banks. First among these are the woollen mills known as Gordon's Mills. Beyond these are Grandholm Works, where Messrs. J. & J. Crombie manufacture winceys, cloths, and tweeds, equal, if not superior, to any in the trade—a large quantity going to London and the other southern markets. The village which lies along the heights, with the dome-like church tower rising out among the clustering roofs, is called Woodside, and is chiefly dependent upon the manufactories I have mentioned, and upon the granite quarries called the Dancing Cairns—whose great mounds of *debris* you can see. This village may be said to stretch for several miles along the Inverurie and Oldmeldrum turnpike roads, under the various names of Cotton, Woodside, Auch-mull, Sclattie, and Stoneywood. By taking this foot-path, we pass the Hermitage which ornaments the grounds of Powis, and crossing above the Great North of Scotland Railway, near the Kittybrewster Station, reach the line of road that leads to Aberdeen either by Broadford or Causewayend. Passing along North Broadford, that large manufactory which you see on the right is the flaxmills of Messrs. Richards & Co., the most extensive of all our public works. In Hutcheon Street, on your left, Messrs. Stewart's large comb manufactory is situated, which, together with the manufactories for flax, jute, paper, cotton, and wool, and the ship-building yards, gives employment to the bulk of our population.

Aberdeen, not being confined to any special industry like some towns, without any great flashes of com-mercial activity, or on the other hand notable depressions, has gone on steadily increasing in population, wealth, and importance for many years. It has two daily newspapers, from the establishments of each of which three editions of evening papers are issued ; and each publish a weekly compendium. There is an advertising paper, with a large guaranteed gratis circulation, published twice a week. In addition to these there are two weekly Scotch newspapers which publish Aberdeen editions, and two illustrated weeklies devoted to the gossipy and comic view of matters. One of these, the *Bon-Accord*, while we write, is only in its infancy of renewed life, the other, the *Northern Figaro*, has reached its eighty-second number. The oldest of these papers, the *Journal*, begun in 1746, was the first Scotch newspaper published north of Edinburgh.

The Registrar's returns show Aberdeen to be the healthiest of any of the large towns in Scotland. The sewerage is effective, and there is abundant supply of pure and excellent water, which flows by gravitation from an intake from the river Dee at Cairnton, about $21\frac{1}{2}$ miles from the City.

It has been presumed, in the foregoing, that the progress through the City and suburbs was being made on foot. Where necessary, however, the most of the places of interest are perfectly accessible by carriage. Tramways, also, have been established, going from the western suburb of Queen's Cross to the Cattle Market, King Street, in almost the extreme north-east of the City ; there are also branches to Woodside, a northern suburb, and to Bloomfield, in the south-west, not far from the Duthie Park. There are also omnibusses run to suburban parts not yet overtaken by the tramways, the local time tables giving all information as to the hours of starting for these various conveyances.

THE PARKS.

For many years there were, on the Low Stocket Road, a series of grass parks belonging to the Corporation, which were let to graziers. It was proposed that these should be joined into one, and laid out as a public park for the recreation of the inhabitants. This good purpose was effected with great taste, at considerable cost. There were a good many fine old trees on the original grounds; these were carefully preserved, and the land having been long in grass, the Victoria Park, as it is called, very soon assumed a mature appearance. The borders are tastefully laid out in flower-plots, and the granite merchants in town jointly contributed a large and elegant fountain for the adornment of the place. This park, which will well repay a visit, can be reached by a 'bus leaving the corner of King Street every half-hour for Rosemount and Richmond Hill.

The Duthie Park lies on the banks of the river Dee. It is a gift to the inhabitants by the late Miss Duthie of Ruthrieston. It has an area of forty-four acres of pleasantly undulating ground, in some parts well wooded, and sloping down to the river, with a direct southern exposure. It has shady walks and sunny; lakes, cascades and fountains; rockeries and rooteries; cricket and croquet grounds; and a large artificial mound, from the top of which a fine view is to be had of the surrounding scenery. Before this little volume is long in the hands of the public this park will be adorned by a colossal statue, in bronze, of Sir William Wallace, by William Grant Stevenson, A.R.S.A., of Edinburgh. The statue, now being cast, is sixteen feet in height, and is the largest and most

important figure yet erected in Scotland.   It is the gift
of the late Mr. John Steill, of Edinburgh.   This park
was opened with royal honours on the 27th September,
1883, the Princess Beatrice taking the chief part in the
ceremony.   There was a great procession of the inhabitants to the park in the forenoon, and at night the
town was illuminated.   This park can be nearly
reached by the Bloomfield branch of the tramway,
but there will soon be a fine drive from the town along
the bank of the river to its southern gate.   I have
already mentioned the great free unrestrained
recreation ground, the Links, by the side of the sea,
and the Union Terrace Gardens.   These last are a
fine cool resting place for the visitor, and being almost
in the heart of the town, and thus always easy of
access, are much used and appreciated.

Having now again reached Union Street, our
perambulations of Aberdeen may be said to be completed.   I have not, to be sure, led you into every
hole and corner of it, but I do not think there is anything of interest or of beauty which we have missed ;
and I trust you have been gratified by your visit.
The inhabitants of Aberdeen are rather proud of
their city, and, like a true Aberdonian, I cannot but
say that I participate in this feeling.   " The city of
Aberdeen "—says Gordon—

Exceeds not onlie the rest of the touns of the north of
Scotland, bot lykewayes any citie quhatsumevr of that same
latitude, for greatnes, bewtie, and frequencie of trading . . . . .
The air is temperate and healthful about it ; and it may be that
the citizens owe the acutenes of their witts therunto, and ther
civil inclinations, the lyke not easie to be fund under so norther-
lie climats, damped for the most pairt with the air of a grosse
consistance.   However, it is sure that Aberdeen is reputed (and
not without just cause) the seminarie of so many quho ather are
or have been remarkable for wisdom, learning, gallantrie, breeding, and civill conversatione.

" You cannot deny, but acknowledge "—says another writer about the same period—

That Aberdeen is sweetly situated, and under the government of well-regulated magistrates : No complaint of poverty, nor luxurious superfluities ; where the houses are filled with hospitality, not with profaneness ; their streets and alleys cleanly swept and paved, and their church and state-houses very curiously kept, after the best methods of the Scottish mode.

"Having spoken of the men "—says Sir Samuel Forbes, already quoted—

It would be a crime not to name the gentler sex. They brought us into the world, and carefully and kindly nourished us. The women of this town are virtuous, sober, frugal, and industrious, never going abroad, but to perform the offices of benignity and friendship ; never seen from the windows ; still employing themselves diligently, about the needs of the family. And it is but just to say of them, that they deserve to be praised for much more than the only virtue which Anacreon ascribes to the women of his town, to wit, beauty :

> For woman she had nought besides.
> What does she give ? Beauty.

They have also modesty, chastity, piety, without which beauty becomes the object of contempt, and not a title of praise ; and thus, since all kind of virtue is *a la mode* here amongst the women, they who, in this city, are not virtuous, are really out of fashion.

Thus do we speak of our town, and thus do we think it deserves to be spoken of. I will conclude with the following, which I have written as expressing the feelings of a native on his return to the place of his birth, and also as an epitome of what is to be seen in and about Aberdeen.

Aberdeen Revisited.

> Man ! I was back to Aberdeen,
> I hadna been for years before.
> It made my heart as fresh and green
> As in the laddie days o' yore.

I frolic'd on as I'd been daft,
   'Mang scenes I lang hae lov'd and kent ;
And sometimes grat, and sometimes laugh'd,
   As ilka mood gat willing vent.

I saw the glad, green, gushing wave,
   Come lapping up the *new* New Pier,
And there sang out a patriot stave,
   Wi' nane but the sea-goos to hear.

My heart lap like the white sea jaw
   That dashed in the Breakwater's face,
Which stretched far out its guardian paw,
   Atween me and the Girdleness.

I ran and row'd on the green Links ;
   Wrote verses on the gowden sands ;
Catch'd bandies in the silver trinks,
   That trickle down frae Powis lands.

I sat upon the benty beach
   And gazed across the morning sea ;
Ilk amber wavelet broke in speech
   And whispered " Cassie " unto me.

I wandered by the mouth o' Don
   Beside its lone, black, tangled piles—
'Twas Ythan that I thought upon
   And silver salmon limn'd by Giles.

I glowr'd on Byron's salmon pool
   Beside Balgownie's Brig that sleeps,
And roar'd—the auld light-hearted fool !
   To see the trouts' and grilses' leaps.

The trees hung down wi' verdant gleam
   Aroun' the auld rock's haffits grey,
And watched their likeness in the stream,
   As they have watched for mony a day.

Syne cam' I by the hoary Pile
   That lifts aloft its sister towers,
And sees a' summer's beauties smile
   On Tillydron, and Seaton's bowers.

Oh, mony thanks to generous hearts,
   And thanks to mony a tastefu' brain,
The grey auld Pile's majestic pairts
   Have got some *braverie* back again !

The grand, tall, wastlin' window's filled
    Wi' pictured glass in glorious gleams !
To see't—the very soul is thrill'd,
    As by the joy o' wizard dreams.

And roun' and roun', on ilka side,
    Are windows stained in fair device,
And *ane* you're sure to mark wi' pride,
    To Philip, Jameson, and to Dyce.

Now the grey College' grand auld croon
    You see between you and the lift,
And inly thank the powers aboon
    For such a mind-exaltin' gift.

And O ! the carvings rich and rare
    The chapel—now restored—displays—
Carved work you'll find where'er you fare,
    But this will fill you with amaze !

O, stilly grey auld-farrent toon !
    I cannot pace your ancient street,
But—some quaint corner turnin' roun—
    The auld-warld carles I think to meet.

Barbour—intent upon " The Bruce "—
    Scougal—that mild and gentle star ;
Bœce—the learned and abstruse ;
    Or Elphinstone or Gawin Dunbar.

The new toon raxin' wide its boun's,
    A'thing seems strange the wanderer meets !
We harried bykes when we were loons
    Whaur now there's thrang o' busy streets.

Gin it spread oot in future time,
    As fast as since I was a bairn,
There will be nought but stane an' lime
    Frae Rub'slaw to the Dancin' Cairn.

And towers and spires rise grand and fair—
    And in the Sabbath mornin' still,
Ane wi' bell-music fills the air—
    As soon, it's hoped, *anither* will !

For rising o'er the auld West Kirk
    St. Nicholas spire's a glorious sight ;
Marble when moonshine lights the mirk,
    And silver in the sweet sunlight.

G

Its dumb tongues may they soon be heard
 Chimin' wi' music sweet and deep,
O'er the green mounds o' the Kirkyard,
 Where the Toon's grey forefathers sleep.

And soon may the auld haunted Aisles
 O' Drum and Collison shine forth,
Decored wi' a' their rescued spoils
 Of ancient dignity and worth.

Beneath a roof of scutcheon'd shields—
 Arms o' the great, the true, the good—
The new Town Hall for ever yields
 A feast of intellectual food.

For works by artists there you'll see,
 Second to none in fame or skill—
Such Brodie, Gordon, Jameson be,
 Philip and Reid, and Pickersgill.

And in the Tarnty Ha', the Trades
 Have shown a taste few could surpass :
Each craft in glowing tints and shades,
 Its legend tells in blazoned glass.

They took me roun' by Duthie's Park—
 A spot to fill your heart wi' glee—
The sky was ringin' wi' the lark ;
 The linties sang on ilka tree.

They pointed out the verdant knoll
 Whaur Wallace' monument's to stand,
And blessed the donor's generous soul,
 And praised the artist's skilful hand.

The Dee cam' twinin' link on link ;
 I saw a net the fishers trail,
And twenty salmon on the brink
 Lap, glitterin' in their silver mail.

Victoria brig, some farther doon,
 Spanning the waters bright I saw,
Linkin' auld Torry to the toon
 Wi' Kemnay granite white as snaw.

Thro' the braif toon where'er you look,
 For stirring sights there's never loss,
Frae Cleave-the-win' to Poynernook,
 Frae Rub'slaw to the Market Cross ! —

The Market Cross ! Aye, it's a treat !
  There's nae the like in Scottish toon :
I love it aye the mair I see't,
  I doated on it when a loon.

It's sculptured busts o' monarchs gane ;
  It's tall shaft unicorn crown'd ;
It's wreathes and gurgoyles carv'd in stane-
  Nae wonder tho' it be renowned.

And glancin' far up Union Street,
  As by Duke George you tak' your stan',
When nicht fa's doon—in sunshine sweet—
  There's nae sic sicht in a' the lan' ;

By day the granite glints and shines,
  And here and there a spire you see ;
By nicht the licht in wavy lines
  Seem stretch'd out to infinity.

But I maun stop my maundering lay—
  Gang north yoursel's to Aberdeen ;
And may your hearts rejoice that day,
  And feel like mine as fresh and green !

FINIS.

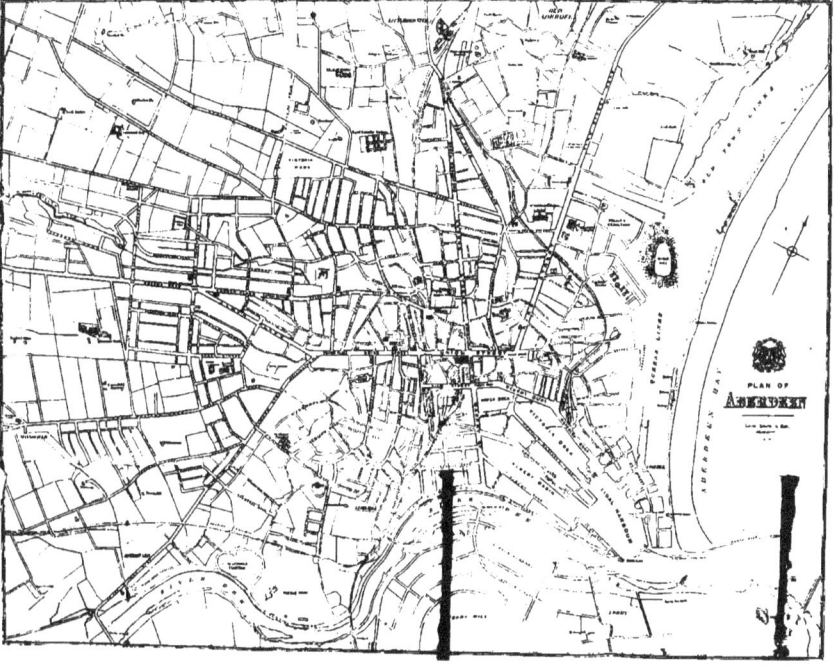

PLAN OF
ABERDEEN

JAMIE FLEEMAN.

THE

LIFE AND DEATH

OF

JAMIE FLEEMAN,

THE LAIRD OF UDNY'S FOOL.

FORTY-THIRD THOUSAND, ENLARGED.

𝕬berdeen:

LEWIS SMITH & SON, M'COMBIE'S COURT.

1883.

Life & Death of Jamie Fleeman.

INTRODUCTION.

HERE are more fools in the world than those publicly accounted such, and in the number many who would be highly offended were the least hint thrown out that their names stood on the list. Idiots, or common fools, whose minds are so framed that it is difficult to determine whether the weak parts or the strong be the more conspicuous, generally view things through a medium peculiar to themselves, and think, speak, and act in a way distinct from the great mass of mankind. While other men allow the world to become acquainted with only the more rational part of their views, the fool reveals all that comes into his thoughts. Both rational men and idiots build castles in the air. The former are accounted wise because they conceal the airy fabrics; the latter are esteemed fools, not because they allow their thoughts to run riot, but because they cannot conceal their vagaries from the public. The one may embark in the wildest schemes, and pursue the most headlong course, and still be reckoned no fool; while the other may say many witty things, and do many rational deeds, and still the world will not account him wise, but will laugh at both his sayings and his doings, because he does not follow exactly the same track, nor view circumstances in the same light as the multitude. But if the

world laugh at the eccentricities of the fool, the fool,
in revenge, seems to hold the notions of the world in
derision ; for, while the more rational part of the
community are carefully keeping in one common and
beaten track, and, individually, would be quite unhappy
were they to be singular in their manners and habits,
the fool fearlessly bounds into a path of his own
formation, and pursues his way through a kind of
fictitious region, wherein he seems to find enjoyments
of no ordinary nature, and beyond the ken of all
ordinary men.

A century or two ago, a *professed* fool was considered a necessary appendage to every family of
distinction. The primitive elements of his character
were the knave—the idiot—the crazed madman.
Wit combined with apparent stupidity, unbending
fidelity mingled with reckless audacity, and a discrim-
inating judgment concealed by a well-dissembled
indifference, were indispensible ingredients in his
composition. When the demand for family fools was
great, the supply appears to have been most abundant.
A curious Act of Parliament shows us that at one
time it was necessary to restrain the assumption
of this character by legislative enactment. It was
"ordainit that shireffs, baylyiss, and officials inquer at
ilk court, *gif thair be ony that maks them foolis that are
nocht ;* and gif ony sic be fundyn, that thai be put in
the king's warde, or in his yrnis, for thair trespass, as
lang as thai haf ony gudes of thair awin to leve upon ;
and fra thai haf nocht to leve upon, that thair eris be
naylt to the trone, or to ane uther tre, and cuttit of,
and bannysit the cuntre ; and gif thairaftir thai be
fundyn again, that they be hangyt." * This laconic
piece of legislation shows that the emoluments of a
fool must have been considerable, since the number of

---

* Act for the away-putting of Fenyet Fules, &c., 19th January, 1449.—
THOMSON'S "Acts of Parliament of Scotland."—Vol. I.

persons feigning to be fools was such as to call forth so
severe an enactment. This is farther evident from a
passage in Dunbar's poem, entitled "Kennedy's
Testament":—

> To Jock the fule, my follie free,
>   Lego post corpus sepultum,
> In faith I am mair fule than he,
>   Licet ostendi bonum multum.
> Of corn and cattle, gold and fee,
>   Ipse habet valde multum,
> And yet he bleirs my Lordis ee,
>   Fingendi eum fore stultum.

Thus it would appear that of their foolishness part
was real and part was feigned. They were generally
at least as much knaves as fools, concealing their
knavery under the best of all cloaks—simplicity.
Their dry sarcastic humour and rude ready wit received
much freshness and zest from their wild craziness.
They were a link between the quiet helpless idiot and
the boisterous madman. They shared of the eccen-
tricity of the latter and of the stupidity of the former,
and added to these the sharp-wittedness of the knave.
They are now almost, if not altogether, extinct. The
fool's cap and bells have long hung untenanted on the
walls, his seat by his lord on the *dais* has long since
disappeared, and it is many a day since his sallies have
been heard in the hall or at the festive board. The
country clachan has still its innocent or idiot, and the
crazed madman still wanders restlessly through his
chosen district; but it would seem as if these also
were soon to disappear. Already they are much less
frequently to be seen than formerly, being concealed
from the public eye in the cells of charitable asylums.
But till within these few years, we have seen several
idiots led about the streets of Aberdeen, or wandering
to and fro under their own guidance. We recollect
one in particular—a most pitiful spectacle—who was
led from door to door of the suburbs by a woman, we

believe his mother. "Feel Peter," "Willie More," and many others, will be remembered by many of our readers. In a country village it is no uncommon sight still to see, on a sunny day, the *innocent* seated bare-headed on the stone-seat by the house door, or sitting for hours motionless as a pillar, or wandering about, sometimes carrying on an unmeaning soliloquy, and sometimes running over the air of a favourite song. The race of madmen continued to appear on our streets to a later date. Indeed, we believe it is not long since "Mourican-roum-roum-roum" discontinued his visits. The backs of some of our readers, we doubt not, will be ready to attest how lately "Jean Carr" brandished her staff, and, single-handed, scoured the streets of a whole schoolful of her tormenters; while the bodies of some of them, perhaps, still ache at the memory of a direful conflict with that renowned amazon, "Lady Leddles."

It was in the fifteenth and sixteenth centuries that family fools were most in request. Before the eighteenth century, about the middle of which Jamie Fleeman flourished, matters wore a very different aspect. Jamie was, perhaps, the *ultimus Romanorum*, the last of the race of Scottish family fools—a class of beings which the author of *Waverley* has rendered so familiar to every one by his picture of "Daft Davie Gellatly." Jamie differed from his brethren and ancestors in this, that whereas the great majority of them were "fenyet fules," he was, in most respects, naturally what he appeared to be, and by chance fell into the very situation in which he was capable of acting the most conspicuous part.

CHAPTER I.

PARENTAGE AND BOYHOOD.

HE author of the Biographical Sketch of Fleeman, which appeared in the number of the *Aberdeen Magazine* for March, 1832, candidly admits that his account of the fool was very imperfect, and in some respects not very correct. This was owing not to any design or inability on the part of the author, but to the scantiness of his materials and the channels of his information. With regard to Jamie's birth, his words are—" Mr. James Fleming was born, as far as can now be ascertained, early in the last century. The place of this great man's birth is so uncertain, that the eighty-and-one parishes of Aberdeenshire may, if they please, contend for that high honour, in like manner as the seven cities of Greece contended for the glory of having been the birth-place of Homer." There is, however, no such uncertainty in the case. Jamie Fleeman first saw the light in the parish of Longside, and braeside of Ludquharn.* There are many still alive who can point out the spot where his parents lived, and still more who can tell how his mother was drowned, near the bridge of Ludquharn, in a deep pool, which at this very day, is known by the name of " Fleeman's Pot." He had a brother who was killed on board one of His Majesty's ships, we believe the *Serapis ;* and it was not till the beginning of the

---

* The Register Books of Longside contain the record of his baptism :—
" Fleming, James, son of James Fleming in Ludquharn, 7th April, 1713."

present century that his sister, Martha,* died at Nether
Kinmundy, in the parish where she was born.

An association of ideas depends, in many instances,
on the most trifling circumstances; and to imagine
that the same effect will be produced, or the same
interest excited, by any other means, is a mistaken
notion. We are of opinion that Jamie's biographer
has erred, in these respects, with regard to his hero's
surname. There is not one who remembers Jamie
that would recognise his old friend by the appellation
of "Mr. Fleming," or even "James Fleming." He
was universally known, and is still mentioned, by the
name of "Jamie Fleeman," a name possessing a charm
sufficient, even at the present day, to arrest the attention of every child in the district of the country which
Jamie frequented.

From the way in which the biographer has introduced his narrative, one would be led to suppose that
Jamie was more "knave than fool," or, in other words,
that he was a fool by profession more than by nature.
From the ample information which we have derived
from those who were personally acquainted with Jamie,
we can scarcely allow that this was really the case.
Although he possessed wit keen as a razor, and
sufficient understanding to take care of himself, yet he
certainly had many of the properties peculiar to an
idiot. His countenance, indescribably or even pain-

---

* Having mentioned Martha, and it being improbable that any one now
alive can be narrowly concerned in the matter, it may not be out of place to
relate that she too had a kind of craze as well as her brother, but of a different
kind. Martha's was of a religious turn. She was a presbyterian of the old
stamp ; and believing that quotations from Scripture were the best seasonings
of common conversation, and the strongest proof of being a chosen vessel,
the good woman had a text ready for every occasion. Once on a time her
daughter (and be it known that Martha Fleeman was a woman of irreproachable character, and twice regularly married) having fallen among rather low
company, on the evening of a market at Longside, the ill-natured women of
the neighbourhood alleged that the maiden's fair fame was somewhat darkened.
Soon after, they were surprised by Martha's running from house to house,
and saluting each goodwife in the words of the prophet—" Rejoice not against
me, O mine enemy ; when I fall, I shall arise : when I sit in darkness, the
Lord shall be a light unto me."

fully striking, wore that expression which at once betrays the absence of sound judgment. His head, large and round—his hair, perhaps naturally brown, but rendered, by constant exposure to the weather, of a dingy fox-colour, and not sleek, but standing on end, as if poor Jamie had been frightened out of his wits—indicated that his foolishness was not assumed but real. In a word, his general appearance, his manner and habits, combined to excite the suspicion that, although the lamp of reason was ever and anon bursting forth in brilliant flashes of wit, yet its light was flickering and unsteady. The lurid gloom which generally prevailed, tended to render those bright gleams more attractive than they otherwise might have been, and invested them with an unnatural sort of character, which rivetted attention, and at the same time amused and amazed the beholder.

The author of the Biographical Sketch has stated that, "either from necessity, or from that love of animals so common to persons of weak intellect, Jamie's bed was in the dog-kennel among the hounds." We have inquired into the correctness of this statement, and have found that, although Fleeman, generally invited the dog to share his bed, there is yet no reason to conclude that he ever passed a single night in a dog-kennel. There are many who allow dogs to sleep in their bedrooms, perhaps in their beds, who would be very unwilling to admit that they were in the habit of sleeping in a dog-kennel. The place where a dog sleeps may be termed a kennel; but still, when we speak of a dog-kennel, our meaning is commonly confined to a place set apart for the habitation of dogs ; and, therefore, an erroneous opinion is apt to be conveyed, when it is said of Fleeman that "his bed was in the dog-kennel among the hounds."

Jamie spent the days of his boyhood about the house of Sir Alexander Guthrie, commonly known in

the country by the appellation of "the Knight of
Ludquharn," and, at a very early period of life, began,
by bluntness of manner and shrewdness of remark, to
attract the notice of his betters. On account of these
peculiarities, young Fleeman was permitted to take
liberties which, in other boys, would have been rigor-
ously repressed ; and being introduced into the
company which commonly visited at Ludquharn, he
never failed to contribute to their amusement, and to
ingratiate himself into their favour. Hence the reason,
that, when Ludquharn no longer afforded him a home,
he found an open door, and, it may be said, a ready
welcome, at every gentleman's mansion in the neighbourhood which he chose to visit.

CHAPTER II.

ATTACHMENTS AND PREJUDICES.

RARELY is a fool pleased with a common
dress, and that which Fleeman chose to
wear was not of usual pattern. With
regard to inexpressibles, accounts do
not well agree, some admitting that he
patronised the modern form of garment,
but most declaring that he was partial to
the more ancient and upland fashion,
and decked himself out in a blue baize
petticoat. Be this as it may, it is certain
that a kind of sackcloth doublet, in place
of a coat and vest, served to protect his
upper man from the weather. As to his
head, it had no great acquaintance with hat, cap, or
bonnet ; and his feet were in much the same state of

slender intimacy with shoes.   If his appearance was calculated to attract notice, his tone of voice was not less so.   It was peculiar to himself—hollow, loud, nasal; so that while his words dropped slowly from his lips, or rather were trumpeted through his nose, and at the same time were accompanied by an air of sottish simplicity or cunning waggery (no one could well have said which), it was next to impossible to be inattentive to his singular remarks and sarcastic witticisms.

Fools are rarely without feelings both of affection and of hatred, and in general these are of a very marked description.   It may be supposed that Jamie's attachments, when once fixed, were strong and unwavering; and an instance corroborative of this is recorded.   When Sir Alexander's family were about to leave the old mansion at Ludquharn, one of the ladies broadly hinted to Fleeman that they would be under the necessity of dispensing with his services, alleging as a reason that they were henceforth to occupy a smaller house, and were compelled by various circum- stances to part with every servant whose labour was not absolutely necessary.   Jamie listened with down- cast look and heavy heart; and having some indistinct notion that the worthy ladies were under the necessity of curtailing their comforts on account of limited means of subsistence, and believing that his services might be of some use to them in their humbler station, he generously resolved to convince them that, to him, worldly considerations were of no value in comparison to the regard which he had for his bene- factors.   In a faltering tone, which showed that the poor creature was really affected, he stammered out— " Ye hae been kind, kind to me, an' I canna leave you in your strait.   I'm gain wi' you, should ye gang to the *ill pairt.*"*   The effect of this speech may be

---

* The Infernal Regions.

gathered from the following kind reply :—" Well, I
believe, Jamie, we have few friends who would venture
so far with us, so we must do something for you."
Even fools may in some things set an example to
wiser men ; and we have here, in a poor simpleton, an
instance of sincere gratitude and noble disinterested-
ness which would embellish any character, and which
many would be proud to reckon in the list of their
virtues. There are numbers who may, perhaps, laugh
at the singular argument which Fleeman used to prove
the regard he felt for the family of Ludquharn ; but
while they ridicule the odd language of the fool, let
them consider his conduct on the occasion, and happily
they may find in it something which commands their
respect and deserves their imitation.

Jamie was recommended to the Laird of Udny,
about whose hand he spent many a day ; but, as far as
we can learn, he was at full liberty to go and come,
just as he liked and when he thought proper—a liberty
of which he not unfrequently availed himself. After
saving the charter-chest at Knockhall, Udny allowed
him a peck of meal and a sixpence a week during his
life. There was likewise some mention made of a
pair of shoes once a-year, but on this part of his
reward he did not very scrupulously insist. Most
people discover a pretty strong memory in cases where
a promise advantageous to themselves has been made ;
and in this respect, at least, Fleeman was like other
men. That he did not wholly forget the shoes which
had been promised, we gather from the following
anecdote :—Having some wish to get a new doublet,
he seated himself on the opposite side of a dyke from
that along which he saw Udny approaching, and, as if
unconscious of the Laird being near, he began to sing
with all his might,—" I'm to get a new coat frae bonny
Udny ; I'm to get a new coat frae bonny Udny." The
Laird listened for some time to this simple and rather

unique ditty, when, looking over the dyke, he said—
" Well, Fleeman, you shall have a new coat." " What !
and sheen tee?" inquired Jamie. The Laird smiled
and assented.

Fidelity towards those whom they esteem is a trait
generally found in the character of fools. They cannot
bear to hear anything to the reproach of their favourites;
and when entrusted by them with any charge, they
seem to have a pride in executing it with fidelity and
precision. Such was the confidence placed in Fleeman
by Lady Mary Hay of Errol,* that, when he was at
the castle, she rarely took any other servant with her
when she rode from home. Jamie was extremely
proud of such distinguished honour, and her ladyship
ran no risk of annoyance from any one while he was
her attendant. A hundred years ago, it was not as it is
at the present day with regard to travelling. No turnpike roads then intersected the country, and it was
only on extraordinary occasions that any one thought
of travelling in a carriage. When Lady Mary had
occasion to go Aberdeen, she mounted her steed,
while Jamie astride on a stick, ran on before. When
they reached Waterside, he usually kept his face towards
his mistress, and, wading the Ythan back foremost,
every now and then called out, " Your ladyship has
nae got afore me yet, I think." He would then laugh
most heartily, as if he had done or said something very
wonderful.

From the indulgence he met with, and the privilege
usually granted to fools, he sometimes took the liberty,
as we have already mentioned, of doing and saying
things to those with whom he resided which no other
person durst have taken. James, Earl of Errol, had
procured a superior breed of cows. His lordship

---

* Not the Countess, as mentioned in the first edition.

B

praised them so highly, that his brother, the Hon. Charles Boyd, then residing at Ludquharn, became particularly anxious to have some of the breed. The Earl would not part with the cows, even to his brother, but at an exorbitant price ; but this being at last agreed to, four of the number were transferred from Slains Castle to Ludquharn. Whether the change of pasture had any effect on the cows, or whether they had been more famous for stock than for milk, or whether any other cause might have been assigned, is a matter which cannot now be explained ; but so it was, that they had not been many weeks at Ludquharn when complaints began to be heard about the quantity of milk which they yielded, and surmises were quietly hazarded that the Earl had cheated his brother. Fleeman was at the time paying a visit to his old quarters, and very soon understood that the cows were not only not answering the high expectations which had been formed concerning them, but that they did not yield a quantity of milk sufficient to supply the family, and therefore could not be kept much longer about the place. Whether or not any hints more direct were given to Fleeman is unknown ; but one fine night in the beginning of harvest, Jamie, after all the people about Ludquharn had retired to rest, stole quietly to the byre, and, having unloosed the cows, was soon past Cairn Catta, with them before him. Arriving at Slains Castle long before daybreak, he got the cows under Lord Errol's bed-room window, when he began to yell and swear among them as if he had been in a violent passion. His lordship, aroused from his slumbers, was much amazed at the unaccountable noise ; but having got up and opened the window, he discovered Fleeman. Still his surprise was by no means removed, when, by means of the dim moonlight, he saw several cows crowded under the window, and Jamie keeping them there with much noise and trouble.

"What do you want, Fleeman? What is the meaning
of this?" demanded his lordship. "Ye canna thrive,
my lord," answered Jamie—"ye canna thrive, my lord.
Ye hae cheated your brother Charlie. Ye hae gi'en
him kye as dry as the bull, an' I hae brought them to
get the milk from your lordship that ye said they had
when in your aught. Ye hae kept the milk to yoursel',
my lord. Ye canna thrive. Ye hae cheated your
brother Charlie." And then, suddenly breaking off
the conversation, he muttered in a low tone of voice,
"D——d yule rumps." His lordship ordered him to
put the cows into the byre until morning, when he
would settle the matter. Jamie did so, but stayed not
to hear his lordship's decision. He was at Ludquharn
by the time the domestics got up, when, as may be
supposed, there was no small stir about the cows.
They were everywhere sought, but could nowhere be
found. No one could tell or even conjecture what
had become of them. Fleeman was profoundly
silent on the subject, till Mr. Boyd was informed of the
inexplicable circumstance, when, in a peculiarly grave
and ludicrous tone, he said, "Faith, the kye are maybe
awa for their milk that they left at the castle." Being
further interrogated, he merely replied, "I'll wager an
ounce of tobacco Errol has ta'en back his yule kye, an'
ordered them into his byre. Keep ye the price, if
ye're a wise man."

Fleeman was a man of strong prejudices. These
had respect to places, persons, and animals, and were
often taken up, one could scarcely have said how, but
always maintained with a degree of determination not
a little uncommon. Sometimes his prejudices were in
favour of the object, and sometimes the reverse.

There are, perhaps, few things in the world about
which men are more capricious than about the beauties
and properties of local situations. One generally
discovers in the place where he has spent his early

days, charms which any other person would, in all
probability, never find out; and instances may be
found of men who are loud in praise of situations
which, to the cursory observer, are both bleak and
uninteresting. It is not to be supposed that we can
give any good reason for Fleeman's partiality to some
places in preference to others. We can merely state
the fact that he showed such partiality. On his way
to Slains Castle, he very frequently called and stayed
a few days at the Nethermill of Cruden, a place of
whose beauty and situation he had so high an opinion,
that it was a common saying of his, "Guid faith, the
king must be a great feel, or he would come and live
at the Nethermill."

With regard to persons, Jamie's prejudices were of
a very singular character. Prejudices have generally some connection with the merits and demerits of
the esteemed or hated object. Fleeman's had none.
Whole classes of the community, and not individuals,
were the objects of his ill-will. Some trifling and
accidental circumstance not unfrequently gave a bias
to his opinion. If a woman had her head adorned
with the golden locks so much admired by the ancients,
no more was needed to reduce her very low in Fleeman's
estimation. "Whare saw ye ever a lady wi' scarlet
hair?" he would growl, and no other reason would he
give for his ill-founded prejudice. The cause was
probably connected with the following circumstance :—
There was at Waterton a cook-maid whose locks were
of the above-mentioned colour. This maiden had a
temperament not of the mildest kind ; and when poor
Fleeman had in any degree been negligent of his duty,
she would have sworn in the most furious way, and
wished him in a bad place. Jamie stood more in awe
of the cook than he did of any other person about a
gentleman's house. Although he often deeply grum-
bled, yet these indications of rebellion were generally

displayed in an indirect way, and just as he was marching off to obey the order against which he was complaining. Thus his expressions of rebellion were generally neutralised by his acts of obedience. It must be allowed, however, that Fleeman had no good-will toward the whole race of cook-maids. He respected their commands more from a dread of their resentment than from a wish to oblige them. Where-ever he went they insisted on having a right to his services, and would give him nothing to eat unless he kept plenty of peats and water about their hands. One day Jamie had allowed either the one or the other of these necessary articles to be wanting. Complaints concerning this negligence were louder than usual, and threats of no ordinary potent were uttered in his hearing. These were continued so long, that Fleeman's anger began to be a little excited, and, his patience being completely exhausted, he ventured to reply in a manner more direct than usual. This new species of offence greatly increased the rage of the maid, and she wished him in h—ll for his impudence, as she formerly wished him with its monarch for his carelessness. "I see your drift, you jade," said Jamie, "Ye expect to be there yoursel', and to torment me wi' your eternal cry of 'Peats, peats, Fleeman; and 'Water, water, Fleeman.' There is an old boy there already that will hold peats enough about your hand. As for water, you may cry till your jaws split, but there will be deil a drap for your use." From that day forward the maidens with golden locks were objects of his aver-sion. The anecdote is perhaps one of the least proper for public notoriety; but as it brings into view a leading feature of Fleeman's character, its impropriety is not so great as to demand its suppression.

It was a trait in Fleeman's character, that he watched every opportunity to annoy those whom he did did not like, and often adopted means as singular as

they were sure. Factors were no favourites with Jamie.
In this case, too, the tide of his prejudices set strongly
against the whole race. One day a proprietor, at
whose house Jamie was staying, was walking out with
his factor, and showing him a field of hill-land which
he had cultivated at considerable expense, but which
had proved very unproductive. "I have," said the
gentleman, "tried many things in this field, but have
succeeded in none, and I know not what to put in it
that would thrive. I should be glad, Mr.——, to
have your advice with regard to the matter." As sometimes happens, the man of business was not very
intelligent in anything with regard to farming but the
collection of the rents. Yet, unwilling to be thought
ignorant, he put on an air of great consequence, and
mused for a time, as if about to give a very sagacious
and useful advice. In the meantime, Jamie, who was
near, was overheard saying, "Od, I could tell you
what would thrive in't."—"Well, Fleeman," said the
laird, "and what might that be?"—"Plant it wi'
factors," said the fool; "they thrive in every place;
but for all that," added he, "d—l curse the crap if it
be very profitable." Both the laird and the factor
were covered with confusion.

Among the crowd of mortals there are not a few
whose minds are so framed that they appear to place
all eminence in some trifling circumstance. Fleeman
occasionally betrayed some symptoms of this singular
disposition. For example, if he heard any one performing on the bagpipes, he almost invariably marched
up to him, and bluntly asked, "Can ye play the
Piper's Maggot?* If the musician replied that he
could play the tune, Fleeman would immediately
request him to do so, and then he would extol him as
an excellent piper, although, perhaps, the most bungling
performer imaginable; while, on the other hand, what-

---

* The name of an old Scotch air.

ever the musician's merits might have been, if he
unfortunately could not play the favourite air, he was
at once degraded in the fool's estimation, who would
henceforth report him as one not worthy of the least
approbation.   "He a piper!" Fleeman would say;
" he's a bummer; he canna play the Piper's Maggot!"

Jamie had a prejudice in favour of dogs and in
hatred of cats, and this, he said, was "*gentlmanny.*"
All the curs in the country knew him well, and were
glad to see him.   Wherever he stayed much, the dog
was generally permitted to share his bed and board.
At Waterton, it is said that he had taught a large house-
dog to observe a line drawn across the pottage pot.
On one side of the line, the pottage belonged to Jamie;
on the other, the dog was permitted to feed.   The cur
knew, from experience, that Jamie's spoon made the
boundary to be duly respected.   As the story has it, the
dog was from home one morning, when Jamie's acquaintance, the cook, insisted that the cat should be
permitted to occupy his place.   It was plainly revealed
by Fleeman's side-long look and heavy brow that he
did not much relish this new messmate.   He did not,
however, venture to remonstrate, and the maid placed
her cat opposite to Jamie.   Poor puss, ignorant of the
laws observed in the domain of the pottage pot,
speedily transgressed, by putting her nose across the
marches.   Jamie viewed her for a moment with an
eye of sovereign contempt.   He even suspended his
own operations for a short space, that he might quietly
observe an act of such daring aggression.   Perceiving
in the cat no signs of either fear or shame on account
of the extraordinary encroachment, he deemed it a
crime of .too grave a nature to be punished in the
usual way, by a slap on the aggressor's face with the
back of his spoon; so, quietly slipping his hand down
on the enemy's head, he, with a sudden jerk, forced
her nose, as far as the ears, among the scalding posset,

gravely remarking—" Desperate diseases require desperate cures, ye d—d wretch." It was some time, and cost some pains, before she cook got her favourite cat well again ; but whether Curry* was at home or not, she never afterwards proposed puss as a messmate to Fleeman.

There are in the many world who, from their endeavours to appear great, render themselves very ridiculous. The truly great and honourable keep from disgraceful and low actions, and are never afraid of their dignity from humble conduct and good-natured condescension ; while those who would be thought great, but whose claims to such distinction are founded on pride rather than merit, and on impudence rather than good sense, are afraid of every action which would place them on an apparent level with humble though honest men, and would consider their dignity compromised, and their honour at stake, were they to treat those who are poorer, or who have been less fortunate than themselves, with any degree of attention or common civility. We have rarely met with an instance where such silly pride met with a severer rebuff than it once received from Fleeman. Jamie being at a harvest-home, the farmer's daughter, a young maiden of lively disposition, and fond of a little innocent frolic, invited him to dance with her. Fleeman, proud of being so honoured, or rather, perhaps, anxious to show his respect for the young lady, who was a great favourite, immediately stood up, when her mother thinking that the whole family would be disgraced by the maiden's frolic with Jamie, interfered and prohibited her from proceeding with the dance. While she was scolding her daughter for her impudence and low behaviour, as she was pleased to term it, some of the party endeavoured to mitigate her rage, and convince her that

---

* Courage, the dog's name.

there would not have been much harm in it, even had her daughter danced a reel with Jamie. "Let the auld owman alane," said Jamie, with a most sarcastic air : "sae nathing mair about her ; she is God's handiwark." We have doubts whether the bitter sarcasm in this remark will be generally apprehended. To give some explanation of its meaning, it may be remarked that, when any person is naturally weak in mind, or deformed in body, in speaking of such an one, the common people say, "He is God's handiwark ;" which means that there is some great blemish, and that it would be improper to say much about it, seeing it is the work of nature rather than the fault of the individual. Fleeman's remark indicated that the gudewife's pride betrayed such imbecility of mind that rational people ought not to say much of the matter.

The author of the Biographical Sketch in the *Aberdeen Magazine* gives the following anecdote :— "The Laird of Waterton, it is told, was held by Mr. Fleeming in especial aversion. One day, when Mr. Fleeming was lolling on a bank of the Ythan, basking himself in the sun, he was hailed from the other side of the water by the laird, who asked him where was the best ford. The malicious knave directed the laird to the deepest pool in the river, and the laird, attempting to cross it, narrowly escaped drowning. When he arrived, sorely drenched, on the other side, he made up to Mr. Fleeming, and, in a voice hoarse with passion and cold water, accused the poor fool of a design to drown him. 'Gosh be here, laird !' said Mr. Fleeming, ' I've seen the geese and the dyeucks hunners o' times crossin' there ; and I'm sure your horse has langer legs than the dyeucks or the geese either.'"

This is not the edition of the story which is commonly told. We have frequently heard the anecdote, but never learned that he hated the laird, or that he was the person whom Fleeman misinformed.

To his benefactors he was always faithful, and it is improbable that the laird could have been ignorant of the state of the river close to his own house. Common report mentions a stranger on a visit at Waterton as the luckless wight. This gentleman had made some ill-natured remarks respecting Jamie.

Fleeman, when intrusted with any message or secret, was never known to betray the confidence reposed in him. Nothing annoyed him more than inquiries whither he was going or what he was about; and many a one, who wished curiously to pry into matters with which he had no concern, met with such rebukes from Fleeman as were calculated to teach him better manners, and remind him to busy himself about his own affairs. The Countess of Errol was well aware of Fleeman's fidelity in this respect, and not unfrequently intrusted him with messages which few so fit could have been found to carry. After Culloden, many of the country gentleman, who had joined the Prince's standard, were lying concealed in the neighbourhood of their former dwellings. As the Countess had taken a very active part in advising all the gentlemen in the north, with whom she had the least influence, to espouse the young Adventurer's cause, so after the defeat of the darling project, she continued to keep up a correspondence with as many of them as possible. She consulted their safety by every means she could devise, and as far as was practicable, administered to their immediate wants, while they lurked in the most sequestered spots, and were in continual danger of falling into the hands of those who scoured the country in quest of them. Fleeman was much employed by the Countess about this time. He could traverse the country without exciting suspicion, and he was capable not only of keeping a secret, but of evading the most searching examination, if any should have taken it into their heads to question him. Lord Pitsligo was at that time lying in close confinement at the house of Auchiries, in the parish of Rathen. The Countess of Errol was well aware of this, and, as often as prudence rendered it advisable, sent in the most private manner to ask the welfare of old Mr. Brown,* and perhaps to correspond with him concerning his safety, or to inform him concerning the fate of his companions in distress. In going from Slains Castle to Auchiries, Jamie had to pass the house of a proprietor who was a determined enemy to the Prince and all who favoured him. Fleeman was well aware of this, and as may be supposed, bore the laird no good will. One morning as he went on his way to Auchiries, this gentleman met him and abruptly accosted him, for the purpose of getting either a little amusement or a little information. "Where are you going, Jamie?" "I'm gaun to hell, sir!" said Fleeman dryly. This did not encourage further colloquy, and the parties went their ways. In the evening, as Fleeman was returning, they chanced again to meet, when the gentleman took up the theme so suddenly laid down in the morning. "What are they doing in hell, Jamie?" "Just fat they're deein' here, sir," answered Fleeman; "lattin' in the rich foulk, an' keepin' out the peer." "What said the devil to you, Jamie?" Ou, he said na muckle to *me*, sir; but he was speerin' sair about *you*." †

He who needlessly and wantonly commits mischief will rarely escape the punishment which such conduct deserves. A travelling pedlar, nicknamed "Berries," ventured on one occasion to play off an ill-natured joke at Fleeman's expense. It was in the winter season, and Berries had taken up his quarters for a few days at Mill of Leask, in the parish of Slains. This was a half-way house of Fleeman's when passing from

---

* John Brown, the name assumed by Lord Pitsligo.
† The particulars connected with this anecdote were kindly furnished by a very old person, who had seen what was printed in the second edition.

Waterton to Slains Castle; and, as Mr. Sangster and
his family were great favourites of his, he often prolonged his visits for several days. Arriving at the
house when Berries was there, one of the maid-servants
asked him if he was hungry. "Ay, an' thirsty tee,"
answered Fleeman. In a few minutes Jamie was
busily employed in refreshing himself with bannocks
and pork, while the servant girl, at the desire of her
mistress, prepared a drink of warm ale for his comfort,
as he had come in shivering with cold, the weather
being excessively stormy. Berries, among other small
articles, carried pepper for sale. Addressing Fleeman,
he said, "Od, Jamie, I think your drink would warm
you more if it had a little black spice in it." Jamie
assented, when, instead of *black spice*, the malicious
knave put in a considerable quantity of *black rappee*.
As Jamie's taste does not appear to have been very
nice, he drank off the beverage without making any
further remark than that Berrie's spice had "a cursed
ill *knegum*."* Drawing near the fire to warm himself
and dry his clothes, he soon began to feel very
uneasy. The strong potation began to give unequivocal
indications that it would not endure close confinement, while Berries, perceiving such evident signs of
the success of his trick, could not contain himself,
but burst out into an immoderate fit of laughter.
Fleeman was not in a state to seek for revenge at that
particular time. He vomited so excessively, that no
small alarm as to the consequence was excited. His
bed was prepared, however, and a more wholesome
beverage administered, and before morning Fleeman
was himsef again. The pedlar, when he saw that his
joke had become more serious than he anticipated,
took a sudden departure, no doubt dreading Jamie's
ire, and perhaps apprehending the severe reproofs of

---

* A disagreeable flavour.

Mr. Sangster and his family. Summer came, and with it Aiky Fair, in which Berries had a flashing stall of little "knick-nacks." Jamie was never in his lifetime absent from Aiky Fair. He soon espied his old acquaintance the pedlar, and as soon set about paying him with interest for his present of black spice. Off he set to John Barnet's tent, where he knew the recruiting party always went a-dramming, and proposed to the sergeant to find him a good recruit, on condition that he himself might be allowed to enlist him, and to march before the party in full uniform. No sooner said than done. Jamie was fully equipped,* and furnished with a shilling. Off he marched, sword in hand, directly to Berries' stall, while the shouts of "attention!—right about face!—quick march!" rent the air. "Roll went the drum and the fife played cheerily," when the party, followed by a rear-guard as motley as ever attended "the knight of the woeful countenance," reached the pedlar's stall. Fleeman gave the word "halt." "Ou, Jamie," said Berries, "are ye turned sodger?"—"Ou ay," quoth Jamie, "will ye list?"—Oh, I dinna care though I list wi' you, Jamie," said the pedlar, never suspecting anything serious. "Here's a shilling, then, in the king's name and authority." The pedlar thoughtlessly took the shilling, when Fleeman, wheeling about, marched his party back to the tent where he had left the sergeant. "Well, Jamie," said the sergeant, "have you enlisted your man?" "Hout ay have I, sergeant, come an' look at him," said Fleeman, in the greatest glee imaginable. On their arrival at the stall, Berries, who knew too well the tricks by which men were *trepanned*, perceived at once that he had allowed himself to be duped.

---

* This was no uncommon occurrence. Fleeman was often seen parading the streets of Peterhead dressed partly as a soldier. The recruiting party indulged and encouraged him in this, as by this means young fellows were attracted to them.

The sergeant told him to dispose of his "all," and prepare to join the party. In vain did the pedlar protest that it was "all for fun" that he had taken the shilling. The sergeant seriously told him that, as he had received the king's money, he was to all intents and purposes enlisted. "Nae jeukin now, Berries," quoth Fleeman, "ye maun just gang, or pay *the smart;* ye made me pay the smart last winter wi' a suddenty, ye mind!" In short, the pedlar had to pay the money, which he did, with many an imprecation upon Fleeman, who gave such vent to his joy when he saw him pay down his guinea, that an immense crowd was attracted to the spot, and joined loudly in the laugh against the poor pedlar. As a parting salute, Fleeman roared out, in his own deep nasal tone, "Deevil care, Berries, that's for garrin' me drink the tobacco bree." *

---

* About the time when Fleeman lived, common swearing, or low expressions partaking of the nature of cursing were rather fashionable among the higher ranks of society, and, as a matter of course, sedulously imitated by thousands of those who moved in a lower sphere. This in some measure accounts for the frequent allusion to the arch fiend which we meet with in Fleeman's sayings. We would, however, put the young readers of this history in mind of the fact, that the practice of interlarding common conversation with oaths has become quite unfashionable in good society. Without reference to the immorality of the practice, the manners of the age are sufficient to induce every one who has any regard for the good opinion of the world to abstain from all low expressions and gross allusions. The manners of the present day are much more refined than were those of the middle of last century. Expressions were then tolerated, the use of which would now be esteemed incontestible evidence of low breeding and a coarse mind; and they are completely banished from the more refined circles of society, and held in detestation by every one who has the least claim to politeness.

CHAPTER III.

FEATS OF STRENGTH.

HAT Jamie was possessed of uncommon bodily strength is sufficiently authenticated. Nature seems to have given him in powers of body for what she denied him in strength of mind. If he was inferior to many in the latter, he was superior to most in the former. His figure indicated extraordinary strength, which his habits may have helped to confirm. He was rather above the middle size, and very broad between the tips of the shoulders; but the most striking peculiarity of his form was its roundness. His chest was not flattened even in an ordinary degree, and yet it would be incorrect to say that he was deformed; while the singularly-shaped sackcloth or serge garment that he wore, left his neck and part of his breast completely bare; and, by this constant exposure of his body to the weather, his constitution seemed to be hardened, and his strength increased.

It is not easy to determine whether Fleeman's uncommon sagacity or extraordinary strength was the more surprising, or whether his dry humour yielded to his acute wit. Upon one occasion he was sent with a letter to the laird, resident at that time in Edinburgh. Jamie arrived in Edinburgh safely, but he was quite ignorant of the Laird's address, and this he set himself to work to discover. As he wandered through the streets, he narrowly inspected every dog he met, and he was at last sufficiently lucky to recognise one of his

old bed-fellows.   Seizing him in his arms, he ran into
a shop, and seizing a coil of ropes, measured off five
or six yards, and fastening this round the dog's neck,
set him down, and giving him a few hearty kicks—
" Hame wi' you, ye scunging tyke, hame !" and thus
he discovered the laird's dwelling-place.   As a proof
of his extraordinary strength, it is added that, though
the rope was what is called " plough-line," which, it
seems, is a very strong sort of rope, he instantly
snapped it in two with his hands—an exhibition of
strength which so terrified the shopkeeper that he
allowed Jamie to take himself off without asking for
payment, or making any demur to this felonious
abduction of his wares.

Fleeman's affection for dogs was, in some measure,
the means of saving the Laird of Udny's charter-chest,
when the house of Knockhall was burned.   On the
night in question, Jamie had sat down on his bed,
and was labouring in one department of his vocation—
namely, boring and tuning a chanter or Scotch whistle,
an instrument on which he could play a little, and with
which he often amused himself.   While thus employed,
his friend the dog came and pulled at part of his dress.
" Haud out by—swithe !" said Jamie, and drove him
away.   Fleeman now betook himself to sleep, but
again the dog came, and would not allow him to rest.
Jamie, at last, assuming a milder tone, said, " *Tyangie*,
fat ails ye ?   Ye're wantin' out, are ye ?   Weel, weel,
I'se eemer (I shall humour) you for ance."   He opened
the door, and discovered that the house was on fire.
Immediately he ran and awoke the gardener, who was
a great favourite of his ; then rushing to the charter-
room, the door of which the flames had already reached,
he broke in, and taking the iron chest in his arms,
dashed it through a window, whose frame-work was
composed of oak.   It is true what the author has said,
that it required three ordinary men to lift the chest.

During this time the gardener had given the alarm to the inmates of the house. By-and-by, Jamie was observed gamboling and frisking about on the green, and apparently in great ecstasy of joy. This very much surprised the gardener and others who were present. At length Jamie's conduct attracted their attention in a particular manner; for, as the raging element acquired strength, Jamie's expressions of delight became more lively. Those who were attracted by his oddities observed that he kept muttering something to himself, and they became anxious to learn what it was that gave him such delight. The gardener stole behind him, and heard the following sentence:—"She aye liket to be speakin' o' hell, but faith she'll get hell at hame the night, and d—l care." It flashed like lightning upon the gardener's recollection that he had forgot to awaken the housekeeper, and he knew that Fleeman's portentous words referred to the poor creature. This domestic was very much disliked by Jamie. Among other reasons of his hatred, one was, as he himself expressed it—"She gives me naething but doups o' candles to kitchen my meat." She was likewise somewhat ill-tempered, and often wished Jamie in warm quarters when he offered to complain of her parsimonious habits, or to resent her unkind treatment. The gardener was in the utmost distress about the object of Fleeman's abhorence; and Jamie's affection for the former overcame his hatred for the latter. When he saw his friend in trouble, and understood the cause, he merely remarked, "He disna ken the natur o' the jade sae weel's I dee;" and immediately he darted through the flames, already roaring at her bed-room door, and gave her the alarm—"Lucky! Lucky! rise, ye auld rudas! or ye'll get a pair o' het hurdies ere lang!"

There was in Aberdeen an English Regiment, whose commanding officer was a gasconading fellow, and constantly bragging of the extraordinary strength

c

of his men. One day the Laird of Udny and this officer were of the same party at dinner. When the glass began to circulate the officer began to boast, and, as usual, got louder and louder in praise of his men, as he became more and more heated with wine. At length Udny, believing that an insult was intended to his countrymen, said rather smartly, "From all accounts these famous grenadiers of yours are the best wrestlers that England can produce. I'll take you a wager of twenty guineas, that the lad who herds my cows, and carries peats and water to the kitchen, will throw the best man in your regiment." The officer was in a paroxysm of rage, but confident that his men were as good as he had represented them to be, he readily took the bet, while he muttered an oath, that "the d —d pride of the Scotch would soon be laid as low as it was on Drummossie Muir. Impudence forsooth! Compare a blackguard Scotch servant to the finest fellows that ever crossed the English border!" Time and place being appointed for the trial, Udny, after ordering his servant to buy half a pound of fine twist tobacco, set off for his residence. Fearing that Jamie might not relish the job, Udny though it necessary to coax him a little; and, knowing that he was passionately fond of tobacco, he presented the half-pound, at the same time saying, "Fleeman, I have got myself into a scrape, and no man but you can take me out of it." Jamie, eyeing the tobacco with a look of great satisfaction, his lip curling into a kind of smile at seeing himself in pos-session of such a treasure, twisted off a couple of inches from the end of it, clapped it into his cheek, and look-ing Udny in the face, said with an air of great serious-ness, "Fat is't, sir?" "You must *shak'-a-fa'* for me, Fleeman," said Udny. "And is that a'?" said Jamie. "But it is with soldiers, Jamie; and if ye throw them, ye shall get another half pound of tobacco," was Udny's reply. Jamie began to gambol and cut capers, as was

his custom when in good humour. Udny had gained
his point, as far as Jamie's consent and assistance were
concerned. On the day appointed, Jamie was seen
standing near the cross, on the plainstones, dressed in
the sackcloth coat which he usually wore. His head
was bare, and his hair standing on end, as on ordinary
occasions. The soldiers not dreaming that they jested
with their antagonist, were playing him all sorts of
tricks, while Jamie sullenly kept his place, and seemed
to heed them not. When the hour approached, the
colonel appeared, and had his men drawn up in order.
Seeing no person with Udny, he asked with an air of
triumph, whether he had forgot that he had promised to
produce a cow-herd who was to throw the best man
that England could produce? Udny beckoned to Jamie,
who came capering forward. The officer looked with
an air of utter contempt on Udny and his cow-boy,
while a broad laugh burst from every soldier in the
ranks, when they saw the poor idiot, whom they had
lately been jeering, brought forward as a match for any
man in the company. As the soldiers were really fine
men and expert wrestlers, their commander, instead of
selecting the strongest of his party, ordered out one of
the weakest, determined, as he thought, to turn the
laugh, as well as the bet, against Udny. But it is sometimes easier to suppose than to do. The soldier seemed
rather averse to degrade himself by contending with
Jamie, or even by touching him. "Do you take the
first shake?" said he to Fleeman. "Na, na," replied
Fleeman, "tak' ye the first shake for fear ye getna
anither;" and he threw the soldier from him as he would
have done a child. Another and more powerful man
shared the same fate. The colonel now began to suspect
that Udny's man was better than he looked. He was
likewise irritated by the smiles which he saw playing on
the faces of the bystanders, and he ordered out the
best man in the regiment. Jamie, too, was beginning

to be in earnest. No ordinary man could bear his powerful grasp, and the poor soldier was dashed to the ground in an instant. Jamie now run up to Udny and inquired, "Od, have I a' that *dyke* o' men to throw? Tell their maister to send twa or three at a time, or I'll be o'er lang in getting hame to tak' out the kye." The Castlegate rang with shouts of laughter.

As Jamie lived a good deal at Slains Castle, and other places whose inhabitants were rather favourable to those who had espoused the cause of Prince Charles, and who were hunted through every corner of the land by the emissaries of the bloodthirsty Cumberland, he imbibed a feeling of no very friendly nature towards "the red coats." In confirmation of this, we might relate two anecdotes, both equally authenticated, but so similar that we think it sufficient to give one. The circumstances on which they originate took place at Udny Market, and at Aiky Fair of Old Deer. We give the latter. Jamie was at Aiky Fair, and having met with a lad of his acquaintance whom he observed to be crying, he looked him earnestly in the face, and in a tone of pity said, "I dinna like to see grown folk greetin'. Fat's the matter?" The lad told him that one of a recruiting party in the market had *trepanned* him, by secretly slipping a shilling into his pocket, and then offering to swear that he was in possession of the king's money. This was a practice of no rare occurrence in Scotland in those days, and hence we are able to account for the circumstance of Jamie being several times engaged in a transaction such as we are now describing. If the poor fellows who were thus unwittingly enlisted offered to remonstrate, they were immediately reported as friends of the prince, and enemies to the sovereign, and thus their last state was worse than their first. Fleeman desired his acquaintance to point out the fellow who had been guilty of such a disgraceful deed, when taking the shilling, he offered it back to the soldier. His

Majesty's servant began to laugh at Jamie, and told him he would enlist him next. "Upstarts should be civil—tak' back your money," said Jamie; but the soldier showing no disposition to comply with the request, Jamie threw the coin in his face. Had the soldier been wise, he would have carried the joke no further; but, assuming a tone of great wrath, he began to threaten Jamie and his friend, and swore that he would make vengeance fall on the head of such rebels. In an instant, Fleeman's "rung" was laid across the soldier's shoulders with such hearty good-will, that the poor "red coat" relled and fell. His companions, gathering round, seemed disposed to assist him; but the market people taking part with Jamie, the recruit-ing party, consisting of a sergeant and four or five men, were glad, after being rather roughly handled, to take a right sudden departure. Report says that, when they were scampering off, Jamie was capering in his usual way when anything pleased him, and muttering to him-self these abrupt and somewhat unintelligible sentences, "Red coats and black coats now-a-days fight under fause colours. They will a' be put to flight yet. Od, how they rin! Right never ran."

Jamie's genius was of a discursive stamp, and led him to various modes of employment. His biographer has neglected to mention one avocation in which he took particular delight. When a wedding or baptism among the gentry, or above all things of this descrip-tion, the placing of a parish minister, was to be cele-brated in the district of country with which Jamie was acquainted, he was sure to make his appearance on the day preceding the *fete;* but he came not to sit idle. He was employed in the capacity of a kind of under-cook, and considered it his peculiar business to turn the spit. Such was his predilection for this office, that during the latter part of his life, when winding-up jacks began to be used, he exerted his genius in no ordinary degree in contriving and executing devices by which the obnoxious machine might be rendered useless; and so sudden and unexpected were his attacks, that, in general, no one could bring home the charge of the jack's destruction to Fleeman. When the cooking was over, and the company assembled, Jamie appeared in a very different character. At the period when he flourished, the country was infested with large gangs of strolling vagrants or gipsies. Wherever there was a wedding, or such-like meeting, a number of these vagabonds were sure to be present. It almost always happened that they became very unruly, and often excessively annoying to the company. In some instances they carried their impudence so far as not only to mingle with their betters, but to take the lead in the amusements of the day, and to maintain their ground in spite of every remonstrance, and in defiance of every threat. It was Fleeman's province to keep these blackguards in order; and so effectually did he execute this office, that when he was present there was never any annoyance on the part of the tag-rag-and-bob-tail gentry. They knew well that Jamie was armed with the authority of the landlord, and as well that he would not hesitate to exercise his commission with little respect for their feelings, were they to encroach in the least degree beyond the boundary to which he was willing to admit them. In a word, there perhaps were few things in the world of whom those lawless banditti stood more in awe than of Fleeman's "rung." Those who had felt its weight knew its effects, and those who saw its size had some guess what these might be.

CHAPTER IV.

ANECDOTES AND WITTICISMS.

HERE are in the world some who make a great noise, have extensive influence, and consider themselves far removed from the ordinary ranks of life. It is sufficient to say that, strange and unaccountable though it be, many of them have scarcely any other way of making future generations aware that such men existed than to employ a painter, and get their picture hung up in the place where they think it will, in all probability, be longest preserved. They seem to have strange forbodings that, with the destruction of the picture the remembrance of their existence will be lost; and they cannot help occasionally thinking, that nothing will live on the breath of fame but distinguished merit or distinguished worthlessness. But a truce with these remarks. They may beget in the breast of some one who is now happy in contemplating the distinguished figure which he imagines he is making, a suspicion that an imperishable name is not to be acquired by assumed greatness or fortuitous influence, but by real merit or transcendant abilities; and we would not for the world deprive any man of his importance during the period of its natural or supposed existence.

It was attempted to hand down to future times the memory of Jamie Fleeman by the simple though common means now referred to, but Fleeman had no hand in this himself. On the contrary, it was with no small trouble, and by much skilful manœuvring, that a likeness of the fool could be obtained. An itinerant limner, named Collie, was for some weeks at Longside, in the way of his vocation. This artist having by accident seen Jamie, was so struck with his singularly strange appearance, that he became desirous, above all things, to sketch his likeness; but Jamie was of a restless turn, and scarcely ever remained in one position, even for a few seconds. Besides this, there was in his disposition a certain waywardness, which made him take great delight in frustrating the designs of all who in any way meddled with him. For these reasons, it was not till several plans had been tried and failed that the limner effected his purpose. One of Fleeman's favourites having got him into the inn at Sandhole, plied him with tobacco and ale, of both of which Jamie was remarkably fond. Word was sent to the painter that now was his time; but the best opportunity is occasionally rendered unavailable by untoward circumstances. The painter had none of his tools at hand. Determined, however, not to lose the only chance which it was likely he would ever have, he drew upon his ingenuity to the account of his mishap, and made a piece of pasteboard and a burnt stick supply the place of canvas and brushes.* Keeping himself concealed in a corner, where he had a full view of his object, he contrived, with his rude implements, to produce a most striking likeness of Fleeman. The history of this rough picture is strange. The Rev. Mr. Skinner of Linshart got it from Collie; Miss Boyd of Ludquharn, afterwards Mrs. Gordon of Wardhouse,

---

* We are under very great obligations to that eminent scholar and antiquarian, John Leith Ross, Esq. of Arnage, for having put it in our power to present the public with a print of Fleeman. Mr. Ross, on looking lately into some of his grandfather's repositories, found a bundle of drawings by Lady Mary Hay, which that gentleman had got from her Ladyship about 1760. Among these was a likeness of Fleeman, done on a piece of stiff paper in pencil. This drawing exhibits all the characteristics of an original. It is from it that our print is copied. It is not improbable that this is the very picture which Collie drew.

having seen it at Linshart, begged it of Mr. Skinner, who made a present of it to her; but neither did it remain long in her possession, for Lady Mary Hay, having seen it, pressed Miss Boyd so much to give it up, that she consented, when Fleeman's picture graced the drawing-room of Slains Castle, as its original so often did the kitchen. Whether Lady Mary took it with her when she married General Scott, or left it at Slains Castle, we cannot tell; nor can we tell whether it be still in existence, or whether, like many things of more value, it has passed away on the wings of time. Certain it is, that is was much prized sixty years ago; but sixty years work wonderful changes. There are many things besides Fleeman's picture that were much esteemed in their day, which are now entirely forgotten or held in utter contempt.

To try if Jamie was proof against the allurements of pelf, some of his acquaintances about the place where he was staying scattered a few copper coins on his way to the well, and kept watch at the time when he was sent out for water. Fleeman, carrying his buckets, came to the place where the coins lay. Eyeing them for a moment, he said to himself, loud enough to be heard by those who watched his conduct, "When I carry water, I carry water—and when I gather bawbees, I gather bawbees," and passed on. This discloses a trait in Fleeman's character which we greatly admire. It showed that he could not be allured from his duty by the most tempting objects, and that he thought it better to attend to the business in hand than to turn aside to an entirely different pursuit.

Fleeman's wit was sometimes of a playful cast, sometimes of a grave and didactic nature, but in either case it rarely failed to effect the object for which it was called forth. A gentleman, whose drollery outran his prudence, and who, perhaps, thought that his rank in life gave him a title to take any liberty he chose with

one so much his inferior, having one day met Fleeman,
asked him in a rather pertinacious manner—"Who's
fool are you?" Jamie, eyeing him for a moment with
a kind of odd stare peculiar to himself, and which
seemed to indicate that he considered the gentleman's
impudence to be fully as conspicuous as his good
breeding, calmly replied, "I'm Udny's fell. Wha's feel
are ye?" It is needless to say that the laugh which
the gentleman meant to raise at Jamie's expense was
turned against himself, and he was taught the lesson,
that the man who neglects the rules of propriety, in
hopes that his rank will command the respect due to
good breeding, lays himself open to the rebukes of
those whose deference he would otherwise command,
and reduces himself to a level with those whom he
may thoroughly despise.

Being at Peterhead, Fleeman was one day on the
shore near the "Wine Well," where several of the
gentlemen belonging to the town were assembled, and
seeing one of them with whom he was acquainted,
looking very earnestly with a perspective glass at some
distant object, his curiosity was excited. When with
the naked eye he could see nothing very remarkable,
he took the liberty of asking the gentleman what it
was that he was so intently surveying. "Oh, Jamie,"
said he, "I am looking at a couple of limpets that are
trying a race on the Skerry!"* Fleeman pretended
to look for a minute with great attention toward the
rock, and remarked, "I canna just say that I see onything particular;" but immediately turning up one
side of his head, as if listening with anxiety, he all of
a sudden assumed an expression of countenance as if
he had made some wonderful discovery, and, with an
archness peculiar to himself, he looked the gentleman
full in the face, and with ludicrous gravity said, "L—d

---

*A rock in the sea nearly two miles distant from Peterhead.

bless me, sir, I hear the soun' o' their feet as they scamper up the face o' the rock!" The gentleman had wished to play off his wit on the fool; but the loud laughter of those who were near plainly indicated that he had extremely little room to boast of his success.

Much in the same way did he silence a man who met him one day near Waterton, and thought to play a little on his credulity. "Ou, Jamie," said he, "have you heard the news?" "Na, faith I," said Jamie, "fat news, man?" "Ou, that seven miles of the sea are burnt at the Newburgh this morning?" "Od, little ferlie," replied Fleeman, "for I saw a flock o' skate about breakfast-time, flying past Waterton to the woods o' Tolquhon, may be to big there." In this way would he put to confusion those who thought they might take the liberty of interfering with him in a way which he did not think proper. His replies on such occasions were so sudden, and so different from what could have been anticipated, that they were sure to confound his opponent, and call forth the admiration of the bystanders. As a farther proof of this, we select the following anecdote from the number of his graver retorts:—A young fellow, servant about a farm house where Fleeman sometimes stayed a few days, had seduced a poor girl in the neighbourhood. With an effrontery not so common in those days as it has since become, the rascal added to his first fault, not only by resolutely denying that he was the father of the child, but also by strenuously endeavouring to make it be believed that the girl's reputation had always been of a very doubtful nature. As the girl was able to lead no collateral evidence by which the charge might be brought home to him, he set her and the members of the Kirk-Session at defiance, and heaped no small abuse on them altogether. The poor girl, who, up to that time, had borne an irreproachable

character, was much dispirited when she found the
author of her disgrace also determined to impeach her
veracity; for he again and again averred before the
church court that he was ready to swear and prove to
the world, as he said, that he was innocent, and that
the woman was both a liar and a strumpet. When
some years had passed by, and no confession could be
drawn from him, the matter was at last referred to his
oath, when, as far as this could do it, his character was
cleared in the eyes of the world. But suspicion was
by no means removed, for many were inclined to give
more credit to the girl's word than to his oath, and
several circumstances combined to prove that they
were not mistaken. Some time after the business had
been thus arranged, Fleeman paid a visit to the farm
house. In the evening, when all were placed round the
kitchen fire, the servants, as was common, were playing
of little jokes upon Jamie, in order to get amusement by
his quick repartee. No one teased him more than he
who had so lately figured before the Kirk-Session. It
was soon evident to all that this man did not stand high
in Fleeman's estimation, whose growling laconic replies,
or no less portentous sullen silence, gave him fair
warning to desist from such a mode of amusement.
But the fellow pertinaciously continued to tease the
poor fool. "Jamie," said he, "ye're sic a feel that I'll
wager ye canna tell whether ye be your father's son or
yer mither's? Fat answer hae ye ta gie? Come, tell
me." And he burst out in a loud fit of laughter, as if
he had got the better of Jamie. "Tell ye me first, then,"
said Fleeman, gravely, "fat answer ye have to gie your
Maker at the last day, when he asks you if ye didna
break the lass's character, and then swear that ye did
nae sic thing. It will maybe then be asked at you if you
can tell whether her boy be not your son as well as his
mither's; and, faith, I'm thinking it will puzzle ye to
mak' it out that his being the son o' the ane hinders

him from being the son o' the ither." It is needless to say that some laughed, and that some looked as if they did not know well what to do. But the upshot of the matter was that, in the course of a few days after, the manwaited on the minister, declared himself mis-sworn, confessed he had purposely endeavoured to injure the girl's character, and begged to be absolved from church censure.

Nothing provoked Jamie more than his auditors pretending, when he was relating some wonderful story, probably of his own invention, to be already intimately acquainted with all the particulars. On one occasion of this kind a person of the name of William Robb was amusing himself at Jamie's expense, by continually interrupting him, in the midst of one of his highest flights, with such exclamations as "Ou, I ken that!" &c. Jamie endured this for a time with some degree of equanimity; but at length, when he could bear it no longer, he took an opportunity of privately ascertaining the name of his tormentor; then, turning to Robb with some asperity, he said, "Dee ye ken, man, 't there's ane Sandy Robb, a brither or some near freen (relation) o' yours, gaun to be hanged at Banff on Munonday? I wager ye dinna ken that." Robb was thus compelled to confess, amidst the laughter of those around, that Jamie's knowledge transcended his.

We have not been able to discover that Fleeman had much sense of religious obligation. He had been brought up about the house of strict Episcopalians, and lived chiefly among those of this persuasion, and so was in some degree impressed with the notions inimical to the Established Church, of which the Episcopalians of those days were so much, and perhaps not altogether unjustly accused; but he did not carry his bigotry farther than an occassional sarcasm; for as often as he found it convenient, he attended the kirk

of the parish where he was residing. In a word, his
religious principles did not seem to give him much
trouble; but when he was asked by any member of
the Established Church how he, who was such a determined advocate of the Episcopalians, would condescend
to enter a Presbyterian place of worship, he would
reply, in the most ironical tone conceivable,"he aye
liket, in this matter, to be in the fashion wi' the multitude, whose religious principles depended on three
things—what would gie greatest satisfaction to their
friends, least trouble to themselves, and maist folk an
opportunity o' seeing their braw claise." It was remarked that, when asked concerning the text, after
being at the parish church, he invariably replied, "in
the *tenth* of Ephesians." "And in what verse?" the
inquirer would ask. "Ye wish to ken a' things," Jamie
would then say, "and therefore you should be tauld
naething. If ye get the chapter there is little fear but
that you will meet with the verse." It is to be recollected that, in the epistle to which Fleeman directed
those anxious to know the text, there are only *six*
chapters.

About the middle of the last century, it was customary for the ministers of the Establishment to extend
their discourses to an inordinate length, during which
many of the congregation were often disposed to go to
sleep. Fleeman, with that singularity which marked
his character in most things, never gave way to the
common failing, but seemed always to be paying the
most marked attention to the sermon, however long or
tedious it might be. In the Kirk of Udny, one Sunday—whether owing to the soporific nature of the
sermon, or the manner of the preacher, we cannot tell
—the disposition to slumber was greater than usual.
Jamie was there, and, as was his wont, apparently all
attention. The minister thought it necessary to ad-
monish his flock with some severity. "My brethren,"

said he, "you should take an example by that fool
there"—pointing to Jamie:—"fool though he be, *he*
keeps awake, while you—think shame of yourselves!
—are nodding and sleeping." "Ay, ay, minister,"
muttered Fleeman to himself, "gin I had nae been a
feel I had been asleep tee." The *double entendre* and
biting sarcasm of this brief soliloquy are inimitable.

In Jamie's day, field-preachings were of rather
common occurrence at the "sacramental occasions" in
the country parishes. Jamie, being present at one of
these, saw many of those who had congregated behaving in a way not altogether in keeping with the pious
motives which may be supposed to have brought them
thither. Among other things, while the preacher was
labouring to impart nourishment to their souls, they
were busy taking refreshment to their bodies. There
was, perhaps, little harm in this, and in the case of
those who had come from a distance, or from other
parishes, there was a kind of necessity to be urged in
favour of such practice; but, on the other hand, there
was certainly something rather unbecoming in the
appearance of a set of people stuffing themselves with
all kinds of food during the time of divine service, and
we are therefore of opinion that there was room for
reproof, as well as need for reformation, in this matter.
Had the people been within the walls of the church, it
is not probable that they would have indulged in such
an unseemly practice; but being in the *field*, they considered themselves to be more at liberty, apparently un-
mindful that the sacred duties which they had come to
discharge demanded equal reverence, whether performed within the walls of the kirk, or under the broad canopy
of heaven. But the plain truth is, that in those days the
mists of ignorance were still hovering over the sequestered parishes; many considered their presence at "an
occasion" to be of more importance than the part
which they took in the services, and believed that they

had performed their duty by travelling a number of miles to hear an eminent preacher, and uttering an occasional groan during the sermon; while they seemed to think that there was little impropriety in eating and drinking, and smoking, and even sleeping, during part of the time they were there.   Fleeman, fool though he was, highly disapproved of such conduct, and on the occasion alluded to, sat with a face as grave as a judge, while numbers around him were busily and differently employed.   At last a dog approached him, and from the expressions of kindness which the animal showed, it was evident that in Jamie he recognised an old acquaintance.   Fleeman always kept a pocket well stored with bread and other eatables, and was never known to be sparing in his bounty towards the numerous curs with which he was in the way of meeting during his peragrinations.   The dog in question tried various methods to excite Jamie's attention and to draw forth his bounty, but they were all in vain.   Jamie sat unmoved.   As may be supposed, the attention of many was in some measure engaged by Fleeman and the dog.   At last Jamie held out his hand, and the dog, expecting to be treated as on ordinary occasions, approached nearer; but instead of a piece of bread, he received a very smart stroke across the nose, which made him scamper off, yelping a very bitter complaint. "Tak' ye that, ye ill-bred brute," said Fleeman, without relaxing his gravity in the least; "it will teach you better manners than to chew and eat in the *kirk*."   It is doubtful whether this sarcasm conveyed a severer animadversion on the practice of eating during the time of sermon, or of leaving the *kirk* to declaim in the *fields*.   The only effect which it produced at the time was a titter which ran through the greater part of the congregation.

To an accident which befell him when following his avocation of cow-herd, is to be ascribed the origin of a proverb very current in Buchan—"The truth aye tells best." Fleeman had, in repelling the invasion of a corn-field by the cattle under his charge, had recourse to the unwarrantable and *unherd-like* expedient of throwing stones. One of his missiles, on an evil day and an hour of woe, broke the leg of a thriving *two-year-old*. Towards sunset, when the hour of driving the cattle to their home had arrived, Jamie was lingering by a dykeside, planning an excuse for the fractured limb of the unfortunate *stot*. " I'll say," he soliloquised, " that he was loupin' a stank an' fell an' broke his leg. Na ! that winna tell! I'll say that the brown stallion gied him a kick and did it. That winna tell either! I'll say that the park yett fell upon't. Na! that winna tell! I'll say—I'll say—what will I say? Od, I'll say that I flung a stane and did it! That'll tell !" Ay, ay, Jamie," cried the Laird, who had been an unseen listener to this soliloquy—" ay, ay, Jamie, the truth aye tells best."

An anecdote related of Fleeman, in his office of guardian of the geese, perhaps exhibits a mixture of the rogue with the wag. He had been sent to Haddo House to fetch some geese thence to Udny Castle. Finding the task of driving them before him a very arduous one, and his patience being completely worn out by the innumerable and perverse digressions they made from the proper road in which they should have walked, Fleeman procured a straw rope, and twisting this about their necks, walked swiftly on, dragging the geese after him, and never casting a look behind. What was his horror, when he arrived at Udny, to find the geese all strangled and stone dead ! As the breed was peculiar, the strictest injunctions had been given to him to be careful in conducting the geese safely home. His ingenuity soon devised a plan to free him from this dilemma. Dragging the victims into the poultry-yard, he stuffed their throats with food, and then boldly entered the castle. " Well, Jamie, have you brought

the geese?" "Ay, have I." "And are they safe?"
"*Safe!* they're gobble, gobble, gobblin' as if they had
nae seen meat for a twalmonth! Safe! Ise warran'
they're safe eneuch, if they hae nae choked themsells!"

The same ingenuity which he displayed in extricating
himself from the scrape of the strangled geese he showed
on another occasion. Loitering one day in the passage
leading to the hall, while the servants were carrying in
the dinner, his appetite was so strongly excited by the
savoury smell of a couple of roasted ducks, that, watching a favourable opportunity, he pounced upon them,
tore off a leg from each, and instantly devoured them.
The servants discovered the theft, accused Fleeman,
and insisted on his carrying the dish to the table.
" These ducks, Jamie," said the Laird, "are very queer
ducks." The deucks!" mumbled Fleeman; "what's
the matter wi' the deucks?" Why, they have only one
leg each!" " Ae leg! od, there's nathing queer about
that. If ye look out o' the window just now ye'll see
the deucks in the yard in dizzens standin' upon ae leg,
and what for shouldna these twa beasties hae but ae
leg tee?"

Fleeman was a good hand at repartee, nor were his
powers of satire and quizzing by any means inconsider-
able. It is recorded that one day, when travelling
along the road, he found a horse-shoe. Shortly after,
Mr. Craigie, minister of St. Fergus, came up to him,
and Jamie, as he was acquainted with him, holding up
the shoe, addressed him thus :—" Minister, can you
tell me what that is?" That!" said the minister, "you
fool, that's a horse-shoe!" " Ah!" said Fleeman with
a sigh—" ae! sic a blessing as it is to be weel learned!
I couldna tell whether it was a horse's shoe or a mare's
shoe!" Mr. Craigie, who delighted much in a joke
himself, used to tell this anecdote with great glee,
and remarked that wise men ought never to meddle
with fools.

One year the Laird of Udny attended the "Perth Races." Jamie, as usual on such occasions, accompanied him. Taking a near cut across the country, he reached St. Johnstone before his master. Having by some means got hold of the largest half of a leg of mutton, he had taken his seat on the bridge of Perth, and was making the best use of a large knife on the *lunch*, when Udny came riding up. As Fleeman had not often had such a joint of meat at his command, he had assumed no small consequence in his own eyes, as he sat refreshing himself like a prince. "Ay, Fleeman, are you here already?" said the Laird. "Ou, ay," quoth Fleeman, with an air of assumed dignity and archness which no one could either imitate or describe, while his eye glanced significantly towards the mutton ; "Ou, ay, ye *ken* a body when he has onything." As much as to say, you recognise me as an acquaintance when you see me well provided with the good things of life ; but would probably have taken no notice of me had I been less so.

The following anecdote displays a degree of good sense and courage which, perhaps, at that period, we should have looked for in vain from persons making greater pretentions to wisdom than "Feel Fleeman." Returning from Aberdeen one evening, Jamie, on arriving at the brig of Udny, found the road occupied by an appearance having all the characteristics of the enemy of man—long tail, hairy hide, and portentous horns. Fleeman attempted to pass this awful vision, but which side soever of the road he took, Satan still confronted him. Fleeman dropped plump on his knees, and besought the foul fiend, saying, "O gweed deevil, let me past ! I'm naething but Udny's feel ! O gweed deevil let me past !" But the "gweed deevil" was inexorable. "Be ye gweed deevil, be ye ill deevil," cried Fleeman with much indignant energy, as he began to gather an armful of stones, "Ise try you wi' a *lea arnot !*" (a cant name for stones), and he commenced to pelt the "arch-angel ruined." Satan fled ingloriously, and in his flight dropped his hide, tail, and horns. Jamie soon after triumphantly entered the castle, and flung down the trophies of victory—the *spolia opima.* "Ye need never fear the deevil now, lads, for there's his skin," cried he in ecstacy of delight. We question if the fellow-servant who personated his infernal majesty would, if placed in Fleeman's shoes, instead of being disguised in the cow's hide, have acted with as much magnanimity.

A story tells that, on one occasion, being requested to deliver a message at some place several miles distant from Udny, he took it into his head that he would not go unless on horseback. It was not thought proper to in-dulge him in this luxury, and Fleeman, alive to a sense of the affront thus offered to him, obstinately refused to go otherwise ; when, at last, a servant luckily bethought himself of an expedient. He procured a stick, and giving it to Fleeman, said, " Here, Jamie, here's a horse for ye." The fool, with characteristic simplicity and great delight, instantly bestrode the proffered stick, and arming his right hand with a stout switch, gave his wooden steed a few stinging blows, and darted away with great rapidity , and we may well suppose that

> The last of human sounds which rose,
> As he was darted from his foes,
> Was the wild shout of savage laughter
> Which on the wind came roaring after.

When Fleeman returned to Udny, he declared, " He's a very rough rider yon beast ! Heigh, sirs, gin it had nae been for the honour o' the thing, I might as well have been on Shank's mare."

Jamie having called at Mill of Leask, one day soon after Christmas, found Mrs. Sangster busy, as usual, knitting stockings. Observing her for some time in silence, he at last broke out in one of his quaintest moods—half-jest, half-earnest, no one could well have

said which—"Noo, guidwife, guid faith I've foun' out
Solomon, wise king and honest man tho' he was, telling
a lee (lie) in ae thing." "Well, Jamie, and what might
that be?" inquired Mrs Sangster. "He says, I'm taul'
that the han' o' the diligent makketh rich ; but faith,
tho' I hae been workin' hard the maist o' a' Yeel, at
the minister's o' Udny, I hae na foun' a word o' truth
in fat he says—the deil ane !" To perceive the full point
of this remark, it must be recollected that, in Jamie's
day, there were few of the inhabitants of the north of
Scotland who did not cease from all sorts of works
during "Yule-tide." It is, as if he had said,—there is
no real advantage to be gained by neglecting those
seasons of festive joy which our forefathers hallowed
by resting from all ordinary labour, in grateful remembrance of some signal blessing.

CHAPTER V.

EXTRAORDINARY LIES.

HE extraordinary relations in which Fleeman occasionally indulged, showed his
love of the marvellous. His talent for
lying was of the first order, and we have
no hesitation in placing him on a level
with the highest geniuses in this line.
His description of "a skate that wad
hae covered seven parishes, which he
saw fleein' in the air," was an idea equal
to the best efforts of the great Munchausen,
and soars far above the happiest concep-
tions of Sir John Mandeville or Ferdinand Mendosa
Pinto. The story upon which a very common byword
is founded, "Hanging in the weathercock, like Flee-

man's mare," or, " Up by carts, like Fleeman's mare."
is nearly the same as one recorded in the work of
Munchausen, Being in Aberdeen ae snawy night, he
said, he tethered his mare to the lumhead, as he
thought ; but a thaw having come during the night, he
in the morning found "the peer beast hanging frae the
steeple of the tolbooth. Ay, faith !" quoth Fleeman,
viewing her, " Yer up by carts this morning !"

At the period when Fleeman lived, ploughs were
generally drawn by oxen, and ten or twelve of these
were commonly yoked to a single plough. The oxen
were yoked by means of bows fixed to their necks, and
the principal plough was held by the guidman himself,
or by a cottar retained for the purpose. To keep all
the oxen at work, a goadman was necessary. As this
office seems to have required some skill, the goadmen
took great delight in telling of the wonders they had
accomplished in making the oxen do their work. Many
an old man yet alive could recount feats of no common
order which he made the oxen perform when he was
a lad. Jamie caught the infection, and seemed
anxious it should be understood that he had been a
first-rate goadman. But if many verged on the very
borders of truth and probability, exalting their character
in this respect, Jamie took a bolder step, and sought
fame by relations altogether extraordinary. " Driving
the oxen in the Laighs of Ludquharn," he said, " the
ground was so swampy that he often saw nothing above
the surface but the nap of the cottar's cap and the tap
of the wyner's* bow ; " and having quarrelled with the
ploughman who was ploughing one fine evening on the
hill of Southfardine, he averred "that he drave the
oxen at so brisk a pace, that the point of the share
coming against a stone,† the ploughman's heels were,

---

* One of the front oxen.
†A large white stone, still to be seen, we believe, is to this day known as
" Fleeman's Stone."

by the jerk which he received, made to fly up and strike the seven stars, when one of these brilliants was knocked down, and has never since been replaced."

But, fond of the marvellous himself, Jamie seemed to have a wonderful pleasure in repressing in others the least symptom of the same predilection, and, as if enraged at those who would dare to use the weapons which he considered as his legitimate property, he wrested them from their impotent hands, and made them heartily ashamed of themselves for having supposed that they could wield them. Sir Arthur Forbes of Fintray was the first in the country who introduced turnips into the list of his husbandry productions ; and soon after the knight, the Laird of Udny turned his attention to the culture of the same useful root. As might be expected, much was said concerning the merits of the turnips, and the size to which they had been raised by each of these proprietors. One day, a person from Sir Arthur's neighbourhood having met Jamie, began to rally him on the superiority of the knight's turnips to Udny's. Jamie allowed him to go on till he had fairly described the wonderful size of the Donside turnip ; and clearly perceiving that he had exaggerated in no ordinary degree, dryly replied, " Gang hame, man, and tell Sir Arthur, that Udny has made byres o' his neeps for his owsen. Ilka owse stands snugly in a neep, and eats round him for owks thegither, and faith ! some o' the big anes would haud twa." The Donside braggart was silent.

It was customary, in Fleeman's day, for tailors to go round to the houses of their employers, and there to perform their work. The present practice of "taking in work " was scarcely known among country tailors sixty years ago. Prevailing practices are generally adapted to the circumstances or convenience of those among whom they are found. It was not till towards the close of the eighteenth century that the inhabitants of Aberdeenshire began to purchase cloth from the merchant. Every family manufactured what was necessary for its own use; and when the web was prepared, the tailor was sent for, who came with his journeymen and apprentices, and remained till the work for which his services were required were completed. Thus, migrating from house to house, the tailors generally became a loquacious race, and delighted much in surprising their employers with wonderful narrations. A company of these tradesmen were employed in a house at which Fleeman chanced to arrive, and, as may be supposed, they were overjoyed when they saw the fool make his appearance. It was in the winter time, and a merry evening was anticipated. Many an incredible story was told by the tailors in order to draw Jamie out; and, it is said, he was not backward to enter the lists with his challengers. He heard their tales, and either told others which eclipsed their best narratives, or made such remarks as might have rebuked the narrators into silence. Perceiving that they could make nothing of Fleeman on ordinary grounds, his tormentors endeavoured to allure him into their own proper territory, no doubt thinking that they might then attack him with more success. One, addressing another, averred that, shutting his eyes, he could thread the finest needle half-a-dozen times in a minute. Another declared that, holding his hands behind his back, he could do the same thing. "I," says a third, "could promise to put a hunner needles on a thread in a minute, if anybody would hand me them." The master-tailor, with a leering look, and in a taunting tone, addressed Fleeman, "Could you thread a needle, Jamie?" Fleeman, assuming a look peculiar to himself when a little nettled, or concious of an affront, replied, with some warmth, "Ye wou'd like to ken, would ye, tailor? Last winter, man, as I was passing

Garpalhead, a ship was lying on the sands. She had been ca'd in by the storm, and she was loaded wi' needles. There were twa men wi' sho'els throwin' them out. Faith, I was wae to see sic a loss o' fine *sharps*. And spyin' a great clue o' sma thread lyin'," quoth Fleeman, " I fell a-threadin' the needles, and I threadit as fast as the men could sho'el them out, an' I missed the deil ane ! Great curse ! that was a threadin' for ye ! "

The allusion to the " Skate " is connected with one of Fleeman's outrageous lies. There lived in Jamie's day, and in the same district of country which he frequented, another fool named Jamie Tam or Thom, who also was noted for telling uncommon lies, and principally concerning things which he had seen. One day the two fools met by chance, and he in whose house the meeting took place, being a man of some humour, thought it a good opportunity of ascertaining which of them could tell the most remarkable lie. Addressing Thom, he said, " Jamie, I'll warrant ye have seen some wonderful things in your day." "Aye," says Thom, " 'tis nae langer syne than yester-day that I saw red cabbage stocks at Ellon so heich that naebody could get up to them without a harrow."* Fleeman eyed his brother fool with a look that bespoke a mixture of contempt and consciousness of superiority, as much as to say, " And is that the greatest lie you can tell ? " And without the least pause or considera-tion, he began—" I've seen a greater won'er than that mysel'. Ae day Countess Mary was wantin' cockle-shells † to a gentleman's supper, an' I gaed out to her Fish Peel ‡‖ to tak' them ; an' divin'," said Fleeman, " I cam' to the boddom. Ye wou'd hae thought it

---

* A harrow, in place of a ladder.
† Oysters, we suppose.
‡ Alias, the German Ocean, which Fleeman often denominated " Countess Mary's fish peel or pond."

anither warl', man. An' sic fearfu' beasts as I saw! Gosh be here! I was nearly fear'd out o' my wit, when a skate, that wou'd hae covered seven parishes, cam' fleein' i' the air abeen my head! Faith, I think I wasna lang o' fillin' my creel wi' cockles, when I took to my heels, an' never halted till I cam' up at the mou' o' the lang haven."* "The deil a marrow!" said Jamie Tam.

At times, when he heard any one relating a circumstance which set probability at defiance, he would listen patiently till he had heard the whole, and then dryly ask the narrator, "Do you ken where the leers gang?" This often produced remarks such as the following:—"Faith, Jamie, I think there is no one that ought to know better than you; I'm sure you do not stick by the truth." "It will never be ask'd at the like o' me," Jamie would retort, "whether I spoke the truth or tauld lies; but when wise folk speak things that would affront feels, it is just makin' a present o' their wit (reason) to Auld Bobby." Thus would the fool reprove wise men.

---

* A creek running up between two rocks close by Slains Castle.

CHAPTER VI.

GRAVE REMARKS.

LITTLE acquaintance with the world will convince us that it is very possible for one man to ruin another, not only without having seriously intended to do him harm, but even without having ever felt any other sentiment towards him than that of kindness. There is a kindness which kills; and instances might be adduced, where marked attention could scarcely be construed into any other meaning than genuine cruelty. This can never happen but where the person on whom favours are heaped is in some sense unfit to receive them, and where the favours themselves have some tendency to bad consequences. One may be worthy of the most marked attention, and yet be unfit to be treated with too great kindness; for if he had not resolution to prevent the friendship of others from interfering with his duty, and to resist the various temptations to which certain modes of discovering kindness insensibly expose him, he may be ruined while he imagines that he is favoured, and lose his reputation while he believes that his company is prized. In such cases the attention of a friend almost assumes the nature of injustice, and his marks of kindness may be said to merge into acts of barbarity; for he fosters the bad propensities of him whom he pretends to favour, and leads him on to wretchedness under the banner of friendship. There lived in the district of country which Jamie Fleeman frequented, a farmer of very amiable disposition, but of little decision of character. This man, by steady attention to business and habitual economy, had raised himself to comparative affluence, He was one of Fleeman's favourites. General Fullarton then resided at Dudwick. A young officer, either an acquaintance or relative, occasionally paid a visit to the General, and often prolonged his stay for two or three months at a time. This man was of easy address and fascinating manners, and, from the account which has come down to us, seems to have been what is commonly called "a real kind-hearted fellow;" but from the gay scenes in which he had mixed, and the example which he had seen in the army, his moral principles were not very high, and his habits, in one or two respects, reflected not much honour on himself, and were rather dangerous to those with whom he associated. He would not seriously have done or even wished ill to any man alive, and yet there was a something about him which most of men had cause to dread. Fond of fishing and coursing, he occasion-ally invited the farmer whom we have mentioned to accompany him in these sports. As they got better acquainted they became more pleased with each other, till at length they were almost inseperable companions. The officer did not relish his sports so much if the farmer was absent, and the farmer was unhappy when anything took place to prevent his attendance. The farmer's enjoyments were so multiplied by the officer's agreeable conversation, that he soon began to feel little regret at leaving the dull routine of business for pleasures so much more agreeable. There was in the neighbourhood what was then termed "an alehouse," where strong home-brewed beer and genuine smuggled gin were sold. Hither the sportsmen generally resorted some time in the course of the day. The officer was generous, and seemed happy in treating the farmer kindly in return for the time which he sacrificed. To

make a long tale as short as possible, the consequence
of all this was, that the farmer's affairs were neglected,
and he contracted a habit of drunkenness. His wife
and family endeavoured to break him off from this
depraved habit; but he, perhaps irritated by the
consciousness of his own misconduct, perhaps no
longer capable of reasoning calmly on any subject,
resisted their attempts with indigation, and seemed to
consider their friendly endeavours as an encroachment
on his liberty, and a reflection on his good sense.
Hence dissension broke out in the family; and where
peace and prosperity, respect and happiness, had been—
quarreling and confusion, and contempt and wretchedness, in the course of a few years, took up their abode.
Fleeman paid a visit to his old acquaintance, and was
evidently sorry when he saw the sad change that had
taken place. Instead of staying a few days, as usual,
he prepared to take his departure in the course of as
many hours. The farmer pressed him to prolong his
stay, but even fools can have little pleasure in the
company of one whose sole delight is to satisfy his
own appetites, and Fleeman would not consent. "Na,
na," said he, in a grave and melancholy tone, "na, na;
ae feel is aneuch at a time about a house. Feels,
Robbie, canna bide lang in ae place. Od, I'm fear'd
ye'll shortly need to be trudging as well as me." Then,
looking earnestly in the farmer's face, he continued,
"Did you ever hear, that for ae feel that God maks,
the deevil maks a score? Faith, Robbie, I doubt
ye're auld Bruickie's handiwork," and having said this,
went away without waiting for a reply. Some time
after, Fleeman was at Dudwick, and by chance while
he was there the General's friend arrived. Jamie
generally claimed the privilege of accompanying in
their walks the gentlemen about whose house he was
staying, and to this little objection was offered, as all
knew that Fleeman never repeated at one place what

he heard at another. In the afternoon, the party at Dudwick were walking about the place, and having come in sight of the farmer's house, the officer made some inquiry concerning his acquaintance. The General, in few words, informed him of the man's altered habits. "I am sorry to receive such an account," said the officer; "he was a good sort of man, and I should have been glad to hear of his success, but, d—n the fellow, I could perceive when I was here some years ago that he was getting to fond of the *Flushing*. I meant to have befriended him, but must now altogether cut his acquaintance." Fleeman, as was often his way, was heard making his own remarks on what had been said. "Od, some folk's friendship is like the Auld Smith's,* the less o't we hae the better for us." "What smith are you talking of, Fleeman?" demanded the officer; but Fleeman, nowise studious to give a direct answer, went on with his soliloquy; "the mair he blaws, the sairer he burns, and then pretends to laugh at folk who say that wind blisters." "What can Fleeman mean?" inquired the officer, looking at the General; but Jamie proceeded: "Faith, I believe it is soldier's trade to kill folk; od; it would have been better for Robbie, and just the same thing to him, had he ta'en Robbie's life wi' his durk,† rather than wi' his kindness." "Fleeman," said the General, interrupting him, "here is a shilling for you to buy tobacco." Jamie thanked the General, and was soon on his way to Udny,

In Jamie's time, smuggling of gin from Holland was carried on to an almost incredible extent. From the Don to the Ugie there was scarcely a farmer or petty merchant within sight of the sea, who did not, more or less, engage in this "free trade" system. Illicit trans-

---

* A quaint term by which Fleeman occasionally designated the enemy of mankind.
† His sword, we suppose.

actions generally display very tempting prospects, but
they rarely fail to inveigle their abettors into evils which
lie deeply concealed ; so, in the "gin trade," as it was
called, men looked only to the money which it promised
to put into their pockets, but considered not the neglect
of more lawful employments which it occasioned, nor
the habits of intemperance and immorality which it
fostered. It placed immediately within their reach the
means of indulgence to excess, and to this they were
tempted as often as they had occasion to rejoice over a
successful "run." When a cargo was safely deposited,
the partners in this speculation rarely failed to make
merry after their toil, and to dissipate over full bowls
that care and solicitude which had harassed their minds
during the time of landing and securing their treasure.
Hence many a sober and industrious man was gradually
betrayed into habits of enebriety and laziness. Among
others was one whom Fleeman had long known. This
man, previous to engaging in smuggling, had borne an
excellent character, but from that time he began to
neglect his business, and to become more and more
attached to his bottle. He still retained his obliging
disposition, which circumstances tended to render his
debauched habits a matter of very general regret. Fleeman was on a visit to his friend, and as his remarks
were generally as unexpected as they were singular, he,
one day, abruptly addressed the farmer as follows :—
" Od, Charlie, they say ye winna gie Auld Nick a lodging ony way about your house, but just in ae place."
" I hope, Jamie," replied his friend, " he gets na
encouragement to tak' up a quiet residence with me in
any place." " Faith, they say he does though," said
Fleeman. ."Od, man, I was tauld that ye let him
lodge in your gin bottle, and that ilka time ye taste the
liquor, he comes out into the glass and gi'es you a kiss.
For the Lord's sake, Charlie, tak' care o' him, he's a
sleekit rascal; and guid faith, I've kent him bite aff three

or four foulk's heads in his fits o' kindness." We have
not heard whether Jamie's strange rebuke had the least
effect in making his friend reflect on the dangerous
course he was pursuing. We suspect not ; for, although
we should imagine that Fleeman's remark would have
some times crossed his mind when about to put the glass
to his lips, yet we are not ignorant how rarely it happens
that one succeeds in conquering a bad habit which he
has allowed to acquire strength. A confirmed drunkard
rather than relinquish his bottle, would almost consent
to salute Satan ; and we are of opinion that Fleeman
got extremely little thanks for his remarkable advice.

Speculation is the greatest stimulus to improvement,
but it is likewise the means of hurrying many a man to
his ruin. If not pushed beyond rational bounds, it
will produce activity, and has every chance of being
attended with success; but employed without prudence,
and urged without caution, its consequences will seldom
fail to be poverty instead of wealth, and redicule in place
of applause. About the middle of the last century,
speculation in agricultural pursuits was scarcely known
in the north of Scotland. Many a good farm was then
lying without a tenant. Even the most unclouded prospects of success could scarcely tempt farmers to hazard
the smallest trifle in improving either the soil or the
implements of their trade, and they were ready to pre-
dict speedy ruin to the man who should have deviated
in the least from the old and rugged track. Men at a
certain stage of knowledge seem incapable of distinguish-
ing between wild speculation and rational enterprise,
and are ever ready to dread the consequences of the
former, if any one recommend the adoption of the later.
In this state was the great proportion of the farmers of
Aberdeenshire about a hundred years ago. So very
different was the system of farming from that which
now prevails, that scarcely a farm could be found of
which great part was not lying waste or covered with

morasses, and in few instances did the farmer think it
worth while to improve the one or drain the other.
What was still more extraordinary, if any one ever
ventured to be a little more forward than his neighbour in correcting such errors, he was looked on by
them with an eye of contempt, if not of ill will.
They could scarcely bear with patience to see any man
departing from the old system, which they held to be
the best possible mode that could be devised—a mode
adopted by the wisdom of former days, and rendered
next to sacred by long-continued usage. The Laird of
Udny was among the first in his district who showed
unequivocal symptoms of hostility to this wretched
system. Regardless of established customs when not
conducive to his interests, and of popular odium when
supported only by senseless prejudice, he adopted a
mode of farming so novel, and on a scale so extensive,
that the rustics stared with astonishment, and even
ventured to surmise that the lands of Udny could not
long bear such reckless expenditure. Fleeman heard
their remarks, and was deceived by their exaggerated
representations. Fearing that what all were predicting
might prove true, he resolved, like a faithful servant,
to give his matser a hint of the issue in which his
speculations were likely to terminate. Watching his
opportunity, he one day saw the Laird pointing out to
a friend what he had already done, and what he still
meant to do on his domain. Fleeman approached, and
for some time seemed to pay great attention to what
Udny was describing, then suddenly mounting upon
the top of a dyke, and there standing on tip-toe, he
looked round him with apparent anxiety. " What is
the matter now, Fleeman?" said Udny; "what are
you looking for?" " Faith sir," replied Fleeman, " I
am looking for places on which we may big win'mills."
·'Windmills!" said Udny; "what do you want with
windmills?" " Od, that ye may rid your head o'

some o' them.　Ilka body says it's fou o' win'mills ;
and, Lord bless me ! how feared I am, aye when the
win' rises, they may turn your head a'thegither ; they
will be your ruin."　"Here is sixpence for you," said
Udny ; "but recollect to keep in order the blockheads
who tell you these things, and not allow them to speak
ill of me or my plans either."　Udny knew well how to
convert Fleeman's opposition into powerful support ;
for, after this, Jamie never failed, not only to ridicule
those who spoke against his master's operations, but
also to maintain that "guid Udny" was setting an
example which every one who wished to become rich
would do well to imitate.

Most people are as ready to give an advice to others,
as they are to consider whether it may not be partly
applicable to themselves.　A rather curious instance
of this is on record, in which Fleeman acted a part.
The Laird of Udny had a friend in Aberdeen, to whom
he frequently sent a present of game.　Fleeman was
generally the bearer, and was not a little chagrined
that he never received anything from the gentleman
for his trouble.　Deeming this a departure from gen-
tleman-like conduct, he resolved to have his revenge
by the neglect of every rule of common courtesy.
Being sent to Aberdeen with a few hares and par-
tridges, when he arrived at the house of his master's
friend, he stopped not at the door to give any information of his arrival, but, marching boldly into the apartment where the gentleman was sitting, threw the
bundle on the floor, growled " Hares frae Udny," and
turned to go away.　The gentleman called him back,
gave him a long lecture concerning the importance of
good breeding, and endeavoured to convince him of
the rudeness and impropriety of his conduct on that
occasion.　Rising up, he said, "Allow me to tell you,
Fleeman, how you ought to behave.　When you come
to the door of a gentleman's house, you ought not to

walk in without further ceremony; but, having knocked, ask if the master be at home; and having waited till he either calls you or comes to you, say, 'With his compliments, Udny sent you this bag of game, Sir.'" At the conclusion of this lecture, Fleeman suddenly took possession of his instructor's chair, and, assuming the air of a gentleman, said, in a very grave and dignified tone, "Give my best respects to Udny, and say I feel particularly indebted to him for his kind attention. And now, my good fellow," continued he, feigning to put his hand into his pocket, "here is half-a-crown to you for your own trouble." We have not learned how the gentleman looked or how he behaved on the occasion, but Fleeman certainly communicated to him the rather curious, though very important intelligence that he who would offer an advice to another nowise indebted to him, must first bribe him to listen, otherwise the best counsel will be disregarded, and he who gives it considered officious and ill-bred.*

At the time when Fleeman lived, religious controversy between those of the Established Church and those who adhered to Episcopacy prevailed to an extent, and was carried on with a degree of acrimony, to which we who live in more peaceful times would scarcely give credit. After the affair at Culloden, Episcopalians were looked on, not only by Presbyterians, but by the Government of the day, as having been the principal friends and abettors of the Prince, and therefore were considered as a dangerous sect, which ought to be put down. These steady adherents to a declining cause were disposed to search deeply into the groundwork of their principles before they would consent to purchase safety at the expense of

---

* It is probable Fleeman had heard the anecdote, similar to this, recorded by Dean Swift.

profession ; and having satisfied themselves on this
head, they exerted themselves in no ordinary degree
to keep their brethern from defection.   None was
more famous in this respect than Mary, Countess of
Errol.   She was in the habit of getting prayer-books
from London, and distributing them privately among
her tenants.   Such attention from such a quarter had
a most powerful effect in making them determined
bigots, and they looked on danger as nought in comparison of what they termed principle.   Fleeman, who
allowed little to pass unobserved, was well aware
that a sure road to favour was to humour the foibles
of those whose good-will he sought.   One day, when
the Countess was about to reward him for some
important service, he refused a pecuniary recompense
which was tendered, and begged that her ladyship
would give him a copy of the " prayer-buik."   As
the Countess knew that Fleeman could not read a
word, she was rather surprised at such a request,
and demanded of Jamie what he meant to do with
the book.   Having satisfied her on this point, he
received a very neatly-bound copy, and immediately
marched off to Whinnyfold, a fishing-village in the
neighbourhood of Slains Castle.   Here Barbara Fleeman, Jamie's niece, had lately come to reside.   Fleeman
appears to have had a particular attachment to this
young woman, and, moreover, to have been of opinion
that his regard could in no way be more effectually
proved that by inducing her to become a bigoted
admirer of the Countess of Errol and her religious
predilections, but, as the sequel will show, Barbara
was not prepared to view these matters in exactly
the same light as her uncle.   Fleeman found her
with two or three of her youthful companions who
had assembled to " weave a wedding "* in the even-

* In the county of Aberdeen, about fourscore years ago, the manufacture
of stockings, or "shanks," as they were provincially called, formed the chief

ing. There are many people who may be willing enough to acknowledge a poor relative in private, but who are almost prepared to disclaim all connection or acquaintance with such before the world. In particular, young people are apt to imagine that they would be disgraced by publicly recognising a relative to whom nature or fortune has not been over propitious ; but as the world is rarely ignorant of the connection, such conduct tends rather to degrade than exalt them in the estimation of every one whose good opinion is worth having. Barbara Fleeman received her uncle with much coldness ; but Jamie, not heeding this much, took his seat among the damsels. After some preliminary observations, he said, " Babie, ye're o' the *gentle persuasion,** and I hae got the book for you ; " and he at the same time drew the book from a fold of his garment. " I'm gaun to the kirk " was the indirect and laconic reply which his niece thought fit to make. " Na, faith ye, lassie," said Fleeman ; " ye can read, and Lady Mary, says that a' that read are o' the ' gentle persuasion.' " Whatever " the lassie "

---

employment of women, and children of both sexes, and even of many men, who thought it no shame to replenish their purses by the proceeds of their labours in knitting during the winter evenings. Crowds of young women frequently assembled to spend their long evenings, when trials of speed in knitting, and "sang about," formed their employment. The "guidwife's" province was to keep these young parties "in order," and to decide all matters with regard to their work during the evening. In the " gloamin'," when the young people were assembled, the guidwife sat down and measured off a "wedding." This was done by putting all their "clues," or ball of worsted in a large dish, and unwinding from each as much as she thought would employ the "lasses " for the evening. Exactly the same length of worsted was unwound from each ball, and a "rose-knot " tied. Sometimes the party divided into pairs for the contest. If they all agreed to try at once for the victory, the guidwife mentioned some young fellow in the neighbourhood who was the known sweetheart of some one present, or a general favourite with all ; or, if they contended in parties, she named one for each. They all started at the same time, and the young maiden who got first to the knot on her worsted was allowed to indulge the hope that she would get for a husband the youth who had been named. She who was accounted his sweetheart wrought most laboriously to make good her claim ; and the other girls, although they cared less for the young man, yet took a pride in annoying their companion, and did everything in their power to get at the "marriage knot " before her.

* A title by which Fleeman, from a wish to flatter the Countess of Errol and his other friends, generally designated Episcopacy.

thought, she made no reply, nor was it for some time that she took the book from her uncle, holding it out to her. At last she snatched it from him and threw it into the fire. Fleeman speedily plucked it from the flames, and, looking his niece sternly in the face, said, " I winna strike you, ye feel, and waur than a feel. Ye think to affront me ; I'm affronted wi' you. Never call me your uncle, nor speak to me again." Then relaxing from rage to grief, he said, " My heart was leal to you, Babie ; but it can be sae nae langer. God forgive you ! " and, as our informant reports, Jamie was moved to teers. His designs were completely thwarted ; his affections met with the most ungrateful return ; and poor Fleeman was overwhelmed with grief and disappointment. The conduct of his niece was not to be commended, but a man of ordinary powers of mind would have looked on all that she did as the thoughtless act of a foolish young girl, and, after an admonition, would have thought no more of the matter; but to Fleeman's eyes it appeared a grave offence, which scarcely left room for pardon. Weak minds always invest trifles with an unbecoming importance. Fleeman muttered something about finding one who would both receive and respect his present, and took an abrupt leave of his niece. He never after entered the house where she resided, nor acknowledged her as a relative ; and when he had occasion to speak of her, he called her " that woman." Barbara Fleeman, when arrived at years of more discretion, no doubt regretted what she had done in a moment of thoughtlessness, when surrounded by her youthful companions, and dreading their scorn on account of her uncle's kindness. In matters of much greater importance than this, a single rash or thoughtless action has not unfrequently been the cause of many evils, which regret can never wholly remove, and of disgrace, which time can with difficulty efface.

The person to whom Fleeman alluded as more worthy than his niece, was a girl whom he had supported almost from her childhood. She was an orphan, and Fleeman had found her, when very young, herding a cow. At that time she was crying for hunger, and in a very pitiable condition. Jamie ministered to her immediate wants from his pocket, and took such a lively interest in her favour, that he soon found means of supplying her with clothes. As he enjoyed a small weekly allowance from Udny, he contrived to maintain and educate this poor child, having placed her with an old woman, with orders that she might be taught to read, sew, spin, and knit stockings. Gratitude demanded of this girl that she should respect her benefactor, and she had good sense enough never to dispute the demand. She treated Jamie with filial regard, and he, in return, looked on "the lassie" with almost more than parental affection. When she was married, Fleeman gave her away; and it is said that, during the whole of the wedding day, he behaved with a degree of decorum and steadiness beyond what any one thought him capable of supporting. The only indication of a disordered mind which he betrayed, was his extreme solicitude that all things should be gone about in "marriage order." * One said to him "Jamie, man,

---

* To one acquainted only with the ceremonies of what may be termed a genteel wedding of the present day, the reason of Fleeman's anxiety about "marriage order" will be altogether unaccountable. It may be interesting to give a brief account of a country wedding, conducted according to the manner of former days. The bridegroom, when inviting his guests, always asked two young men to do him the favour to bring home his bride. These were termed "the sends;" he who was principally entrusted with the charge being called the "best send." He likewise invited two young girls to lead him to the place where the marriage ceremony was to be performed, and these were called "the bridegroom's maidens;" the "best" and the "worst" respectively as each was to lead him by the "right" or "left" hand. In like manner the bride asked two young men to lead her to the place of marriage; the one called "the bride's best young man," the other her "worst young man." She had likewise two young women termed her "maidens;" the one the "best," the other "the worst bride's maid." When the day appointed arrived, these repaired to the houses of the bridegroom and bride, respectively, as they had been invited, and at an hour rather earlier than the

the bride owes you much." "Her freens has paid it a' the day," replied Fleeman. On the man looking surprised, and remarking that he was not aware that

---

other guests. There business was to see that the parties about to be wedded were neatly and properly decked out for the occasion. According to the time requisite for bringing the bride to the place appointed for the marriage, "the sends" took their departure from the bridegroom's house, and proceeded to that of the bride. Having arrived at the door, the "best send" knocked, and the bride, with her maids, having made her appearance, he asked, in case of not being acquainted with her, if she was the bride of such a man, and, on her answering in the affirmative, he told her that the bridegroom had his complements to her, and requested that she would attend to the appointment agreed upon betwixt them at their meeting last past. He then saluted first the bride and then her maids, an example which was followed by his companion ; after which, the bride invited them into the house, where they were treated with something to eat and drink : and, when there was music and dancing, they danced with the bride and her best maid. That done, they shook hands with the bride, mentioned the exact time that the bridegroom expected her, and took their leave. Proceeding till they met the bridegroom and his party on the way to the place appointed for the marriage, they reported to him that his request had been complied with, and that his bride was a-coming. The marriage ceremony over, the "sends" now lead the bride to her new habitation, and the bridesmaids lead home the bridegroom, while the bridegroom's maids, and the bride's "young men" generally walk in pairs. The person who first arrives is said to "win the brose." Having reached the bridegroom's, some matron appointed for the purpose, stood ready with a basket full of "buns," or, in absence of this, of bread and cheese, which being placed on the bride's head, the buns or the bread and cheese were broken, and handed round among the company. The bride was then "welcomed" into the house by the bridegroom's mother or some other relative appointed for the purpose, who generally took care either to compliment or taunt her according as the match was agreeable to the friends or not. This matron then led the bride to the fire-place, and gave her the tongs, by which ceremony she was considered to be established in the possession of her house. All now hastened to the dinner-table, at which it was considered altogether contrary to "marriage order," and even rather unlucky, if the "officials" did not arrange themselves as follows :—The bride at the head of the table ; on her left hand, first, her best maid, then her best young man, after him the bridegroom's second or worst maid, and last of all the bride's worst young man ; and, on her right hand, first the "best send," next to him the bridegroom's best maid, then the "worst send," and, to the right of all, the bride's second maid. Dinner over, the bride takes a glass in her hand, stands up, drinks to the health of the company : then the bridegroom's best man or send does the same, and, in the bridegroom's name assures them of being welcome : after which the bride's best maid does the same thing, and in the bride's name tells them that they are welcome guests. When tired at the table, they rise to the dance. This, too, is a matter of great ceremony, and four reels are completed before any of the ordinary company are allowed to begin. The fifth dance is always considered by young fellows as a high honour, and is, therefore, sought by every device, while not unfrequently the fiddler decides the matter by declaring who has paid him for the tune. The dances are arranged thus :—

1st. The bride is partner to the best send, and her maid to the other send.

she had any nearly related to her, Jamie said, " Poor thing, her good manners are her nearest kin.   Faith ! they have not proved bad freens to Mary, I think."

CHAPTER VII.

HARDSHIPS AND DEATH.

HERE are few whose lives pass on from youth to age without misfortune and without trouble, and poor Fleeman did not escape the fate most common to mortals.   The part of his biography which remains to be recorded compels us to leave the gay and frolicsome scenes in which we have hitherto found him mingling, and to accompany him into others of a sadder and more distressing nature.   In the early part of the summer of 1778, Jamie was one day exposed to a very heavy rain.   As a poor wanderer rarely meets with much attention, so Fleeman found no kind friend who thought of giving him a stitch of clothes, or an opportunity of drying those which he wore.   He arrived at one of his favourite haunts late in the evening.   Drenched with

---

2nd.   The bridegroom's best maid and best send, and bride's second maid and other send.

3rd.   The bride is partner to her best young man, and her maid to the bride's worst young man.

4th.   The bridesmaid and best young man, and the bridegroom's second maid with the bride's second young man.

5th.   The bride and her maid, and any two young men of the company.

Before each dance, the men claim a kiss from their partners ; and at the end of the first, third, and fifth dances, the bride and her maid tie a "favour" of blue ribbon on their partner's arm.

rain, and shivering with cold, he was, as usual, shown
to his bed in an out-house. His constitution, which
had long been proof against the worst usage, was, for
the first time, forced to yield. He passed a sleepless
night, and in the morning feverish symptoms were
apparent. Had he met with the attention of any kind
friend, he might have recovered; but of such he had
none. All were glad to see him when he contributed
to their amusement, and required not their aid; but
now that he was incapable of the former, and stood in
need of the latter, there were few whose pity he excited
—few whose kindness he received. The world, taken
as a whole, is selfish and ungrateful. There are many
noble exceptions, but its general character is cold and
unfeeling. It loads those with kindness who stand in
no need of its favours, while it carelessly and cruelly
overlooks those who would be glad of its least attention.
While Fleeman could move their mirth, he was
welcomed by all, and pressed to prolong his visits;
now that he deserved their pity, he met with a cold
reception from most, and none asked him to stay till
he should recover his health. Jaundice succeeded to
a severe cold, and Fleeman's robust frame gradually
became weak and emaciated. In this diseased state
he wandered from house to house, till, at last, he
reached Little Ardiffery, in the parish of Cruden. It
has been remarked by some, that misfortunes, when
they begin to appear, generally crowd thick upon each
other. Poor Fleeman experienced the truth of this.
Having taken up his lodgings for the night in the
barn, he shook some straw on the floor immediately
opposite the door. Before laying himself down on
his humble couch, he secured the door by placing
against it a large oaken plank, which he found in the
barn. At that period there were no thrashing-machines
in the country, and the servant lads had to rise early
to provide provender for the cattle. In the morning,

when Fleeman had fallen into a kind of slumber, the lads came to the barn door, and not recollecting that Jamie was there, they wondered what hindered the door from being opened, applied their strength to it, and, with a sudden jerk, overturned the plank which Jamie had placed behind the door. It fell with a fearful weight on the poor creature's head, and not only cut him severely, but almost stunned him. He was able to crawl to a corner where the sheaves of corn were packed, and there he laid him down, weak from disease, and in pain from his wound. The blood continued to flow, but no one was present who sought to stem it. He was sick and parched with thirst, but no friendly voice spoke comfort—no kind hand ministered assistance. The servants plied their work, and thought little of the fool. The din of their instruments was incessant, although Jamie had never before stood more in need of quiet. In this state he continued till breakfast time, when the lads having mentioned the misfortune with which he had met, Mr. Johnston's daughter lost not a moment in showing him every attention, and administering every comfort in their power. The lads were not aware of the extent of the injury which he had received. They described the cut in his head as trifling; and, as they had heard no complaints from poor Fleeman, they concluded that little was the matter. The young ladies were much horrified when they ascertained the extent of the wound, the quantity of blood which he had lost, and the feeble state in which he was. They had him immediately removed to the kitchen; and as one of them was cutting off some locks of his hair, in order to have the wound properly dressed, he for the first time. faintly exclaimed, "Alas!"

Poor Fleeman now felt that the cold hand of death was upon him, and he said to Mr. Johnston, "When I am gane, ye winna lay me at Cruden ; but tak' me to

Langside, and bury me among my friends!" Mr.
Johnston, perhaps not imagining that Jamie's death
was yet at hand, replied, "Na, na, Jamie, we'll try you
here first; and if you winna lie, we shall then be
forced to carry you across the hill." The tear came
into the poor creature's eye, and he heaved a deep
sigh, which made Mr. Johnston repent of what he had
said, for he plainly perceived that the time for jesting
with Jamie was gone by. Fleeman without saying a
word, and in spite of every remonstrance, prepared for
his journey to Longside. He thanked those who had
shown him kindness, and said he forgave every injury
which he ever had received. Then summoning the
last remains of that strength which, for many a day,
had enabled him to consider all ordinary exertions as
nought, he found it scarcely sufficient for the task he
had now to perform. The distance which he proposed
to walk was about eight miles. This, at one time,
would have soon been accomplished; but now it was
the work of a whole day. He found it necessary to
call at every house in his way, that he might rest his
weary limbs, and often had he to sit down on the road-
side for the same purpose. A month previous to this
and he was scarcely aware that the vigour of youth
had left him; now he found himself labouring under
the imbecility of extreme old age. Such are the
sudden changes which disease can produce—the direful effects which the neglect of the ordinary means of
preserving health may cause. The shadows of the
evening had fallen thick before Jamie reached his
sister's cottage at Kinmundy. Martha prepared a bed
for him, on which he might wear out his remaining
days. They were not many. On the second, his
strength was so far gone that the neighbours were
called in to see him take his leave of the world. While
standing round his bed, one said to another, "I wonder if he has any sense of another world, or a future

reckoning?" "Oh no, he is a fool!" replied the other; "what can *he* know of such things?" Jamie opened his eyes, and looking this man in the face, said, "I never heard that God seeks where he did not give." The bystanders' unseasonable reasonings were cut short. Fleeman lay quiet for a short time, when he again opened his eyes, and looking at one whom he respected, and who stood near, he said, in a firm tone, "I am a Christian, dinna bury me like a beast."* These were his last words. In the course of a few minutes after he had uttered them, he quietly breathed his last.

His funeral was numerously attended. The Messrs. Kilgour at that time employed a number of wool-combers and weavers at Kinmundy, all of whom they sent to assist in carrying the body of Fleeman to the grave, and they generously treated those who attended the funeral with porter and cakes; so that the poor creature, who died almost friendless, had a decent burial. His remains lie near the north dyke of the churchyard of Longside.

Jamie's grave no longer remains unmarked. An Aberdeen gentleman, while on a visit to Longside, in 1861, having been taken to see the Rev. Mr. Skinner's (Tullochgorum) grave, was informed by the schoolmaster that Fleeman was buried near the musical divine, and being then struck with the idea that a plain tombstone to indicate Jamie's grave should be erected, he, in a quiet way, assisted by one or two friends, collected in the course of a week or two, a sum of about £14, in shilling subscriptions. With the money, a pillar of polished Aberdeen granite, resting on a rustic base, was provided, the work being exe-

---

* One who resided in Kinmundy at the time, says Fleeman's last words were, "I'm of the GENTLE PERSUASION, dinna bury me like a beast.

cuted by Mr. George Donaldson, sculptor, Aberdeen, an old residenter in the parish, who, out of respect for Jamie, requested to be allowed to perform the work. The inscription on the Stone is—

ERECTED IN 1861,

TO INDICATE THE GRAVE OF

JAMIE FLEEMAN

IN ANSWER TO HIS PRAYER,

"DINNA BURY ME LIKE A BEAST."

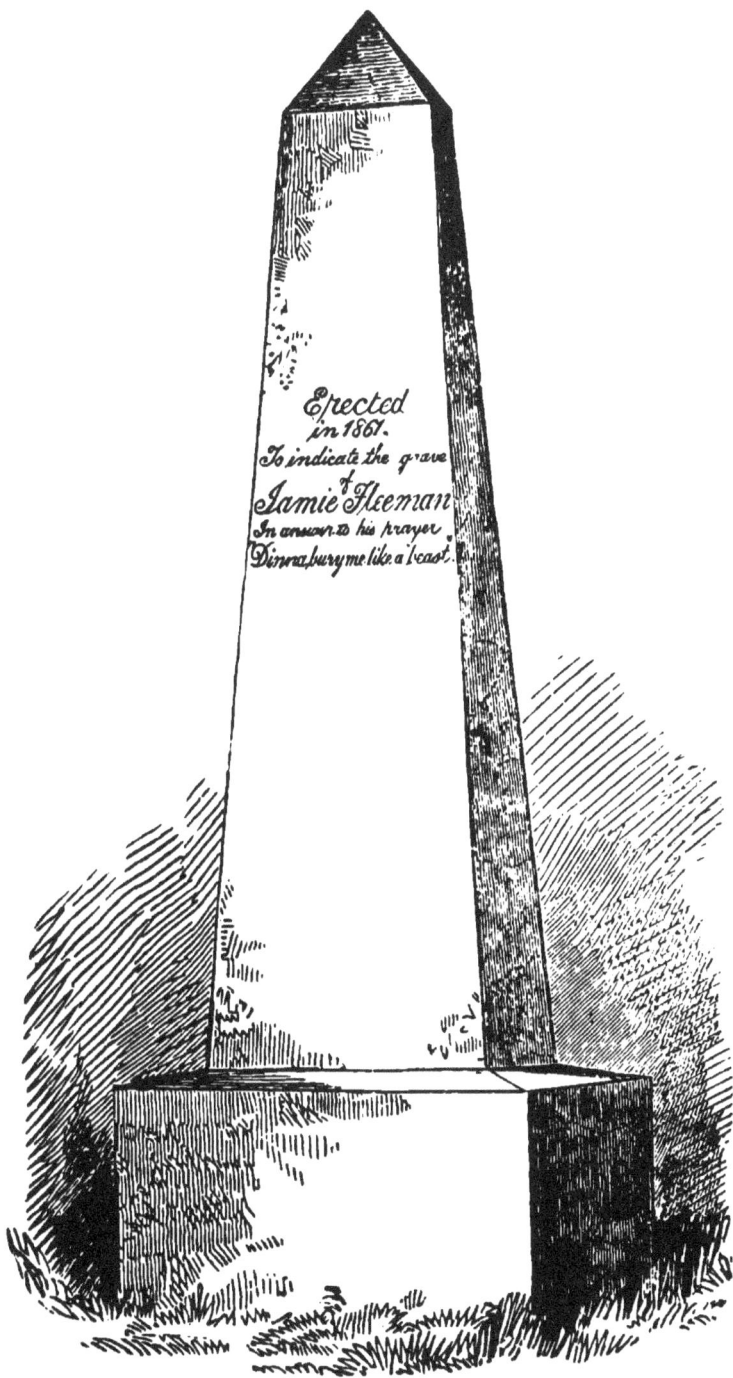

Erected
in 1861.
To indicate the grave
of
Jamie Fleeman
In answer to his prayer
"Dinna bury me like a beast."

THE LIFE

AND

CURIOUS ADVENTURES

OF

PETER WILLIAMSON,

Who was carried off from Aberdeen,
and sold for a Slave.

A NEW EDITION.

ABERDEEN: LEWIS SMITH & SON,

AND ALL BOOKSELLERS.

1885.

ABERDEEN :

PRINTED BY LEWIS SMITH & SON.

PREFACE.

HE who reads the life of Peter Williamson will find it fraught with much useful instruction. The language in which it is narrated is a sufficient proof that its author was no designing man, who intended to impose on the credulity of the vulgar, and satiate their appetite for the marvellous, by the account of his sufferings. Were not the facts sufficiently vouched for, we would almost suppose that, while reading his hair-breadth escapes, we were perusing some tale of romance, or the fanciful production of some ingenious novelist. But the tale is too true; the crime of kidnapping made more sufferers than Williamson, and Aberdeen was not the only place disgraced by this horrible traffic. It is useless—it is worse than useless—it is absolutely criminal to argue, that children of nine or ten years were able to indent themselves, and to implement articles of agreement which were never meant to be fulfilled—nay, where personal liberty is concerned, even although the person had arrived at the years of maturity, it is a right which he could neither give nor sell; in corroboration of this I shall adduce the opinion of the celebrated Rousseau, in his treaty on the Social Compact, he thus writes: " To renounce one's personal liberty is to renounce one's very being as a man; it is to renounce not only the rights but also the duties of humanity. And what possible indemnification can be made to the man who thus gives up his all? Such a remuneration is incompatible with our very nature; for to deprive us of the liberty of will, is to take away all morality from our actions. In a word, a convention which, on the one part stipulates absolute authority, and on the other implicit obedience, is in itself futile and contradictory." Such then is a just view of those indentures for life, which were held out by the kidnappers as just and lawful. But here let us observe, that their crime assumes a blacker die when we take into consideration the circumstance that these indentures were never proposed until they had actual possession of the bodies of their victims; it matters not how this possession was obtained, whether by cajoling artifices, or absolute violence, they were in durance, and no opposition would have availed, nor would resistance have frustrated the designs of their enslavers. When the prisoners were landed in Virginia or Carolina, they discovered their true situation ; driven like beasts of burden to a market place, they were exposed for sale, and given accordingly to the highest bidder, let his character or principles be what they may. Think, reader, for a moment, that your brother, the companion of your sports, the friend of your heart, one night disappeared and was seen no more—that the grief and sorrow of your parents were bringing them fast to the grave ; and that, though years might roll, they brought no tidings of their lost child ; and that their last prayers were breathed for the ever-lost boy. And this was many a brother's—many a parent's lot. Or did chance, at some long future period, bring the doubtful intelligence that he was alive on some far distant shore—a mother's heart would yearn, and a father's grief would be in vain supprest—they would mourn for the living as the dead—to them he would be dead; and, dreading, doubting, hoping, they would die, with the sad, yet consoling anticipation, that a few years after and they would embrace their child in that happy land where oppressors could no more part them, but where "God the Lord would wipe all tears from their eyes." One thought more on this subject, those who were kidnapped were persons who, having felt the blessings of liberty, would therefore be more susceptible of the horrors of slavery : they were fit for the enjoyment of a state of liberty by education and by birth, and the awful novelty of being slaves would therefore present itself to their view in its most aggravated form. All their high hopes would be crushed, all their youthful day-dreams would vanish as airy phantoms, and the cruel reality of their hopeless situation would mock all their fancied prospects of future worldly bliss. Well may we congratulate ourselves that these days have gone by, and that no oppressor, however rich and powerful, can devote us at the ALTAR OF SLAVERY.

It would be well if we could say as much of every class of subjects. There is a race whose only crime is their complexion, and whose only vice is their want of education—a want which their iron-hearted oppressors will not allow to be supplied—and this race is liable to tenfold greater calamities than did ever befal our infatuate fellow-citizens of Aberdeen, even when the practice of kidnapping was carried on in its most villainous extent. The slaves in the West Indies—for it is to them we allude—are the objects of the sympathy of Christendom. Already have the most of its states declared the crime of man-stealing to be piracy, and therefore punishable with death ; but still the nefarious traffic is pursued, and in spite of the vigilance evinced by our cruisers, thousands are dragged from their homes to wear out a listless life of dreary solitude. In vain are laws enacted when interest and prejudice so strongly warp the minds of the planters, that justice and morality are excluded, and rapine and oppression necessarily domineer in their breasts. It has been often argued that the slaves in the West Indies are not the victims of oppression, that they are well treated, and, in many cases, that they live more comfortably than our artisans do at home. But granting that it were the case that the slaves were well treated, what does it bear against the general argument? Nothing at all; for it will not matter whether the chain with which he is fettered be made of iron or of gold, it is equally strong. The wretch who is secured with a silken cord is as much a prisoner as he who is bound with hemp.

THE

LIFE AND CURIOUS ADVENTURES

OF

PETER WILLIAMSON.

INTRODUCTION.

HE reader is not here to expect a large
and useless detail of the transactions of
late years, in that part of the world where,
ever since my infancy, it has been my
misfortune to have lived. Was it in my
power, indeed, to set off with pompous
diction, and embellish with artificial
descriptions, what has so engrossed the attention of
Europe, as well as the scenes of action for some years
past, perhaps I might; but my poor pen being wholly
unfit for such a task, and never otherwise employed
than just for my own affairs and amusement, while I
had the pleasure of living tranquil and undisturbed, I
must beg leave to desist from such an attempt; and if
such is expected from me, claim the indulgence of that
pardon which is never refused to those incapacitated
of performing what may be desired of them. And as
a plain, impartial, and succinct narrative of my own
life, and various vicissitudes of fortune, is all that I
now shall aim at, I shall herein confine myself to plain
simple truth, and, in the dictates resulting from an
honest heart, give the reader no other entertainment

than what shall be matter of fact; and of such things as have actually happened to me, or come to my own knowledge in the sphere of life in which it has been my lot to be placed. Not but I hope I may be allowed, now and then, to carry on my narrative from the information I have received of such things as relate to my design, though they have not been done or transacted in my presence.

It being usual in narratives like this, to give a short account of the author's birth, education, and juvenile exploits, the same being looked upon as necessary, or at least a satisfactory piece of information to the curious and inquisitive reader, I shall, without boasting of a family I am no way entitled to, or recounting adventures in my youth to which I was entirely a stranger, in a short manner gratify such curiosity; not expecting, as I said before, to be admired for that elegance of style, and profusion of words, so universally made use of in details and histories of those adventurers who have of late years obliged the world with their anecdotes and memoirs, and which have had scarce any other existence than in the brains of a bookseller's or printer's garreteer, who, from fewer incidents, and less surprising matter, than will be found in this short narrative, have been, and are daily enabled to spin and work out their elaborate performances to three or four volumes.

THE AUTHOR'S BIRTH, &c.

KNOW, therefore, that I was born in Hirnlay, in the Parish of Aboyne, and County of Aberdeen, North Britain, if not of rich, yet of reputable parents, who supported me in the best manner they could, as long as they had the happiness of having me under their inspection; but fatally for me, and to their great grief, as it afterwards proved, I was sent to live with an aunt at Aberdeen. When under the years of pupillarity, playing on the quay, with others of my companions, being of a stout, robust constitution, I was taken notice of by two fellows belonging to a vessel in the harbour, employed (as the trade then was) by some of the worthy merchants in the town, in that villainous and execrable practice called *Kidnapping;* that is, stealing young children from their parents, and selling them as slaves in the plantations abroad. Being marked out by these monsters of impiety as their prey, I was cajoled on board the ship by them, where I was no sooner got, than they conducted me between the decks to some others they had kidnapped in the same manner. At that time I had no sense of the fate that was destined for me, and spent the time in childish amusements with my fellow sufferers in the steerage, being never suffered to go upon deck whilst the vessel lay in the harbour, which was until such a time as they had got in their loading, with a complement of unhappy youths for carrying on their wicked commerce.

In about a month's time the ship set sail for America. The treatment we met with, and the trifling incidents which happened during the voyage, I hope I may be excused from relating, as not being at that time of an age sufficient to remark anything more than what must occur to everyone on such an occasion. However, I cannot forget that, when we arrived on the coast we were destined for, a hard gale of wind sprung up from the S.E., and, to the captain's great surprise (he not thinking he was near land) although having been eleven weeks on the passage, about twelve o'clock at night the ship struck on a sand-bank off Cape May, near the Capes of Delaware, and to the great terror and affright of the ship's company, in a short time was almost full of water. The boat was then hoisted out, into which the captain, and his fellow villains—the crew—got with some difficulty, leaving me, and my deluded companions, to perish, as they then naturally concluded inevitable death to be our fate. Often, in my distresses and miseries since, have I wished that such had been the consequence, when in a state of innocence ; but Providence though proper to reserve me for future trials of its goodness. Thus abandoned and deserted, without the least prospect of relief, but threatened every moment with death, did these villains leave us. The cries, the shrieks, and tears of a parcel of infants, had no effect on, or caused the least remorse in the breasts of these merciless wretches. Scarce need I say, to which to give the preference ; whether to such as these who have had the opportunity of knowing the Christian religion ; or to the savages hereinafter described, who profane not the gospel, or boast of humanity, and if they act in a more brutal and butcherly manner, yet it is to their enemies, for the sake of plunder and the rewards offered them, for their principles are alike, the love of sordid gain being both their motives. The ship being on a sandbank, which did not give way to let her deeper, we lay in the same deplorable condition until morning, when, though we saw the land of Cape May, at about a mile's distance, we knew no what would be our fate.

The wind at length abated, and the captain (unwilling to lose all her cargo), about ten o'clock, sent some of his crew in a boat to the ship's side to bring us on shore, where we lay in a sort of a camp, made of the sails of the vessel, and such other things as we could get. The provisions lasted us until we were taken in by a vessel bound to Philadelphia, lying on this island, as well as I can recollect, near three weeks. Very little of the cargo was saved undamaged, and the vessel entirely lost.

When arrived and landed at Philadelphia, the capital of Pennsylvania, the captain had soon people enough who came to buy us. He, making the most of his villainous loading, after his disaster, sold us at about £16 per head. What became of my unhappy companions I never knew; but it was my lot to be sold to one of my countrymen, whose name was Hugh Wilson, a North Briton, for the term of seven years, who had in his youth undergone the same fate as myself, having been kidnapped from St. Johnstown, in Scotland. As I shall often have occasion to mention Philadelphia during the course of my adventures, I shall, in this place, give a short and concise description of the finest city of America, and one of the best laid out in the world.

DESCRIPTION OF PHILADELPHIA.

THIS city would have been a capital fit for an empire had it been built and inhabited according to the proprietor's plan. Considering its late foundation, it is a large city, and most commodiously situated between the Delaware and Schuylkill, two navigable rivers. The former being two miles broad, and navigable 300 miles for small vessels. It extends in length two miles from the one river to the other. There are eight long streets two miles in length, all straight and spacious. The houses are stately, very numerous (being near 3000), and still increasing, and all carried on regularly according to the first plan. It has two fronts to the water, one on the east side facing the Schuylkill, and that on the west facing the Delaware. The Schuylkill being navigable 800 miles above the falls, the eastern part is most populous, where the warehouses (some three stories high), and wharfs are numerous and convenient. All the houses have large orchards and gardens belonging to them. The merchants that reside here are numerous and wealthy, many of them keeping their coaches, &c. In the centre of the city there is a space of ten acres, whereon are built the state-house, market-house, and school-house. The former is built of brick, and has a prison under it. The streets have their names from the several sorts of timber common in Pennsylvania; as Mulberry Street, Saffafras Street, Chestnut Street, Beech Street, and Cedar Street. The oldest church is Christ Church, and has a numerous congregation; but the major part of the inhabitants, being at first Quakers, still continue so, who have several meeting-houses, and may not improperly be called the church, as by law established, being the originals. The quay is beautiful, and 200 feet square, to which a ship of 200 tons may lay her broadside. Near the town, and on the spot which separates it from the Schuylkill, where that river falls into the Delaware, is found black earth of a great depth, and covered with vegetation; and which, it is evident, has been recently left by the water; It has all the character of land perfectly new, and as yet scarcely raised from the bed of the river. This land is used for meadows, and is in great estimation. It is acknowledged, however, to be extremely unhealthy. Between that and Wilmington, the quality of the stone is quartzose; ocher is also to be found in an imperfect state. As the advantages this city may boast of has rendered it one of the best trading towns out of the British empire, so in all probability it will increase in commerce and riches, if not prevented by party, faction, and religious feuds, which of late years have made it suffer considerably. The assemblies and courts of judicature are held here, as in all capitals. The French have no city like in all America.

Happy was my lot in falling into my countryman's power, as he was, contrary to many others of his calling, a humane, worthy, honest man. Having no children of his own, and commiserating my unhappy condition, he took great care of me until I was fit for business, and about the 12th year of my age sent me about little trifles, in which state I continued until my 14th year, when I was more fit for harder work. During such my idle state, seeing my fellow-servants often reading and writing, it incited in me an inclination to learn, which I intimated to my master, telling him I should be very willing to serve a year longer than the contract by which I was bound, if he would indulge me in going to school; this he readily agreed to, saying that winter would be the best time. It being then summer, I waited with impatience for the other season; but to make some progress in my design, I got a primer, and learned as much from my fellow-servants as I could. At school, where I went every winter for five years, I made tolerable proficiency, and have ever since been improving myself at leisure hours.

With this good master I continued till I was seventeen years old, when he died, and, as a reward for my faithful service, he left me £200 currency, which was then about £150 sterling, his best horse, saddle, and all his wearing apparel.

Being now my own master, having money in my pocket, and all other necessaries, I employed myself in jobbing about the country, working for any one that would employ me, for near seven years, when thinking I had money sufficient to follow some better way of life, I resolved to settle, but thought one step necessary thereto was to be married, for which purpose I applied to the daughter of a substantial planter, and found my suit was not unacceptable to her or her father, so that matters were soon concluded upon, and we married. My father-in-law, in order to establish us in the world in an easy, if not affluent manner, made me a deed of gift of a track of land, that lay (unhappily for me as it has since proved) on the frontiers of the province of Pennsylvania, near the forks of Delaware, in Berks county, containing about 200 acres, 30 of which were well cleared, and fit for immediate use, whereon was a good house and barn. The place pleasing me well, I settled on it, though it cost me the major part of my money in buying stock, household furniture, and implements for out-door work; and happy as I was in a good wife, yet did my felicity last me not long, for about the year 1754 the Indians, in the French interest, who had for a long time before ravaged and destroyed other parts of America unmolested, I may very properly say, began to be very troublesome on the frontiers of our province, where they generally appeared in small skulking parties, with yellings, shoutings, and antic postures, instead of trumpets and drums, committing great devastations. The Pennsylvanians little imagined at first that the Indians, guilty of such outrages and violence, were some of those who pretended to be in the English interest, which, alas! proved to be too true to many of us, for, like the French in Europe, without regard to faith or treaties, they suddenly break out into furious, rapid outrages and devastations, but soon retire precipitately, having no stores or provisions but what they meet with in their incursions. Some, indeed, carry a bag with biscuit or Indian corn therein, but not unless they have a long march to their destined place of action. And those French, who were sent to dispossess us in that part of the world, being indefatigable in their duty, and continually contriving and using all manner of ways and means to win the Indians to their interest, many of whom had been too negligent, and sometimes, I may say, cruelly treated by those who pretend to be their proctectors and friends, found it no very difficult matter to get over to their interest many who belonged to those nations in amity with us, especially as the rewards they gave them were so great, they paying for every scalp of an English person £15 sterling.

Terrible and shocking to human nature were the barbarities daily committed by the savages, and are not to be paralleled in all the volumes of history! Scarce did a day pass but some unhappy family or other fell victims to *French chicanery* and savage cruelty. Terrible indeed it proved to me as well as to many others; I that was now happy in an easy state of life, blessed with an affectionate and tender wife, who was possessed of all amiable qualities, to enable me to go through the world with that peace and serenity of mind which every Christian wishes to possess, became on a sudden one of the most unhappy and deplorable of mankind; scarce can I sustain the shock, which forever recoils on me, at thinking on the last time of seeing that good woman. The fatal 2nd of October, 1754, she that day went from home to visit some of her relations. As I staid up later than usual, expecting her return, none being in the house besides myself, how great was my surprise, terror, and affright, when about eleven o'clock at night I heard the dismal war-cry or war-whoop of the savages, which they make on such occasions, and may be expressed, *Woach, woach, ha, ha, hach, woach,* and to my inexpressible grief, soon found my house was attacked by them; I flew to my chamber-window, and perceived them to be twelve in number. They making several attempts to get in, I asked them what they wanted. They gave me no answer, but continued beating, and trying to get the door open. Judge, then, the condition I must be in, knowing the cruelty and merciless disposition of those savages should I fall into their hands. To escape which dreadful misfortune, having my gun loaded in my hand, I threatened them with death if they should not desist. But how vain and fruitless are the efforts of one man against the united force of so many, and of such merciless, undaunted, and bloodthirsty monsters as I had here to deal with. One of them that could speak a little English, threatened me in return, "That if I did not come out, they would burn me alive in the house;" telling me further, what I unfortunately perceived, "That they were no friends to the English, but if I would come out and surrender myself prisoner, they would not kill me." My terror and distraction at hearing this is not to be expressed by words, nor easily imagined by any person, unless in the same condition. Little could I depend on the promises of such creatures, and yet if I did not, inevitable death, by being burned alive, must be my lot. Distracted as I was in such deplorable circumstances, I chose to rely on the uncertainty of their fallacious promises, rather than meet with certain death by rejecting them; and accordingly went out of my house with my gun in my hand, not knowing what I did, or that I had it. Immediately on my approach, they rushed on me like so many tigers, and instantly disarmed me. Having me thus in their power the merciless villains bound me to a tree near the door; they then went into the house, and plundered and destroyed everything there was in it, carrying off what moveables they could; the rest, together with the house, which they set fire to, was consumed before my eyes. The barbarians, not satisfied with this, set fire to my barn, stable, and outhouses, wherein were about 200 bushels of wheat, six cows, four horses, and five sheep, which underwent the same fate, being all entirely consumed to ashes. During the conflagration, to describe the thoughts, the fears, and misery that I felt, is utterly impossible, as it is even now to mention what I feel at the remembrance thereof.

Having thus finished the execrable business about which they came, one of the monsters came to me with a *tomahawk** in his hand, threatening me with the worst of deaths if I would not willingly go with them, and be contented with their way of living. This I seemingly agreed to, promising to do everything for them that lay in my power, trusting to Providence for the time when I might be delivered out of their hands. Upon this they untied me, and gave me a great load to carry on my back, under which I travelled all that night with them, full of the most terrible apprehensions, and oppressed with the greatest anxiety of mind lest my unhappy wife should likewise have fallen a prey to these cruel monsters. At daybreak, my infernal masters ordered me to lay down my load, when, tying my hands again round a tree with a small cord, they then forced the blood out of my finger-ends. They then kindled a fire near the tree whereto I was bound, which filled me with the most dreadful agonies, concluding I was going to be made a sacrifice to their barbarity.

This narrative, O reader! may seem dry and tedious

---

*Tomahawk is a kind of hatchet, made something like our plasterers' hammers, about two feet long, handle and all. To take up the hatchet (or tomakawk) among them, is to declare war. They generally use it after firing their guns, by rushing on their enemies, and fracturing or cleaving their skulls with it, and very seldom fail of killing at the first blow.

to you : my miseries and misfortunes, great as they
have been, may be considered only as what others have
daily met with for years past ; yet, on reflection, you
cannot help indulging me in the recital of them, for
to the unfortunate and distressed, recounting our
miseries is, in some sort, an alleviation of them.

Permit me therefore to proceed : not by recounting
to you the deplorable condition I was then in, for that
is more than can be described to you, by one who
thought of nothing less than being immediately put to
death in the most excruciating manner these devils
could invent. The fire being thus made, they for some
time danced round me after their manner, with various
odd motions and antic gestures, whooping, hallooing,
and crying in a frightful manner, as it is their custom.
Having satisfied themselves in this sort of their mirth,
they proceeded in a more tragical manner, taking the
burning coals and sticks, flaming with fire at the ends,
holding them near my face, head, hands, and feet, with
a deal of monstrous pleasure and satisfaction, and at
the same time threatening to burn me entirely if I
made the least noise or cried out. Thus tortured as
I was, almost to death, I suffered their brutal pleasure
without being allowed to vent my inexpressible anguish
otherwise than by shedding tears, even which, when
those inhuman tormentors observed, with a shocking
pleasure and alacrity, they would take fresh coals, and
apply near my eyes, telling me my face was wet, and
that they would dry it for me, which indeed they
cruelly did. How I underwent these tortures I have
here faintly described, has been matter of wonder
to me many times ; but God enabled me to wait with
more than common patience for a deliverance I daily
prayed for.

Having at length satisfied their brutal pleasure, they
sat down round the fire, and roasted their meat, of

which they had robbed my dwelling. When they had prepared it, and satisfied their voracious appetites, they offered some to me ; though it is easily imagined I had but little appetite to eat, after the tortures and miseries I had undergone, yet was I forced to seem pleased with what they offered me, lest, by refusing it, they had again resumed their hellish practices. What I could not eat I contrived to get between the bark and the tree where I was fixed, they having unbound my hands until they imagined I had eat all they gave me ; but then they again bound me as before, in which deplorable condition was I forced to continue all that day. When the sun was set they put out the fire, and covered the ashes with leaves, as is their usual custom, that the white people might not discover any traces or signs of their having been there.

Thus had these barbarous wretches finished their last diabolical piece of work, and shocking as it may seem to the humane English heart, yet what I underwent was but trifling, in comparison to the torments and miseries which I was afterwards an eye-witness of being inflicted on others of my unhappy fellow creatures.

Going from thence along by the river Susquehana for the space of six miles, loaded as I was before, we arrived at a spot near the Apalachian mountains, or Blue Hills, where they hid their plunder under logs of wood. And, oh, shocking to relate ! from thence did these hellish monsters proceed to a neighbouring house, occupied by one Joseph Snider and his unhappy family, consisting of his wife, five children, and a young man, his servant. They soon got admittance into the unfortunate man's house, where they immediately, without the least remorse, and with more than brutal cruelty, *scalped** the tender parents and the unhappy children :

---

* Scalping is taking off the skin from the top of the head, which they perform with a long knife which they hang round their necks, and always carry

nor could the tears, the shrieks, or cries of these unhappy victims, prevent their horrid massacre ; for having thus scalped them, and plundered the house of every thing that was moveable, they set fire to the same, where the poor creatures met their final doom amidst the flames, the hellish miscreants standing at the door, or as near the house as the flames would permit them, rejoicing, and echoing back in their diabolical manner, the piercing cries, heart-rending groans, and paternal and affectionate soothings, which issued from this most horrid sacrifice of an innocent family. Sacrifice ! I think I may properly call it, to the aggrandizing the ambition of a king who wrongly styles himself *Most Christian !* For, had these savages been never tempted with the alluring bait of all-powerful gold, myself, as well as hundreds of others, might still have lived most happily in our stations. If Christians countenance, nay, hire those wretches to live in a continual repetition of plunder, rapine, murder, and conflagration, in vain are missionaries sent, or sums expended, for the propogation of the gospel. But these sentiments, with many others, must, before the end of this narrative, occur to every humane heart. Therefore to proceed—Not contented with what these infernals had already done, they still continued their inordinate villainy, in making a general conflagratoin of the barn and stables, together with all the corn, horses, cows, and every thing on the place.

Thinking the young man belonging to this unhappy family would be of some service to them in carrying

---

with them. They cut the skin round as much of the head as they think proper, sometimes quite round from the neck and forehead, then take it in their fingers and pluck it off, and often leave the unhappy creatures, so served, to die in a most miserable manner. Some who are not cut too deep in the temples and skull, live in horrid torments many hours, and sometimes a day or two after. The scalps, or skins thus taken off, they preserve and carry home in triumph, where they receive, as is said before, a considerable sum for every one.

part of their hellish acquired plunder, they spared his life, and loaded him and myself with what they had here got, and again marched to the Blue Hills, where they stowed their goods as before. My fellow-sufferer could not long bear the cruel treatment which we were both obliged to suffer, and complaining bitterly to me of his being unable to proceed any farther, I endeavoured to condole him as much as lay in my power, to bear up under his afflictions, and wait with patience till by the divine assistance we should be delivered out of their clutches; but all in vain, for he still continued his moans and tears, which, one of the savages perceiving, as we travelled on, instantly came up to us, and with his tomahawk gave him a blow on the head, which felled the unhappy youth to the ground, where they immediately scalped and left him. The suddenness of this murder shocked me to that degree, that I was in a manner like a statue, being quite motionless, expecting my fate would soon be the same : however, recovering my distracted thoughts, I dissembled the uneasiness and anguish which I felt, as well as I could, from the barbarians; but still, such was the terror that I was under, that for some time I scarce knew the days of the week, or what I did, so that, at this period, life indeed became a burden to me, and I regretted being saved from my first persecutors, the sailors.

The horrid fact being completed, they kept on their course near the mountains, where they lay skulking four or five days, rejoicing at the plunder and store they had got. When provisions became scarce, they made their way towards Susquehana, where still, to add to the many barbarities they had already committed, passing near another house inhabited by an unhappy old man, whose name was John Adams, with his wife and four small children; and, meeting with no resistance, they immediately scalped the unhappy wife and her four children, before the good old man's eyes. Inhuman and horrid as this was, it did not satiate them; for when they had murdered the poor woman, they acted with her in such a brutal manner, as decency, or the remembrance of the crime, will not permit me to mention; and this even before the unhappy husband, who, not being able to avoid the sight, and incapable of affording her the least relief, entreated them to put an end to his miserable being; but they were as deaf and regardless to the tears, prayers, and entreaties of this venerable sufferer, as they had been to those of the others, and proceeded in their hellish purpose of burning and destroying his house, barn, cattle, hay, corn, and every thing the poor man a few hours before was master of. Having saved what they thought proper from the flames, they gave the old man, feeble, weak, and in the miserable condition he then was, as well as myself, burdens to carry, and loading themselves likewise with bread and meat, pursued their journey on towards the Great Swamp, where, being arrived, they lay for eight or nine days, sometimes diverting themselves in exercising the most atrocious and barbarous cruelties on their unhappy victim, the old man: sometimes they would strip him naked, and paint him all over with various sorts of colours, which they extracted, or made from, herbs and roots: at other times they would pluck the white hairs from his venerable beard, and tauntingly tell him *he was a fool for living so long, and that they would shew him kindness in putting him out of the world;* to all which the poor creature could but vent his sighs, his tears, his moans, and entreaties, that, to my affrighted imagination, were enough to penetrate a heart of adamant, and soften the most obdurate savage. In vain, alas! were all his tears, for daily did they tire themselves with the various means they tried to torment him; sometimes tying

him to a tree, and whipping him; at others, scorching
his furrowed cheeks with red-hot coals, and burning
his legs, quite to the knees; but the good old man,
instead of repining, or wickedly arraigning the divine
justice, like many others in such cases, even in the
greatest agonies, incessantly offered up his prayers to
the Almighty, with the most fervent thanksgivings for
his former mercies, and hoping the flames, then surrounding and burning his aged limbs, would soon send
him to the blissful mansions of the just, to be a partaker
of the blessings there. And during such his pious
ejaculations, his infernal plagues would come round
him, mimicking his heart-rending groans and piteous
wailings. One night after he had thus been tormented,
whilst he and I were sitting together condoling each
other at the misfortunes and miseries we daily suffered,
twenty scalps and three prisoners were brought in by
another party of Indians. They had unhappily fallen
in their hands in Cannocojigge, a small town near the
river Susquehana, chiefly inhabited by the Irish.
These prisoners gave us some shocking accounts of
the murders and devastations committed in their parts.
The various and complicated actions of these barbarians
would entirely fill a large volume, but what I have
already written, with a few other instances which I
shall select from their information, will enable the
reader to guess at the horrid treatment the English,
and Indians in their interest, suffered for many years
past. I shall therefore only mention in a brief manner
those that suffered near the same time with myself.
This party, who now joined us, had it not, I found, in
their power to begin their wickedness as soon as those
who visited my habitation, the first of their tragedies
being on the 25th day of October, 1754, when John
Lewis, with his wife and three small children, fell
sacrifices to their cruelty, and were miserably scalped

and murdered, his house, barn, and everything he possessed, being burned and destroyed. On the 28th, Jacob Miller, with his wife and six of his family, together with everything on his plantation, underwent the same fate. The 30th, the house, mill, barn, twenty head of cattle, two teams of horses, and everything belonging to the unhappy George Folke, met with the like treatment; himself, wife, and all his miserable family, consisting of nine in number, being inhumanly scalped, then cut in pieces and given to the swine, which devoured them. I shall give another instance of the numberless and unheard-of barbarities they related of these savages, and proceed to their own tragical end. In short, one of the substantial traders belonging to the province, having business that called him some miles up the country, fell into the hands of these devils, who not only scalped him, but immediately roasted him before he was dead; then, like cannibals for want of other food, eat his whole body, and of his head made what they called an Indian pudding.

From these few instances of savage cruelty, the deplorable situation of the defenceless inhabitants, and what they hourly suffered in that part of the globe, must strike the utmost horror to a human soul, and cause in every breast the utmost detestation, not only against the authors of such tragic scenes, but against those who through perfidy, inattention, or pusillanimous and erroneous principles, suffered these savages at first, unrepelled, or even unmolested, to commit such outrages and incredible depredations and murders: for no torments, no barbarities that can be exercised on the human sacrifices they get into their power, are left untried or omitted.

The three prisoners that were brought with these additional forces, constantly repining at their lot, and almost dead with their excessive hard treatment, contrived at last to make their escape ; but being far from their own settlements, and not knowing the country, were soon after met by some others of the tribes or nations at war with us, and brought back to their diabolical masters, who greatly rejoiced at having them again in their infernal power. The poor creatures, almost famished for want of sustenance, having had none during the time of their elopement, were no sooner in the clutches of the barbarians, than two of them were tied to a tree, and a great fire made round them, where they remained till they were terribly scorched and burnt ; when one of the villains, with his scalping knife, ript open their bellies, took out their entrails, and burnt them before their eyes, whilst the others were cutting, piercing, and tearing the flesh from their breasts, hands, arms, and legs, with red hot irons, till they were dead. The third unhappy victim was reserved a few hours longer, to be, if possible, sacrificed in a more cruel manner : his arms were tied close to his body, and a hole being dug deep enough for him to stand upright, he was put therein, and earth rammed and beat in all round his body, up to the neck, so that his head only appeared above the ground ; they then scalped him, and there let him remain for three or four hours in the greatest agonies, after which they made a small fire near his head, causing him to suffer the most excruicating torments imaginable, whilst the poor creature could only cry for mercy in killing him immediately, for his brains were boiling in his head. Inexorable to all his plaints, they continued the fire, whilst, shocking to behold, his eyes gushed out of their sockets, and such agonising torments did the unhappy creature suffer for near two hours, till he was quite dead ! They then cut of his head and buried it with the other bodies, my task being to dig the graves, which, feeble and terrified as I was, the dread of suffering the same fate enabled me to do. I shall not here take up the reader's time, in vainly attempting to describe what I felt on such an occasion, but continue my narrative as more equal to my abilities.

A great snow now falling, the barbarians were a little fearful lest the white people should, by their traces, find out their skulking retreats, which obliged them to make the best of their way to their winter quarters, about two hundred miles farther from any plantations or inhabitants; where, after a long and tedious journey, being almost starved, I arrived with this infernal crew. The place where we were to rest, in their tongue, is called Alamingo. There were found a number of wigwams* full of their women and children. Dancing, shooting, and shouting were their general amusements; and in all their festivals and dances they relate what successes they have had, and what damages they have sustained in their expeditions, in which I became part of their theme. The severity of the cold increasing, they stript me of my clothes for their own use, and gave me such as they usually wore themselves, being a piece of blanket, a pair of *mogganes*, or shoes, with a yard of coarse cloth to put round me instead of breeches. To describe their dress and manner of living may not be altogether unacceptable.

That they in general wear a white blanket, which, in war time, they paint with various figures, but particularly the leaves of trees, in order to deceive their enemies when in the woods. Their mogganes are made of deer-skins, and the best sort have them bound round the edges with little beads and ribbands. On their legs they wear pieces of blue cloth for stockings,

---

* Wigwams are the names they give their houses, which are no more than little huts, made with three or four forked stakes drove into the ground, and covered with deer or other skins, or, for want of them, with large leaves and earth.

some like our soldiers spatterdashes—they reach higher than their knees, but not lower than their ankles. They esteem them easy to run in. Breeches they never wear, but instead thereof two pieces of linen, one before and another behind. The better sort have shirts of the finest linen they can get, and to these some wear ruffles; but these they never put on till they have painted them of various colours which they get from the pecone root and bark of trees, and never pull them off to wash, but wear them till they fall to pieces. They are very proud, and take great delight in wearing trinkets, such as silver plates round their wrists and necks, with several strings of wampum (which is made of cotton, interwoven with pebbles, cockle-shells, &c.), down to their breasts; and from their ears and noses they have rings or beads which hang dangling an inch or two. The men have no beards, to prevent which they use certain instruments and tricks as soon as it begins to grow. The hair of their heads is managed differently, some pluck out and destroy all, except a lock hanging from the crown of the head, which they interweave with wampum and feathers of various colours. The women wear it very long twisted down their backs, with beads, feathers, and wampum, and on their heads most of them wear little coronets of brass or copper; round their middle they wear a blanket instead of a petticoat. The females are very chaste, and constant to their husbands, and if any young maiden should happen to have a child before marriage, she is never esteemed afterwards. As for their food they get it chiefly by hunting and shooting, and boil or roast all the meat they eat. Their standing dish consists of Indian corn soaked, then bruised and boiled over a gentle fire for ten or twelve hours. Their bread is likewise made of wild oats, or sun-flower seeds. Set meals they never regard, but eat when they are hungry. Their gun, tomahawk, scalping knife, powder and shot, are all they have to carry with them in time of war—bows and arrows being seldom used by them. They generally in war decline open engagements; bush fighting or skulking is their discipline; and they are brave when engaged, having great fortitude in enduring tortures and death. No people have a greater love of liberty or affection to their neighbours; but are the most implacably vindictive people upon the earth; for they revenge the death of any relation, or any great affront, whenever occasion presents, let the distance of time or place be never so remote. To all which I may add, and which the reader has already observed, that they are inhumanly cruel. But some other nations might be more happy, if in some instances they copied them, and made *wise conduct, courage,* and *personal strength,* the *chief* recommendations for war captains, or *werowances,* as they call them. In times of peace they visit the plantations inhabited by the whites, to whom they sell baskets, ladles, spoons, and other such trifles, which they are very expert in making. When night comes, if admitted into any house, they beg leave to lie down by the fire-side, choosing that place rather than any other, which is seldom refused them, if sober, for then they are honest; but if drunk, are very dangerous and troublesome, if people enough are not in the house to quell them. Nor would they at any time be guilty of such barbarous depredations as they are, did not those calling themselves Christians entice them thereto with strong liquors, which they are vastly fond of, as well as by the pecuniary rewards which they gave for the scalps. If ambition cannot be gratified, or superiority obtained, otherwise than by the death of thousands, would it not, in those who seek such airy phantoms, and are so inordinately fond of their fellow creatures' lives, savour a little more of humanity, to have them killed instantly, and, if they must have proofs of murder, scalped afterwards, than by allowing and encouraging such merciless treatment, render themselves as obnoxious, cruel, and barbarous, to a humane mind, as the very savages themselves? However, they sometimes suffer by their plots and chicanery laid for the destruction of others, it often happening that the traders or emissaries sent to allure them to the execution of their schemes, rightly fall victims themselves; for, as they always carry with them horse-loads of rum, which the Indians are fond of, they soon get drunk, quarrelsome, and wicked, and in their fury often kill and destroy their tempters: a just reward for their wicked designs; nay, it had such an effect on them, that when so intoxicated, they even burn and consume all their own effects, beating, wounding, and sometimes killing their wives and children; but, in disputes among themselves, when sober, they are very tenacious of decorum, never allowing more than one to speak at a time. Profane swearing they know not in their own language how to express, but are very fond of the French and English oaths.

The old people, who are by age and infirmities rendered incapable of being serviceable to the community, they put out of the world in a barbarous and extraordinary manner; an instance of which I had, whilst among them, an opportunity of seeing practised on an old Indian. He being, through age, feeble and weak, and his eyes failing him, so that he was unable to get his living either by hunting or shooting, was summoned to appear before several of the leading ones, who were to be his judges. Before whom being come, and having nothing to say for himself (as how indeed could he prove himself young?) they very formally, and with a seeming degree of compassion, passed sentence on him to be put to death. This was soon after executed on him in the following manner : he was tied naked to a tree, and a boy, who was to be his executioner, stood ready with a tomahawk in his hands, to beat his brains out ; but when the young monster came to inflict the sentence, he was so short of stature that he could not lift the tomahawk high enough, upon which he was was held up by some others, a great concourse being present ; and then, though the young devil laid on with all his strength, he was not for some time able to fracture the old man's skull, so that it was near an hour before he was dead ; thus are they, from their youth, inured to barbarity ! When they found no remains of life in him, they put him into a hole dug in the ground for that purpose, in which he stood upright. Into his left hand they put an old gun, and hung a small powder-horn and shot-bag about his shoulders, and a string of wampum round his neck ; and into his right hand a little silk purse with a bit of money in it ; then filled the hole round, and covered him over with earth. This I found to be the usual manner of treating the old of both sexes ; only that the women are killed by young girls, and put into the ground with nothing but a ladle in one hand, and a wooden dish in the other.

They are very strict in punishing offenders, especially such as commit crimes against any of the royal families. They never hang any ; but those sentenced to death are generally bound to a stake, and a great fire made round them, but not so near as to burn them immediately ; for they sometimes remain roasting in the middle of the flames for two or three days before they are dead.

After this long digression, it is time to return to the detail of my own affairs. At Alamingo was I kept near two months, until the snow was off the ground. A long time to be amongst such creatures, and naked as I almost was ! whatever thoughts I might have of making my escape, to carry them into execution was impracticable, being so far from any plantations or white people, and the severe weather rendering my limbs in a manner quite stiff and motionless: however, I contrived to defend myself against the inclemency of the weather as well as I could, by making myself a little wigwam, with the bark of the trees, covering the same with earth, which made it resemble a cave ; and to prevent the ill effects of the cold which penetrated into it, I was forced to keep a good fire always near the door. Thus did I for near two months endure such hardships of cold and hunger as had hitherto been unknown to me. My liberty of going about was indeed more than I could have expected, but they well knew the impracticability of my eloping from them. Seeing me outwardly easy and submissive, they would sometimes give me a little meat, but my chief food was Indian corn, dressed as I have above described. Notwithstanding such their civility, the time passed so tedious on, that I almost began to despair of ever regaining my liberty, or seeing my few relations again ; which, with the anxiety and pain I suffered, on account of my dear wife, often gave me inexpressible concern.

At length the time arrived when they were preparing themselves for another expedition against the planters and white people ; but before they set out they were joined by many other Indians from Fort Du Quesne, well stored with powder and ball they had received from the French.

As soon as the snow was quite gone, and no traces of their vile footsteps could be perceived, they set forward on their journey toward the back parts of the province of Pennsylvania, leaving their wives and children behind in their wigwams. They were now a terrible and formidable body, amounting nearly to 150. My duty was to carry what they thought proper to load me with, but they never entrusted me with a gun. We marched on several days without any thing particular occurring, almost famished for want of provisions; for my part I had nothing but a few stalks of Indian corn, which I was glad to eat dry; nor did the Indians themselves fare much better, for as we drew near the plantations they were afraid to kill any game, lest the noise of their guns should alarm the inhabitants.

When we again arrived at the Blue Hills, about thirty miles from Cannocojigge, the Irish settlement before mentioned, we encamped for three days, though, God knows, we had neither tents, nor any thing else to defend us from the inclemency of the air, having nothing to lie on by night but the grass. Their usual method of lodging, pitching, or camping by night, being in parcels of ten or twelve men to a fire, where they lie upon the grass or bushes, wrapt up in a blanket, with their feet to the fire.

During our stay here a sort of council of war was held, when it was agreed to divide themselves into companies of about twenty men each; after which, every captain marched with his party where he thought proper. I still belonged to my old masters, but was left behind on the mountains with ten Indians, to stay until the rest should return; not thinking it proper to carry me nearer Cannocojigge, or the other plantations.

Here being left, I began to meditate on my escape; and though I knew the country round extremely well, having been often thereabouts with my companions, hunting deer and other beasts, yet was I very cautious of giving the least suspicion of such my intention. However, the third day after the grand body left us, my companions or keepers thought proper to visit the mountains in search of game for their subsistence, leaving me bound in such a manner, that I could not escape. At night, when they returned, having unbound me, we all sat down together to supper on two polecats, being what they had killed, and soon after (being greatly fatigued with their day's excursion) they composed themselves to rest as usual. Observing them to be in that somniferous state, I tried various ways to see whether it was a scheme to prove my intentions or not ; but after making a noise and walking about, sometimes touching them with my feet, I found there was no fallacy. My heart then exulted with joy at seeing a time come that I might in all probability be delivered from my captivity, but the joy was soon damped by the dread of being discovered by them, or taken by any straggling parties. To prevent which, I resolved, if possible, to get one of their guns, and if discovered, to die in my defence rather than be taken ; for that purpose I made various efforts to get one from under their heads (where they usually secured them) but in vain. Frustrated in this my first essay regarding my liberty, I dreaded the thoughts of carrying my new design into execution ; yet after a little considera-tion, and trusting myself to the Divine protection, I set forward, naked and defenceless as I was. A rash and dangerous enterprise ! Such was my terror, however, that in going from them I halted and paused every four or five yards, looking fearfully towards the spot where I had left them, lest they should awake and miss me ; but when I was about two hundred yards from them I mended my pace, and made as much haste as I could to the foot of the mountains, when on a sudden I was struck with the greatest terror and amaze at hearing the wood-cry, as it is called, and may be expressed *Jo hau ! Jo hau !* which the savages I had left were making, accompanied with the most hideous cries and howling they could utter. The bellowing of lions, the shrieks of hyenas, or the roarings of tigers, would have been music to my ears in comparison to the sounds that then saluted them. They having now missed their charge, I concluded that they would soon separate themselves, and hie in quest of me. The more my terror increased, the faster did I push on; and scarce knowing where I trod, drove through the woods with the utmost precipitation, sometimes falling and bruising myself, cutting my feet and legs against the stones in a miserable manner, but though faint and maimed, I continued my flight until break of day, when, without having any thing to sustain nature but a little corn left, I crept into a hollow tree, in which I lay very snug, and returned my prayers and thanks to the Divine Being, that had thus far favoured my escape. But my repose was in a few hours destroyed at hearing the voices of savages near the place where I was hid, threatening and talking how they would use me if they got me again—that I was before too sensible of to have the least rest either in body or mind since I had left them. However, they at last left the spot where I had heard them, and I remained in my circular asylum all that day without further molestation.

At night I ventured forward again, frightened and trembling at every bush I past, thinking each twig that touched me to be a savage. The third day I concealed myself in the like manner, and at night I travelled on in the same deplorable condition, keeping off the main road used by the Indians as much as possible, which made my journey many miles longer, and more painful and irksome than I can express. But how shall I describe the fear, terror, and shock that I felt on the fourth night, when, by the rustling I made among the leaves, a party of Indians, that lay round a small fire, which I did not perceive, started from the ground, and seizing their arms, ran from the

fire amongst the woods. Whether to move forward or
to rest where I was I knew not, so distracted was my
imagination. In this melancholy state, revolving in
my thoughts the now inevitable fate I thought waited
on me, to my great consternation and joy, I was relieved
by a parcel of swine that made towards the place I
guessed the savages to be, who on seeing the hogs,
conjectured that their alarm had been caused by them,
and very merrily returned to the fire, and lay down to
sleep as before. As soon as I perceived my enemies so
disposed of, with more cautious step and silent tread I
pursued my course, sweating (though winter, and
severely cold) with the fear I had just been relieved
from. Bruised, cut, mangled, and terrified as I was,
I still, through the divine assistance, was enabled to
pursue my journey until break of day, when thinking
myself far off from any of those miscreants I so much
dreaded, I lay down under a great log, and slept
undisturbed till about noon, when getting up, I reached
the summit of a great hill with some difficulty, and
looking out if I could spy any inhabitants of white
people, to my unutterable joy I saw some, which I
guessed to be about ten miles distant.

This pleasure was in some measure abated by my not
being able to get among them that night; therefore,
when evening approached, I again recommended myself
to the Almighty, and composed my weary mangled
limbs to rest. In the morning, as soon as I awoke, I
continued my journey towards the nearest cleared lands
I had seen the day before, and about four o'clock in the
afternoon arrived at the house of John Bell, an old
acquaintance, where knocking at the door, his wife, who
opened it, seeing me in such a frightful condition, flew
from me like lightning, screaming into the house. This
alarmed the whole family, who immediately fled to their
arms, and I was soon accosted by the master with his

gun in his hand. But on my assuring him of my innocence as to any wicked intentions, and making myself known (for he before took me to be an Indian), he immediately caressed me, as did also his family, with a deal of friendship, at finding me alive, they having all been informed of my being murdered by the savages some months before. No longer able to support my fatigued and worn out spirits, I fainted and fell to the ground. From which state having recovered me, and perceiving the weak and famished condition I then was in, they soon gave me some refreshment, but let me partake of it very sparingly, fearing the ill effects too much would have on me. They for two or three nights very affectionately supplied me with all necessaries, and carefully attended me until my spirits and limbs were pretty well recruited, and I thought myself able to ride, when I borrowed of these good people (whose kindness merits my most grateful return) a horse and some clothes, and set forward for my father-in-law's house in Chester county, about 140 miles from thence, where I arrived on the fourth day of January, 1755; but scarce one of the family could credit their eyes, believing, with the people I had lately left, that I had fallen a prey to the Indians.

Great was the joy and satisfaction wherewith I was received and embraced by the whole family; but oh, what was my anguish and trouble, when inquiring for my dear wife, I found she had been dead near two months! This fatal news, as every humane reader must imagine, greatly lessened the joy and rapture I otherwise should have felt at my deliverance from the dreadful state of captivity I had been in.

The news of my happy arrival at my father-in-law's house, after so long and strange an absence, was soon spread round the neighbouring plantations by the country people who continually visited me, being very desirous of hearing and eagerly inquiring an account of my treatment and manner of living among the Indians, in all which I satisfied them. Soon after this my arrival, I was sent for by his excellency Mr. Morris, the governor, a worthy gentleman, who examined me very particularly as to all incidents relating to my captivity, and especially in regard to the Indians, who had first taken me away, whether they were French or English parties. I assured his excellency they were of those who professed themselves to be friends of the former; and informed him of the many barbarous and inhuman actions I had been witness to among them, on the frontiers of the province; and also that they were daily increasing, by others of our pretended friends joining them; that they were all well supplied by the French with arms and ammunition, and greatly encouraged by them in their continual excursions and barbarities, not only in having extraordinary premiums for such scalps as they should take and carry home with them at their return, but great presents of all kinds, besides rum, powder, ball, &c., before they sallied forth. Having satisfied his excellency in such particulars as he requested, the same being put into writing, I swore to the contents thereof, as may be seen by those who doubt of my veracity, in the public papers of that time, as well in England as in Philadelphia. Having done with me, Mr. Morris gave me three pounds, and sent the affidavit to the assembly, who were then sitting in the state-house at Philadelphia, concluding on proper measures to check the depredations of the savages, and put a stop to their barbarous hostilities on the distressed inhabitants, who daily suffered death in a most deplorable condition; besides being obliged to abscond their plantations, and the country being left desolate for several hundred miles on the frontiers, and the poor sufferers could have no relief, by reason of the disputes between the governor and the assembly. The former was led by the instructions of the proprietor, which was entirely against the interest of the province, so that it caused great confusion among the people to see the country so destroyed, and no preparations making for its defence.

However, on receiving this intelligence from his excellency, they immediately sent for me. When I arrived, I was conducted into the lower house, where the assembly then sat, and was there interrogated by the speaker, very particularly, as to all I had before given the governor an account of. This my first examination lasted three hours. The next day I underwent a second for about an hour and a half, when I was courteously dismissed, with a promise that all proper methods should be taken, not only to accommodate and reimburse all those who had suffered by the savages, but to prevent them from committing the like hostilities for the future.

Now returned, and once more at liberty to pursue my own inclinations, I was persuaded by my father-in-law and friends to follow some employment or other; but the plantation from whence I was taken, though an exceeding good one, could not tempt me to settle on it again. What my fate would have been if I had, may easily be conceived. And there being at this time (as the assembly too late for many of us found) a necessity for raising men to check those barbarians in their ravaging depredations, I enlisted myself as one, with the greatest alacrity and most determined resolution to exert the utmost of my power in being revenged on the hellish authors of my ruin. General Shirley, governor of New England, and commander-in-chief of his Majesty's land forces in North America, was pitched upon to direct the operations of the war in that part of the world.

Into a regiment immediately under the command of

this general, was it my lot to be placed for three years. This regiment was intended for the frontiers, to destroy the forts erected by the French, as soon as it should be completely furnished with arms, &c., at Boston, in New England, where it was ordered for that purpose. Being then very weak and infirm in body, though possessed of my resolution, it was thought advisable to leave me for two months in winter quarters, at the end of which, being pretty well recruited in strength, I set out for Boston to join the regiment, with some others likewise left behind ; and after crossing the river Delaware, we arrived at New Jersey, and from thence proceeded through the same by New York, Middleton, Mendon in Connecticut, to Boston, where we arrived about the end of March, and found the regiment ready to receive us.

Boston being the capital of New England, and the largest city in America, except two or three on the Spanish continent, I shall here subjoin a short account of it.

DESCRIPTION OF BOSTON.

IT is pleasantly stituated, and about four miles in com- pass, at the bottom of Massachuset's Bay, into which there is but one common and safe passage, and not very broad, there being scarce room for the anchorage of 500 sail. It is guarded by several rocks, and above a dozen islands ; the most remarkable of these islands is Castle Island, which stands about a league from the town, and so situated that no ship of burden can approach the town, without the hazard of being shattered in pieces by its cannon. It is now called Fort William, and mounted with 100 pieces of ordnance ; 200 more, which were given to the province by Queen Anne, are placed on a platform, so as to rake a ship fore and aft, before she can bring about her broadsides to bear against the castle. Some of these cannon are 42 pounders; 500 able men are exempted from all military duty in time of war, to be ready, at an hour's warning, to attend the services of the castle, upon a signal of the approach of an enemy, which there seems to be no great danger of at Boston, where, in 24 hours time, 10,000 effective men, well armed, might be ready for its defence. According to a computation of the collectors of the light-house, it appeared there were 24,000 tons of shipping cleared annually.

The pier is at the bottom of the bay, 2,000 feet long, and runs so far into the bay, that ships of the greatest burden may unload without the help of boats or lighters. At the upper end of the chief street in the town, which comes down to the head of the pier, is the Town House, or Exchange, a fine building, containing, besides the walk for merchants, the Council Chamber, the House of Commons, and a spacious room for the Courts of Justice. The Exchange is surrounded with booksellers' shops that have a good trade—here being five printing-houses, and the presses generally full of work, which is in a great measure owing to the colleges and schools in New England; and likewise at New York and Phila-delphia, there are several printing-houses lately erected, and booksellers constantly employed, as well as at Virginia, Maryland, South Carolina, Barbadoes, and the Sugar Islands.

The town lies in the form of a half-moon, round the harbour, and consisting of about 4,000 houses, must make an agreeable prospect, the surrounding shore being high, the streets long, and the buildings beautiful. The pavement is kept in so good order, that to gallop a horse on it is 3s. 4d. forfeit. The number of inhabitants is computed at about 24,000.

There are eight churches, the chief of which is called

the Church of England church, besides the Baptist Meeting, and the Quaker Meeting.

The conversation in this town is as polite as in most of the cities and towns in England. A gentleman of London would fancy himself at home at Boston, when he observes the number of people, their furniture, their tables, and dresses, which perhaps is as splendid and showy as that of most tradesmen in London.

In this city, learning military discipline, and waiting for an opportunity of carrying our schemes into execution, we lay till the 1st of July, during all which time great outrages and devastations were committed by the savages in the back parts of the province. One instance of which, in particular, I shall relate, as being concerned in rewarding, according to desert, the wicked authors thereof.

Joseph Long, Esq., a gentleman of large fortune in those parts, who had in his time been a great warrior among the Indians, and frequently joined in expeditions with those in our interest, against the others. His many exploits and great influence among several of the nations, were too well known to pass unrevenged by the savages against whom he had exerted his abilities. Accordingly, in April, 1756, a body of them came down on his plantation, about 30 miles from Boston, and, skulking in the woods for some time, at last seized an opportunity to attack his house, in which, unhappily proving successful, they scalped, mangled, and cut to pieces the unfortunate gentleman, his wife, and nine servants, and then made a general conflagration of his houses, barns, cattle, and every thing he possessed, which, with the mangled bodies, were all consumed in one blaze. But his more unfortunate son and daughter were made prisoners, and carried off by them to be reserved for greater tortures. Alarmed and terrified at this inhuman butchery, the neighbourhood, as well as the people of Boston, quickly assembled themselves to think of proper measures to be revenged on these execrable monsters. Among the first of those who offered themselves to go against the savages, was James Crawford, Esq., who was then at Boston, and heard of this tragedy. He was a young gentleman who had for some years paid his addresses to Miss Long, and was in a very little time to have been married to her. Distracted, raving, and shocked as he was, he lost no time, but instantly raised 100 resolute and bold young fellows, to go in quest of the villains. As I had been so long among them, and was pretty well acquainted with their manners and customs, and particularly their skulking places in the woods, I was recommended to him as one proper for his expedition ; he immediately applied to my officers, and got liberty for me. Never did I go on any enterprise with half that alacrity and cheerfulness I now went with this party. My wrongs and sufferings were too recent in my memory to suffer me to hesitate a moment in taking an opportunity of being revenged to the utmost of my power.

Being quickly armed and provided, we hastened forward for Mr. Long's plantation on the 29th, and after travelling the most remote and intricate paths through the woods, arrived there on the 2nd of May, dubious of our success, and almost despairing of meeting with the savages, as we had heard or could discover nothing of them in our march. In the afternoon, some of our men being sent to the top of a hill to look out for them, soon perceived a great smoke in a part of the low grounds. This we immediately and rightly conjectured to proceed from a fire made by them. We accordingly put ourselves into regular order, and marched forwards, resolving, let their number have been what it might, to give them battle.

Arriving within a mile of the place, Captain Crawford,

whose anxiety and pain made him quicker sighted than any of the rest, soon perceived them, and guessed their number to be about 50. Upon this we halted, and secreted ourselves as well as we could, till twelve o'clock at night. At which time, supposing them to be at rest, we divided our men into two divisions, 50 in each, and marched on ; when coming within twenty yards of them, the captain fired his gun, which was immediately followed by both divisions in succession, who, instantly rushing on them with bayonets fixed, killed every man of them.

Great as our joy was, and flushed with success as we were at this sudden victory, no heart among us but was ready to burst at the sight of the young lady. What must the thoughts, torments, and senstations of our brave captain then be, if even we, who knew her not, were so sensibly affected! For oh! what breast, though of the brutal savage race we had just destroyed, could, without feeling the most exquisite grief and pain, behold in such infernal power, a lady in the bloom of youth, blest with every female accomplishment that could set off the most exquisite beauty ! Beauty which rendered her the envy of her own sex and the delight of ours, enduring the severity of a windy, rainy night ! Behold one nurtured in the most tender manner, and by the most indulgent parents, quite naked, and in the open woods, encircling with her alabaster arms and hands a cold rough tree, whereto she was bound, with cords so straitly pulled that the blood trickled from her finger ends ! Her lovely tender body, and delicate limbs, cut, bruised, and torn with stones and boughs of trees, · as she had been dragged along, and all besmeared with blood ! What heart can even now, unmoved, think of her distress, in such a deplorable condition, having no creature, with the least sensation of humanity, near to succour or relieve her, or even pity

or regard her flowing tears, and lamentable wailings!
The very remembrance of the sight has, at this
instant, such an effect on me that I almost want
words to go on. Such then was the condition in which
we found this wretched fair, both faint and speechless
with the shock our firing had given her tender frame.
The captain, for a long time, could do nothing but
gaze upon and clasp her to his bosom, crying, raving, and
tearing his hair like one bereft of his senses; nor did
he for some time perceive the lifeless condition she was
in, until one of the men had untied her lovely mangled
arms, and she fell to the ground. Finding among the
villains' plunder the unhappy lady's clothes, he gently
put some of them about her; and after various trials,
and much time spent, recovered her dissipated spirits,
the repossession of which she first manifested by eagerly
fixing her eyes on her dear deliverer, and, smiling with
the most complacent joy, blessed the Almighty and him
for her miraculous deliverance.

During this pleasing, painful interview, our men
were busily employed in cutting, hacking, and scalping
the dead Indians; and so desirous was every man to
have a share in wreaking his revenge on them, that
disputes happened among ourselves, who should be the
instruments of further shewing it on their lifeless trunks,
there not being enough for every man to have one
wherewith to satiate himself. The captain observing
the animosity between us on this occasion, ordered that
the two divisions should cast lots for this bloody, though
agreeable piece of work, which, being accordingly done,
the party whose lot it was to be excluded from this
business stood by with half-pleased countenances,
looking on the rest, who, with the utmost cheerfulness
and activity, pursued their revenge, in scalping and
otherwise treating their dead bodies as the most
inveterate hatred and detestation could suggest.

The work being done, we thought of steering home-wards triumphant with the scalps ; but how to get the lady forward, who was in such a condition as rendered her incapable of walking further, gave us some pain, and retarded us a little, until we made a sort of carriage to seat her on, and then, with the greatest readiness, we took our turns, four at a time, and carried her along. This, in some measure, made the captain cheerful, who all the way endeavoured to comfort and revive his desponding afflicted mistress ; but, alas ! in vain, for the miseries she had lately felt, and the terrible fate of her poor brother, of whom I doubt not but the tender-hearted reader is anxious to hear, rendered even her most pleasing thoughts, notwithstanding his soothing words, corroding and insufferable.

The account she gave of their disastrous fate and dire catastrophe, besides what I have already mentioned, was, that the savages had no sooner seen all consumed, but they hurried off with her and her brother, pushing, and sometimes dragging them on, for four or five miles, when they stopt, and stripping her naked, treated her in a shocking manner, whilst others were stripping and cruelly whipping her unhappy brother. After which, they, in the same manner, pursued their journey, regardless of the tears, prayers, or entreaties of this wretched pair; but with the most infernal pleasure laughed and rejoiced at the calamities and distresses they had brought them to, and saw them suffer, until they arrived at the place we found them, where they had that day butchered her beloved brother in the following execrable and cruel manner: they first scalped him alive, and after mocking his agonizing groans and torments for some hours, ripped open his belly, into which they put splinters and chips of pine trees, and set fire thereto, the same (on account of the turpentine wherewith these trees abound) burnt with great quickness and fury for a little time, during which, he remained in a manner alive, as she could sometimes perceive him move his head and groan. They then piled a great quantity of wood all around his body, and consumed it to ashes.

Thus did these barbarians put an end to the being of this unhappy young gentleman, who was only twenty-two years of age when he met his calamitous fate. She continued her relation by acquainting us that the next day was to have seen her perish in the like manner, after suffering worse than even such a terrible death, the satisfying these diabolical miscreants in their brutal lust. But it pleased the Almighty to permit us to rescue her, and entirely to extirpate this crew of devils !

Marching easily on her account, we returned to the captain's plantation on the 6th of May, where, as well as at Boston, we were joyfully received, and rewarded handsomely for the scalps of those savages we had brought with us. Mr. Crawford and Miss Long were soon after married, and, in gratitude for the services we had done them, the whole party was invited to the wedding, and nobly entertained ; but no riotous or noisy mirth was allowed, the young lady, we may well imagine, being still under great affliction, and in a weak state of health.

Nothing further material, that I now remember happened during my stay at Boston. To proceed therefore, with the continuation of our intended expedition.

On the 1st of July, the regiment began their march for Oswego. The 21st we arrived at Albany, in New York, through Cambridge, Northampton, and Hadfield, in New England. From thence, marching about 20 miles farther, we encamped near the mouth of the Mohawk river, by a town called Schenectady, not far from the Endless Mountains. Here did we lie some time, until batteaux (a sort of flat-bottomed boats, very small, and sharp at both ends) could be got to carry our stores and provisions to Oswego, each of which would contain about six barrels of pork, or in proportion thereto. Two men belonged to every batteaux, who made use of strong scutting poles, with iron at the ends, to prevent their being too soon destroyed by the stones in the river (one of the sources of the Ohio), which abounded with many, and large ones, and in some places was so shallow, that the men were forced to wade and drag their batteaux after them. Which, together with some cataracts, or great falls of water, rendered this duty very hard and fatiguing, not being able to travel more than seven or eight English miles a-day, until they came to the great carrying place, at Wood's Creek, where the provisions and batteaux were taken out, and carried about four miles to Allegany, or Ohio great river, that runs quite to Oswego, to which place General Shirley got with part of the forces on the 8th of August ; but Colonel Mercer with the remainder did not arrive until the 31st. Here we found Colonel Schuyler with his regiment of New Jersey provincials, who had arrived some time before. A short description of a place which has afforded so much occasion for animadversion, may not here be altogether disagreeable to those unacquainted with our settlements in that part of the world.

DESCRIPTION OF OSWEGO.

OSWEGO is situated in N. lat. 43 deg. 20 min., near the mouth of the river Onondago, on the south side of the lake Ontario, or Cataraque. There was generally a fort and constant garrison of regular troops kept before our arrival. In the proper seasons a fair for the Indian trade is kept here : Indians of about twenty different nations have been observed here at a time. The greatest part of the trade between Canada and the Indians of the

Great Lakes, and some parts of the Mississippi, pass near this fort—the nearest and safest way of carrying goods upon this lake being along the south side of it. The distance from Albany to Oswego fort is about 300 miles west, to render which march more comfortable, we met with many good farms and settlements by the way. The Outawaes, a great and powerful nation, living upon the Outawae river, which joins the Cataraque river (the outlet of the great lake), deal considerably with the New York trading houses here.

The different nations trading to Oswego are distinguishable by the variety and different fashions of their canoes; the very remote Indians are clothed in skins of various sorts, and have all fire-arms; some come so far north as Port Nelson in Hudson's Bay N. lat. 57 deg.; and some from the Cherokees west of South Carolina, in N. lat. 32 deg. This seems indeed to be a vast extent of inland water carriage, but it is only for canoes and the smallest of craft.

Nor will it in this place be improper to give some accounts of our friends in these parts, whom we call the Mohawks, viz., the Iroquois, commonly called the Mohawks, the Oneiades, the Onendagues, the Cayugaes, and the Senekaes. In all accounts they are called the Six Nations of the New York Friendly Indians; the Tuscaroroes, stragglers from the old Turcaroroes of North Carolina, lately are reckoned as the sixth. I shall here reckon them as I have been informed they were formerly. (1). The Mohawks: they live upon the Mohawk's or Schenectady river, and head or lie north of New York, Pennsylvania, Maryland, and some part of Virginia; having a castle or village, westward from Albany 40 miles, and another 65 miles west, and about 160 fencible men. (2). The Oneiades, about 80 miles from the Mohawks' second village, consisting of about 200 fighting men. (3). The Onondagues, about 25 miles farther (the famous Oswego, a trading place on the lake Ontario, is in their country), consisting of about 250 men. (4). The Cayugaes, about 70 miles farther, of about 130 men; and, (5), the Senekaes, who reach a great way down the river Susquehana, consist of about 700 marching, fighting men, so that the fighting men of the five or six nations of Mohawks may be reckoned at 1500 men, and extend from Albany, west, 400 miles, lying in about 30 tribes or governments. Besides these, there is settled above Montreal, which lies N. E. of Oswego, a tribe of scoundrels, runaways from the Mohawks—they are called Kahnuages, consisting of about 80 men. This short account of these nations I think necessary to make the English reader acquainted with, as I may have occasion to mention things concerning some of them.

It may not be improper here also, to give a succinct detail of the education, manners, religion, &c., of the natives. The Indians are born tolerably white; but they take a great deal of pains to darken their complexion by anointing themselves with grease, and lying in the sun. Their features are good, especially those of the women. Their limbs clean, straight, and well proportioned, and a crooked and deformed person is a great rarity amongst them. They are very ingenious in their way, being neither so ignorant nor so innocent as some people imagine. On the contrary, a very understanding generation are they, quick of apprehension, sudden in despatch, subtle in their dealings, exquisite in their inventions, and in labour assiduous. The world has no better marksmen with guns, or bows and arrows, than the natives, who can kill birds flying, fishes swimming, and wild beasts running; nay, with such prodigious force do they discharge their arrows, that one of them will shoot a man quite through, and nail both his arms to his body with the same arrow.

E

As to their religion, in order to reconcile the different accounts exhibited by travellers, we must suppose that different tribes may have different notions and different rites, and though I do not think myself capable of determining the case with the precision and accuracy I could wish, yet, with what I have collected from my own observation when among them, and the information of my brother captives, who have been longer conversant with the Indians than I was, I shall readily give the public all the satisfaction I can.

Some assure us the Indians worship the images of some inferior deities, whose anger they seem to dread, on which account the generality of our travellers denominate the objects of their devotion devils, though at the same time, it is allowed, they pray to their inferior deities for success in all their undertakings, for plenty of food, and other necessaries of life. It appears too, that they acknowledge one Supreme Being; but him they adore not, because they believe he is too far exalted above them, and too happy in himself, to be concerned about the trifling affairs of poor mortals. They seem also to believe in a future state, and that after death, they will be removed to their friends who have gone before them, to an Elysium or Paradise beyond the Western Mountains. Others again, allow them either no religion at all, or at most, very faint ideas of a deity; but all agree that they are extravagantly superstitious, and exceedingly afraid of evil spirits. To these demons they make oblations every new moon, for the space of seven days, during which time they cast lots, and sacrifice one of themselves, putting the person devoted to the most exquisite misery they can invent, in order to satisfy the devil for that moon, for they think, if they please but the evil spirit, God will do them no hurt.

Certain, however, it is, that those Indians whom the

French priests have had an opportunity of ministering unto, are induced to believe "That the Son of God came into the world to save all mankind, and destroy all evil spirits that now trouble them ; that the English have killed him ; and that ever since, the evil spirits are permitted to walk on the earth, that if the English were all destroyed, the Son of the Good Man, who is God, would come again, and banish all evil spirits from their lands, and then they would have nothing to fear or disturb them." Cajoled by these false but artful insinuations of the French Jesuits, the Indians from that time have endeavoured to massacre all the English, in order that the Son of God might come again on the earth, and rid them from their slavish fears and terrible apprehensions, by exterminating the objects thereof.

Being now at Oswego, the principal object that gave at that time any concern to the Americans, I shall, before I continue my own account, give a short recital of what had been done in these parts, in regard to the defence and preservation of the fort and the colonies thereabouts, before I came upon such authorities as I got from those who had been long at Oswego, and I can well depend upon for truth.

General Shirley, in 1754, having erected two new forts on the river Onondago, it seemed probable that he intended to winter at Oswego with his whole army, that he might the more readily proceed to action the ensuing spring. What produced his inactivity afterwards, and how it was that Fort Oswego was not taken by the French in the spring of 1755, are things my penetration will not enable me to discuss. But Oswego is now lost, and would have been so in the spring of 1755, if more important affairs had not made the French neglect it. At this time the garrison of Oswego consisted only of 100 men, under Captain King. The old fort being their only protection, which mounted only eight four-pounders, was incapable of defence, because it was commanded by an eminence directly across a narrow river, the banks of which were covered with thick wood.

In May, 1755, Oswego being in this condition, and thus garrisoned, thirty French batteaux were seen to pass, and two days after eleven more ; each batteau (being much larger than ours) containing fifteen men ; so this fleet consisted of near 600 men, a force which, with a single mortar, might soon have taken possession of the place.

A resolution was now taken to make the fort larger, and erect some new ones ; to build vessels upon the lake ; to increase the garrison; and provide every thing necessary to annoy the enemy, so as they may render the place tenable. Captain Broadstreet arriving on the 27th of May at the fort, with two companies, some small swivel guns, and the first parcel of workmen, made some imagine that a stop would be put to the French in their carrying men in the sight of the garrison—yet they still permitted eleven more French batteaux to pass by, though we were then superior to them in these boats, or at least in number. The reason our forces *could not* attack them was, because they were four miles in the offing, on board large vessels, in which the soldiers could stand to fire without being overset; and our batteaux, in which we must have attacked them, were so small, that they would contain only six men each, and so critical, that the inadvertent motion of one man would overset them. No care, however, was taken to provide larger boats against another emergency of the same kind. At Oswego, indeed, it was impracticable for want of *iron work ;* such being the provident forecast of those who had the management of affairs, that though there were smiths enough, yet there was at this place but one pair of bellows, so that the first accident that should happen to that necessary instrument would stop all the operations of the forge at once.

The beginning of June, the ship-carpenters arrived from Boston, and on the 28th of the same month the first vessel we ever had on the Lake Ontario was launched and fitted out. She was a schooner, forty feet in the keel, had fourteen oars, and twelve swivel guns. This vessel, and 320 men, was all the force we had at Oswego the beginning of July, and was victualled at the expense of the province of New York. Happy indeed it was that the colony provisions were there, for so little care had been taken to get the king's provisions sent up, that, when we arrived, we must have perished with famine, had not we found a supply which we had little reason to expect.

About the middle of July, an attack was again expected, when we (the forces under General Shirley) were still near 300 miles distant. And if the attack had been made with the force the enemy was known to have had at hand, it must, for the reason I have just before given, have fallen into their possession.

Such was the state of Oswego when we arrived there. Where we had been but a short time before, provisions began to be very scarce, and the king's allowance being still delayed, the provincial stores were soon exhausted, and we were in danger of being soon famished, being on less than half allowance. The men being likewise worn out and fatigued with the long march they had suffered, and being without rum (or allowed none at least), and other proper nutriment, many fell sick of the flux, and died, so that our regiment was greatly reduced in six weeks' time. A party that we left at the important carrying place, at Wood's Creek, were absolutely obliged to desert it for want of necessaries.

Sickness, death, and desertion had at length so far reduced us, that we had scarce men enough to perform duty, and protect those that were daily at work. The Indians keeping a strict look-out, rendered every one who passed the out-guards or sentinels, in danger of being scalped or murdered. To prevent consequences like these, a captain's guard of sixteen men, with two lieutenants, two serjeants, two corporals, and one drum, besides two flank guards of a serjeant, corporal, and twelve men in each, were daily mounted, and did duty as well as they were able. Scouting parties were likewise sent out every day; but the sickness still continuing, and having 300 men at work, we were obliged to lessen our guards, till General Pepperell's regiment joined us.

A little diligence being now made use of, about the middle of September four other vessels were got ready, viz., a decked sloop of eight guns, four-pounders, and thirty swivels; a decked schooner, eight guns, four-pounders, and twenty-eight swivels; one undecked schooner of fourteen swivels, and fourteen oars; and another of twelve swivels and fourteen oars—about 150 tons each.

On the 24th of October, with this armament, and a considerable number of batteaux, which were too small to live upon the lake in moderate weather, we were preparing to attack Niagara; though (notwithstanding we had taken all the provisions we could find in Oswego, and had left the garrison behind with scarce enough for three days) the fleet had not provisions sufficient on board to carry them within sight of the enemy, and supplies were not to be got within 300 miles of the place we were going against. However, the impracticability of succeeding in an expedition undertaken without victuals, was discovered in time enough to prevent our march or embarkation, or whatever it might be called; but not before nine batteaux, laden with officers' baggage were sent forward, four men in each batteau, in one of which it was my lot to be. The men being weak, and in low spirits with continual harassing and low feeding, rendered our progress very tedious and difficult—add to this the places we had to ascend, for in many parts the cataracts or falls of water which descended near the head of the river Onondago (in some places near 100 feet perpendicular), rendered it almost impossible for us to proceed—for the current running from the bottom was so rapid, that the efforts of twenty or thirty men were sometimes required to drag the boats along, and especially to get them up the hills or cataracts, which we were forced to do with ropes. Sometimes, when with great labour and difficulty we had got them up, we carried them by land near a quarter of a mile before we came to any water. In short, we found four men to a batteau were insufficient, for the men belonging to one batteau were so fatigued and worn out that they could not manage her, so that she lay behind almost a league.

The captain that was with us observing this, as soon as we had got the others over the most difficult falls, ordered two besides myself to go and help her forward. Accordingly I got into her, in order to steer her, whilst my two comrades and her own crew dragged her along. When we got her into any cataracts, I remained in her to fasten the ropes and keep all safe whilst they hauled her up ; but drawing her to the summit of the last cataract the ropes gave way, and down she fell into a very rapid and boisterous stream, where, not being able by myself to work her, she stove to pieces on a small rock, on which some part of her remaining till morning, I miraculously saved myself. Never was my life in greater danger than in this situation, the night being quite dark, and no assistance to be obtained from any of my comrades, though, many of them, as I afterwards learned, made diligent search for me ; but the fall of the water rendered the noise that they, as well as myself made, to be heard by one another, quite ineffectual.

In the morning, they, indeed, found me, but in a wretched condition, quite benumbed, and almost dead with cold, having nothing on but my shirt.

After various efforts, having with great difficulty got me up, they used all proper means to recover my worn out spirits; but the fire had a fatal effect to what they intended, for my flesh swelled all over my body and limbs, and caused such a deprivation of my senses, that I fainted, and was thought by all to be dead. However, after some time, they pretty well recovered my scattered senses, and fatigued body, and with proper care conducted me, with some others (who were weak and ill of the flux), to Albany, where the hospital received our poor debilitated bodies.

The rest, not able to proceed, or being countermanded, bent their course back again to Oswego, where, a friendly storm preventing an embarkation, when a stock of provisions was got together (sufficient to prevent them from eating one another, during the first twelve days), all thoughts of attacking Niagara were laid aside.

Thus ended this formidable campaign. The vessels that we had built (as I afterwards learned) were unrigged and laid up, without having been put to any use, while a French vessel was cruising on the lake, and carrying supplies to Niagara without interruption—five others, as large as ours, being almost ready to launch at Frontenac, which lies across Lake Ontario, north of Oswego.

The General, whatever appearances might have led others, as well as myself, to think otherwise, soon indicated his intention of not wintering at Oswego, for he left the place before the additional works were completed, and the garrison, by insensible degrees, decreased. The 1100 men still living in perpetual terror, on the brink of famine, and become mutinous for want of their pay, which, in the *hurry of military business*, during a year that was crowned with great events, had been forgotten, for, from my first enlisting, to the time I was laid up at Albany, I never had received above six weeks pay.

A little, indeed, may be offered in vindication of the General, in regard to the numberless delays of this campaign, viz., that it took some time to raise the two regiments which were in British pay, as the name of enlisting for life is somewhat forbidding to the Americans (a few of whom, as well as myself, made our agreement for three years; but soon after that time, I doubt we must have depended on his pleasure for our being discharged, according to our contract, had it not fallen out otherwise). The unusual dryness of the summer rendered the rivers down to Oswego in some places impassable, or very difficult for the batteaux to proceed; and it was whispered that a gentleman lately in an eminent station in New York, did all in his power to hinder the undertaking, from a pique at the General. By these disadvantages, he was detained at Albany till August, and even when he did reach Oswego, he found himself put to no little difficulty to maintain his ground for want of provisions, and the men being so reduced, more than once, to short allowance, as you have seen, became troubled with the flux, and had not anything necessary, not even rum sufficient for the common men, to prevent the fatal effects of that disorder.

In this manner the summer was spent on our side, and the reason why the French did not this year take Oswego, when they might with so little trouble, was, as many beside myself conjectured, that they thought it more their interest to pursue their projects on the Ohio, and preserve the friendship of the confidential Indians, which an attack upon Oswego at that time would have destroyed.

How far they succeeded in such their projects, and the reason of their successes, a little animadversion on our own transactions will let us into the light of it. For, as appearances on our side were very favourable in the spring, General Braddock's defeat greatly increased the gloom which sat on the countenances of the Americans.

Great things being expected from him, he arrived early in the spring at Virginia, with a considerable land force, and Fort Du Quesne seemed to be ours, if we did but go and demand it. The attacks designed against Niagara and Fort Frederick, at Crown Point, were planned in the winter, and the troops employed against the French in Nova Scotia, embarked at Boston in April. Let us view the events besides those already mentioned. General Braddock was ready to march in April ; but, through ignorance or neglect, or a misunderstanding with the governor of Virginia, had neither fresh provisions, horses, nor waggons provided, and so late as the latter end of May, it was necessary to apply to Pennsylvania for the most part of these. This neglect created a most pernicious diffidence and discredit of the Americans, in the mind of the General, and prevented their usefulness, where their advice was wanted, and produced very bad effects. He was a man (as it is now too well known and believed) by no means quick of apprehension, and could not conceive that such a people could instruct him ; and his young counsellors prejudiced him still more, so as to slight his officers, and what was worse, his enemy, as it was treated as an absurdity to suppose the Indians would ever attack regulars, and, of course, no care was taken to instruct the men to resist their peculiar manner of fighting. Had this circumstance been attended to, I am fully persuaded 400 Indians, about the number that defeated him, would have given him very little annoyance; sure I am, 400 of our people, rightly managed, would have made no difficulty of driving before them four times that handful, to whom he owed his defeat and death.

The undertaking of the eastern provinces, to reduce the fort at Crown Point, met that fate which the jarring councils of a divided people commonly meet with, for, though the plan was concerted in the winter of 1754, it was August before these petty governments could bring together their troops. In short, it must be owned by all, that delays were the banes of our undertakings, except in the Bay of Fundy in Nova Scotia, where secrecy and expedition were rewarded with success, and that province reduced.

The General continued inactive, from the time he left Oswego, to March, 1756, when he was about to resume the execution of his scheme to attack Frontenac and Niagara. What would have been the issue of this project, neither myself nor any other person can now pretend to say, for, just at this crisis, he received orders from England to attempt nothing till Lord Loudon should arrive, which was said should be early in the spring. However, his Lordship did not get there until the middle of July, so that by this delay time was given to the Marquis de Montcalm (Major-General Dieskan's successor) to arrive from France at Canada with 3000 regular forces, and take the field before us.

But to return from this digression to other transactions. When I was pretty well recovered again, I embarked on board a vessel from Albany for New York, where, when I arrived, I found to my sorrow, Captain John Shirley, the General's son, had been dead for some time. He was a very promising worthy young gentleman, and universally regretted. His company was given to Major James Kinnair, who ordered that none of his men should go out on the recruiting parties, as was at first intended by his predecessor; but that the private men should either return to Oswego, or do duty in the fort at New York. Not liking my station here, I entreated the General, who was now arrived, for a furlough, to see my friends at Pennsylvania, which he, having then no great occasion for me at New York, granted for three months.

As I have here mentioned New York, and before given a short account of the cities of Philadelphia and Boston, it would be a disrespect shown to this elegant one not to take notice of it, as well as, in some measure, debarring the reader from such information as may not be disagreeable; but not being of that note or consequence with the others, I shall briefly observe that

NEW YORK

Is a very fine city, and the capital of the province of that name. It contains about 3000 houses, and near 9000 inhabitants. The houses are all well built, and the meanest of them said to be worth £100 sterling, which cannot be said of the city of the same name, nor of any other in England. Their conversation is polite, and their furniture, dress, and manner of living, quite elegant. In drinking and gallantry they exceed any city in America.

The great church is a very handsome edifice, and built in 1695. Here is also a Dutch church, a French church, and a Lutheran church. The inhabitants of Dutch extraction make a considerable part of the town, and most of them speak English.

Having obtained my furlough, I immediately set out

for Pennsylvania, and arriving at Philadelphia, found the consternation and terror of the inhabitants was greatly increased to what it was when I left them. They had made several treaties of friendship with the Indians, who, when well supplied with arms, ammunition, clothes, and other necessaries, through the pacific measures and defenceless state of the Philadelphians, soon revolted to the French, and committed great ravages on the back parts of the province, destroying and massacring men, women, and children, and every thing that unhappily lay in their way.

A few instances of which, together with the behaviour of the Philadelphians on these occasions, I shall here present the reader with, who, of whatever sect or profession, I am well assured, must condemn the pacific disposition, and private factions that then reigned, not only in the army, but among the magistrates themselves, who were a long time before they could agree on proper petitions, to rouse the assembly from the lethargic and inactive condition they absolutely remained in. For, about the middle of October, a large body of Indians, chiefly Shawonoese, Delawares, &c., fell upon this province from several quarters, almost at the same instant, murdering, burning, and laying waste all where-ever they came—so that in the five counties of Cumberland, York, Lancaster, Berks, and Northampton, which compose more than half the province, nothing but scenes of destruction and desolation were to be seen.

The damages which these counties had sustained by the desertion of plantations, is not to be reckoned up, nor are the miseries of the poor inhabitants to be described, many of whom, though escaping with life, were, without a moment's warning, driven from these habitations, where they enjoyed every necessary of life, and were then exposed to all the severity of a hard winter, and obliged to solicit their very bread at the cold hand of charity, or perish with hunger, under the inclement air.

To these barbarities I have already mentioned, I cannot pass over the following, as introductory causes of the Philadelphians at last withstanding the outrages of the barbarians.

At Guadenhutten, a small Moravian settlement in Northampton county, the poor unhappy sufferers were sitting round their peaceful supper, when the inhuman murderers, muffled in the shades of the night, dark and horrid as the infernal purposes of their diabolical souls, stole upon them, butchered, scalped them, and consumed their bodies, together with their horses, stock, and upwards of sixty head of fat cattle (intended for the subsistence of the brethren at Bethlehem), all in one general flame, so that next morning furnished only a melancholy spectacle of their mingled ashes.

At the Great Cove in Cumberland, at Tulpehockin, in Berks, and in several other places, their barbarities were stilll greater if possible. Men, women, children, and brute beasts shared one common destruction ; and where they were not burned to ashes, their mangled limbs were found promiscuously thrown upon the ground—those appertaining to the human form scarce to be distinguished from the brute !

But of all the instances of the barbarities I heard of in these parts, I could not help being most affected with the following :—One family, consisting of the husband, his wife, and a child only a few hours old, were all found murdered and scalped in this manner : the mother, stretched on the bed, with her new-born child horribly mangled and put under her head for a pillow, while the husband lay on the ground hard by, with his belly ript up, and his bowels laid open.

In another place, a woman, with her sucking child, finding that she had fallen into the hands of the enemy, fell flat on her face, prompted by the strong call of nature to cover and shelter her innocent child with her own body. The accursed savage rushed from his lurking place, struck her on the head with his tomahawk, tore off her scalp, and scoured back into the woods, without observing the child, being apprehensive that he was discovered. The child was found some time afterwards under the body of its mother, and was then alive.

Many of their young women were carried by the savages into captivity, reserved perhaps for a worse fate than those who suffered death in all its horrid shapes, and no wonder, since they were reserved by savages whose tender mercies might be counted more cruel than their very cruelty itself.

Yet even during all this time, this province (had things been properly ordered) need but, in comparison to her strength, have lifted her foot and crushed all the French force on the borders ; but unused to such undertakings, and bound by non-resisting principles from exerting her strength, and involved in disputes with the proprietors, they stood still, vainly hoping the French would be so moderate as to be content with their victory over Braddock, or at least confine their attacks to Virginia ; but they then saw and felt all this was delusion, and the barbarities of the Indian parties, headed by French officers, notwithstanding all which, they continued in domestic debates, without a soldier in pay, or a penny in the treasury. In short, if the enemy had then had but 1500 men at the Ohio, and would have attempted it, no rashness could have been perceived in their marching down to the city of Philadelphia.

Thus stood our affairs on the Ohio, when an old

captain of the warriors, in the interest of the Philadelphians, and their ever faithful friend, whose name
was Scarooyada, alias Manokatoathy, on the first
notice of these misfortunes, came hastening to Philadelphia, together with Colonel Weiser, the provincial
interpreter, and two other Indian chiefs. Scarooyada
immediately demanded an audience of the assembly,
who were then sitting, to whom he spoke in a very
affecting manner. His speeches being printed, and
sold about Philadelphia, I procured one of them, which
was as follows—

" BRETHREN,
    "We are once more come among you, and sincerely condole with
you on account of the late bloodshed, and the awful cloud that hangs over
you and over us. Brethren, you may be undoubtedly assured, that these
horrid actions were committed by none of those nations that have any fellow-
ship with us, but by certain false-hearted and treacherous brethren. It grieves
us more than all our other misfortunes, that any of our good friends the
English should suspect us of having false hearts.
    "If you were not an infatuated people, we are 300 warriors firm to your
interest, and if you are so unjust to us as to retain any doubts of our sincerity,
we offer to put our wives, our children, and all we have into your hands, to
deal with them as seemeth good to you, if we are found in the least to swerve
from you. But, brethren, you must support and assist us, for we are not
able to fight alone against the powerful nations who are coming against you,
and you must this moment resolve, and give us an explicit answer what you
will do, for these nations have sent to desire us, as old friends, either to join
them, or get out of their way, and shift for ourselves. Alas! brethren, we
are sorry to leave you! We remember the many tokens of your friendship
to us; but what shall we do? We cannot stand alone, and you will not stand
with us!
    "The time is precious. While we are here consulting with you, we know
not what may be the fate of our brethren at home. We do, therefore, once
more invite and request you to act like men, and be no longer as women,
pursuing weak measures that render your names despicable. If you will put
the hatchet into your hands, and send out a number of your young men, in
conjunction with our warriors, and provide the necessary arms, ammunition,
and provisions, and likewise build some strong houses for the protection of
our old men, women, and children, while we are absent in war, we shall soon
wipe the tears from your eyes, and make these false-hearted brethren repent
their treachery and baseness towards you and towards us.
    "But we must at the same time solemnly assure you, that if you delay
any longer to act in conjunction with us, or think to put us off, as usual, with
uncertain hopes, you must not expect to see our faces under this roof any
more. We must shift for our own safety, and leave you to the mercy of our enemies, as an infatuated people, upon whom we can have no longer dependence."

The tears stood in the old man's eyes, while he
delivered this last part, and no wonder, since the very

being of his nation depended upon their joining the enemy, or our enabling them immediately to make head against them.

It was some time, however, before the assembly could be brought to consent to any vigorous measures for their own defence. The black inhabitants lost all patience at their conduct, until, at length, the Governor exerted his utmost power, and procured the militia and money bills to pass. By virtue of the former, the freemen of the province were enabled to form themselves into companies, and each company, by a majority of votes, by way of ballot, to choose its own officers, viz., a captain, lieutenant, and ensign, who, if approved of, were to be commissioned by the Governor. So that the Philadelphians were, at last, permitted to raise and arm themselves in their own defence. They accordingly formed themselves into companies, the Governor signing to all gentlemen qualified, who had been regularly balloted, commissions for that purpose.

Captain Davis was one of the first who had a company, and being desirous of my service, in order to instruct the irregulars in their discipline, obtained from the Governor a certificate to indemnify me from any punishment which might be adjudged by the regiment to which I already belonged, for without that I had not gone. Our company, which consisted of 100 men, was not completed until the 24th of December, 1755, when, losing no time, we next morning marched from Philadelphia in high spirits, resolving to shew as little quarter to the savages as they had to many of us.

Colonel Armstrong had been more expeditious, for he had raised 280 provincial irregulars, and marched a little time before against the Ohio Moravians; but of him more hereafter.

We arrived on the 26th of December at Bethlehem, in the forks of the river Delaware, where, being kindly received by the Moravians, we loaded six waggons with provisions, and proceeded on to the Apalachian Mountains, or Blue Hills, to a town called Kennorton-head, which the Moravians had deserted on account of the Indians. Fifty of our men, of whom I made one, were ordered before the rest, to see whether the town was destroyed or not. Disposing them to the best advantage, we marched on till we came within five miles of the place, which we found standing entire.

Having a very uneven rugged road to it, and not above four men able to go abreast, we were on a sudden alarmed by the firing of the flank guards, which were a little in the rear of our van. The savages briskly returned fire, and killed the ensign and ten of the men, and wounded several others.

Finding this, I being chief in command (having acted as lieutenant, and received pay as such from my first entrance, for my trouble and duty in learning the company), ordered the men to march on with all expedition to the town, and all the way to keep a running fire on the enemy, as they had fallen on our rear.

We would have got there in very good order, had it not been for a river we had to cross, and the weather being so excessively cold, our clothes froze to our bodies as soon as we got out of the water. However, with great difficulty we reached the town, and got into the church, with the loss of 27 men. There we made as good preparations for our defence as possibly we could, making a great fire of the benches, seats, and what we could find therein, to dry our clothes, not esteeming it the least sacrilege or crime upon such an emergency.

The Indians soon followed us into the town, and surrounding us, tried all methods to burn the church, but our continual firing kept them off for about six hours, until our powder and ball were all expended. In the night they set several houses on fire, and we, dreading the consequences of being detained there, resolved to make one bold effort, and push ourselves through the savage forces, which was accordingly done with the most undaunted courage. The enemy fired continually on us during our retreat, and killed many of our men, but in their confusion many of themselves also, it being so very dark that we were not able to discern our own party, so that only five of us kept together, and got into the woods. The rest, whom we left behind, I doubt, fell sacrifices to the savages.

The night being so excessively cold, and having but few clothes with us out of the church, two of my comrades froze to death before we could reach any inhabited place. In short, we did not get any relief till four o'clock in the morning, when we arrived at a house that lay in the gap of the Blue Hills, where our captain had arrived with the remainder of the men and waggons the day before.

The captain enquiring our success, I gave him the melancholy detail of our unfortunate expedition, upon which, an express was immediately sent to the Governor with the account, who ordered 1600 men to march the next morning for the same place, under the command of General Franklin, not only to bury the dead and build a fort there, but to extirpate the savages who infested these parts, and were too powerful for our small number under Captain Davis.

The remainder of our little party were now building a fort at the place where we lay for our defence, until more assistance should arrive—for we were under continual apprehensions of the Indians pursuing and attacking us again.

On the 9th of January, 1756, we were reinforced by General Franklin and his body, and the next day set out again for Kennorton-head, where, when we arrived, to our great consternation, we found little occasion to bury our unhappy comrades, the swine (which in that country are vastly numerous in the woods), having devoured their bodies, and nothing but bones strewed up and down were to be seen. We there built a fort in the place where the old church had stood, and gave it the name of Fort Allen. This was finished in six days, and in so good a manner, that 100 men would make great resistance against a much greater number of Indians.

On the 18th, 1400 of us were ordered about fifteen miles distant from thence, on the frontiers of the province, where we built another fort, called Fort Norris. In our way thither we found six men scalped and murdered in a most cruel manner. By what we could discern, they had made a vigorous defence, the barrels and stocks of their guns being broke to pieces, and themselves cut and mangled in a terrible manner.

From thence we were ordered to march towards a place called the Minnisinks, but this journey proved longer than we were aware of, the Indians committing great outrages in these parts, having burned and destroyed all the houses, &c., in our way. These tragic actions caused us to divide ourselves into several parties, who were ordered divers ways, to cut off as many of these savages as possible.

The day after this scheme was put into execution, we met with a small party which we put to the rout, killing fourteen of them. We then made all possible despatch to save some houses we saw on fire; but on our nearer approach, found our endeavour in vain— John Swisher and his family having been before scalped and burnt to ashes in their own house. On the following night, the house of James Wallis underwent the same fate, himself, wife, seven children, and the rest of the family being scalped, and burnt therein.

The houses and families of Philip Green and Abraham Nairne suffered in the like manner. Nor did the cruelty of these barbarians stop here, but attacked the dwelling-house of George Hunter, Esq., a gentleman of considerable wealth, and a justice of the peace, who made a brave resistance, and rather than fall into the hands of these miscreants, choose to meet death in the flames, which he, his wife, and all his household, consisting of sixteen in number, did with the utmost bravery, before any assistance could be received from our General, who had despatched 500 of us for that purpose, on an express being sent to him that morning.

From thence we marched to the Minnisinks, and built Fort Norris. On the 9th of March, we set out with 1000 men to the head of the Minnisinks, and built another fort, which we named Franklin, in honour of our General—all which forts were garrisoned with as many men as we could possibly spare.

After this we were daily employed in scouring the woods, from fort to fort, of these noxious creatures the Indians, and in getting as much of the corn together as we could find, to prevent the savages from having any benefit therefrom.

Notwithstanding our vigilance, these villains, on the 15th, attacked the house of James Graham, but by Providence, he, with his wife, who had just lain in, and the young infant in her arms (with nothing about her but her shift), made their escape to Fort Allen, about fifteen miles distant. The child perished by the way, and it was matter of wonder to the whole garrison to find either of them alive—indeed, they were in a deplorable condition, and we imagined they would expire every moment. The wife, however, to our great astonishment, recovered, but the husband did not survive above six hours after their arrival.

The house of Isaac Cook suffered by the flames—himself, his wife, and eight children being scalped and burnt in it.

Tedious and shocking would it be to enumerate half the murders, conflagrations, and outrages committed by these hellish infidels—let it suffice, therefore, that from the year 1753, when they first began their barbarities, they had murdered, burned, scalped, and destroyed above 3500, above 1000 of which were unhappy inhabitants of the western part of Philadelphia. Men, women, and children, fell alike a prey to the savages, no regard being had by them to the tender entreaties of an affectionate parent for a beloved child, or the infant's prayers in behalf of his aged father and mother. Such are the miserable calamities attendant on schemes for gratifying the ambition of a tyrannic monarchy like France, or the weak contrivances or indolent measures of blundering ministers or negotiators.

The time of my furlough at length expiring, I prepared to set out for my regiment. Having a recommendatory letter from General Franklin to Major Kinnair, as to my services, I marched forward for New York, where, having arrived, I waited on the Major—he being a worthy gentleman, universally beloved by the whole regiment—and after giving him an account of all our transactions, and the hardships and labours we had gone through, I was dismissed.

After some stay there, I was ordered to proceed on my march for Oswego once more. But before I go further with my affairs, I shall just recount the result of those provincials who went, as I mentioned before, to quell the savages, under the command of Colonel Armstrong.

He having under his command 280 provincials, destined against the Ohio Moravians, against whom nothing had been attempted, notwithstanding their frequent incursions and murders, penetrated 140 miles through the woods, from Fort Shirley, on Juniata river, to Kittanning, an Indian town on the Ohio, about 25 miles above Fort du Quesne, belonging to the French. He soon joined the advanced party at the Beaver-Dams, and on the fourth evening after, being within six miles of Kittanning, the scouts discovered a fire in the road, and reported that there were but three or four Indians at it. At that time it was not thought proper to attempt surprising these Indians, lest if one should escape, the town might be alarmed. Lieutenant Hogg, with twelve men, were therefore left to watch them, with orders not to fall upon them until day-break; and our forces turned out of the path, to pass their fire, without disturbing them.

About three in the morning, having been guided by the whooping of the Indian warriors, at a dance in the town, they reached the river at about 100 perches below it. As soon as day appeared, the attack began. Captain Jacobs, chief of the Indians, gave the war-whoop, and defended his house bravely through the loopholes in the logs. The Indians generally refusing quarter, Colonel Armstrong ordered their houses to be set on fire, which was done by the officers and soldiers with great alacrity. On this, some burst out of the houses, and attempted to reach the river, but were instantly shot. Captain Jacobs, in getting out of a window, was shot and scalped, as were also his squaw, and a lad they called the king's son. The Indians had a number of spare arms in their houses loaded, which went off in quick succession as the fire came to them; and quantities of gunpowder, which had been stored in every house, blew up from time to time, throwing their bodies into the air.

Eleven English prisoners were released, who informed

the Colonel that that very day two batteaux of French-
men, with a large party of Delaware and French
Indians, were to have joined Captain Jacobs, to march
and take Fort Shirley ; and that twenty-four warriors
had set out before them the preceding evening, which
proved to be the party that had kindled the fire the
preceding night—for our people returning, found Lieutenant Hogg wounded in three places, and learned that
he had attacked the supposed party of three or four at
the fire, but found them too strong for him. He killed
three of them, however, at the first fire, and fought
them an hour, when, having lost three of his men, the
rest, as he lay wounded, abandoned him and fled, the
enemy pursuing. Lieutenant Hogg died soon after of
his wounds.

Enough of these two expeditions has been said, nor
can I well tell which of the two was most successful,
both losing more of their own men than they killed of
the enemy.

A little retrospection again on the actions and behaviour of the Philadelphians, and the other provinces,
and places in conjunction with them, may here be
something necessary, for, when I arrived at Philadelphia, I found, however melancholy their situation had
been of late, this good effect had been obtained, that
the most prejudiced and ignorant individual was
feelingly convinced of the necessity of vigorous
measures ; and, besides national and public views, then
the more prevailing ones of revenge and self-interest,
gave a spur to their counsels. They were accordingly
raising men with the utmost expedition, and had, before
the end of the summer, a considerable number, though
not equal to what they could furnish, having at least
45,000 men in Pennsylvania able to fight.

And, pursuant to agreement some months before,
the four governments of New England, in conjunction

with New York (which last furnished 1300), had now assembled 8000 men (for the attack of Fort Frederick) at Albany, 150 miles N. of New York, and about 130 from Crown Point, under the command of General Winslow. But many people dreading the cruelty of the French, were not so very eager to join them this year as the last—an impress therefore of part of the militia was ordered in New York government. To prevent which, subscriptions were set on foot to engage volunteers by high bounties, so loath were they, that some got nine or twelve pounds sterling to enlist.

The 44th, 48th, 50th, and 51st regiments of Great Britain were destined for the campaign on the great lake Ontario, and mostly marched for Oswego, thence to be carried over in 200 great whale boats, which were then at the lake, and were built at Schenectady, on Mohawk's river, and were long, round, and light, as the batteaux, being flat-bottomed and small, would not answer the navigation of the lake, where the waves were often very high. They were then, at last, intended to attack Fort Frontenac, mentioned before, and the other French forts on the lake. Upwards of 2000 batteaux-men were employed to navigate the batteaux, each a ton burthen, laden with provisions and stores from Albany, by the Mohawk river, then through Oneyda lake and river, down to Oswego. There were likewise 300 sailors hired and gone up from New York (as I found, when I arrived there) to navigate the four armed ships on the lake, built there, as I have before mentioned, the last year, for the king's service, and two others were then building—smiths, carpenters, and other artificers having gone there for that purpose some weeks before. Such were the preparations and armaments for this campaign; but how fruitless, to our disgrace, was soon known all over the world!

I shall not trouble the reader with a long account of

a long march I had to take from New York to Oswego, to join my regiment—suffice it therefore, that I arrived there about the middle of July. • In my march thither, with some recruits, we joined Colonel Broadstreet at Albany, and on the 6th of May, at the great carrying place, had a skirmish with the French and Indians, wherein several were killed and wounded on both sides —of the latter I made one. Receiving a shot through my left hand, which entirely disabled my third and fourth fingers; and having no hospital, or any conveniences for the sick there, I was, after having my hand dressed in a wretched manner, sent with the next batteaux to Albany to get it cured.

As soon as I was well, I set out for Oswego again. And, when I arrived there, I began to make what observations I could, as to the alterations that had been made since the month of October preceding. The works of Oswego, at this time, consisted of three forts, viz., the Old Fort, built many years before, whose chief strength was a weak stone wall, about two feet thick, so ill cemented, that it could not resist the force of a four pound ball, and situated on the east side of the harbour. The two other forts, called Fort Ontario and Fort George, were each of them at the distance of about 450 yards from the Old Fort, and situated on two eminences, which commanded it. Both these, as I have already observed, were begun to be built last year, upon plans which made them defensible against musketry, and cannon of three or four pound ball only, the time not allowing works of a stronger nature to be then undertaken.

For our defence against large cannon, we entirely depended on a superior naval force upon the lake, which might have put it in our power to prevent the French from bringing heavy artillery against the place, as that could only be done by water carriage, which is my opinion, as well as many others. If the naval force had but done their duty, Oswego might have been ours to this very day, and entirely cut off the communication of the French from Canada to the Ohio ; but if I would insist on this, as the particulars require, I perhaps should affront some, and injure myself, all to no purpose, or of any beneficial service to recall our former losses.

A day or two after, being at Oswego, the fort was alarmed by hearing a firing, when, on despatching proper scouts, it was found to be the French and Indians engaging the batteaux-men and sailors, conveying the provisions to Oswego from one river to another. On this, a detachment of 500 men were ordered out in pursuit of them, whereof I was one. We had a narrow pass in the woods to go through, where we were attacked by a great number of Indians, when a desperate fight began on both sides, that lasted about two hours. However, at last we gained a complete victory, and put them entirely to the rout, killing fourteen of them, and wounding above forty. On our side we had but two men killed and six wounded. Many more would have been killed of both parties, had it not been for the thickness of the woods.

I cannot here omit recounting a most singular transaction that happened during this my second time of being there, which, though scarce credible, is absolutely true, and can be testified by hundreds who know and have often seen the man. In short, one Moglasky, of the 50th regiment, an Irishman, being placed as sentinel over the rum which had arrived, and being curious to know its goodness, pierced the cask, and drank till he was quite intoxicated, when, not knowing what he did, he rambled from his post, and fell asleep a good way from the garrison. An Indian skulking that way for prey (as is conjectured) found him, and made free with his scalp, which he plucked and carried off. The serjeant, in the morning, finding him prostrate on his face, and seeing his scalp off, imagined him to be dead; but on his nearer approach, and raising him from the ground, the fellow awakened from the sound sleep he had been in, and asked the serjeant what he wanted. The serjeant, quite surprised at the strange behaviour of the fellow, interrogated him, how he came there in that condition? he replied, *he could not tell; but that he had got very drunk, and rambled he knew not whither.* The serjeant advised him to prepare for death, not having many hours to live, as he had lost his scalp. *Arrah, my dear now,* cries he, *and are you joking me?* for he really knew nothing of his being served in the manner he was, and would not believe any accident had happened him, until seeing his clothes bloody, he felt his head, and found it to be too true, as well as having a cut from his mouth to his ear. He was immediately carried before the Governor, who asked him how he came to leave his post? He replied, *that being very thirsty, he had broached a cask of rum, and drank about a pint, which made him drunk; but if his Honour would forgive him he'd never be guilty of the like again.* The Governor told him it was very probable he never would, as he was now no better than a dead man. However, the surgeons dressed his head there as well as they could, and then sent him in a batteau to Albany, where he was perfectly cured, and to the great surprise of everybody, was living when I left the country. This, though so extraordinary and unparalled an affair, I aver to be true, having several times seen the man after this accident happened to him. How his life was preserved seems a miracle, as no instance of the like was ever known.

I had forgot to mention, that before I left Albany,

the last time, upon Colonel Broadstreet's arrival there, on his way to Oswego with the provisions and forces, consisting of about 500 whale-boats and batteaux, intended for the campaign on the great lake Ontario, mentioned before, I joined his corps, and proceeded on with the batteaux, &c.

Going up the river Onondago towards Oswego, the batteaux-men were, on the 29th of June, attacked near the falls, about nine miles from Oswego, by 500 French and Indians, who killed and wounded 74 of our men, before we could get on shore, which, as soon as we did, the French were routed, with the loss of 130 men killed, and several wounded, whom we took prisoners.

Had we known of their lying in ambush, or of their intent to attack us, the victory would have been much more complete on our side, as the troops Colonel Broadstreet commanded were regular, well disciplined, and in tolerable health—whereas the French, by a long passage at sea, and living hard after their arrival at Canada, were much harassed and fatigued.

However, we got all safe to Oswego with the batteaux and provisions, together with the rigging and stores for the large vessels, excepting twenty-four cannon, six-pounders, that were then at the great carrying place, which Colonel Broadstreet was to bring with him, upon his next passage from Schenectady, to which place, as soon as he had delivered to the Quarter-master all the stores under his care, he was ordered to return with the batteaux and men to receive the orders of Major-General Abercromby. On his return from Schenectady, it was expected that Halket's and Dunbar's regiment would have come with him, in order to take Fort Frontenac, and the other French forts on lake Ontario. But, alas! as schemes for building castles in the air always prove abortive for want of proper architecture and foundation, so did this scheme of ours, for want of due knowledge of our own situation.

On the arrival of these forces, a new brigantine and sloop were fitted out, and about the same time, a large snow was also launched and rigged, and only waited for her guns and some running rigging, which they expected every day by Colonel Broadstreet; and had he returned in time with the cannon and batteaux-men under his command, the French would not dared to have appeared on the lake; but Colonel Broadstreet happened to be detained with the batteaux at Schenectady for above a month, waiting for the 44th regiment to march with him. The dilatoriness of his embarkation at Schenectady cannot be imputed to Colonel Broadstreet, because General Shirley waited with impatience for the arrival of Lord Loudon Campbell from England; and when his lordship landed at New York, he, in a few days after, proceeded to Albany, where his lordship took the command of the army from General Shirley, and upon comparing, and considering how bad a situation his forces, and the different governments upon the continent were in, his lordship, with the advice of several other experienced officers, thought himself not in a condition to proceed on any enterprise for that season, no farther than to maintain our ground at Oswego—for which purpose Colonel Broadstreet was immediately ordered off with the batteaux and provisions, as also the aforesaid regiments; but before Broadstreet arrived at the great carrying place, Oswego was taken, with all the ships of war, although our naval force was far superior to the French.

Before I relate the attack of Oswego, I shall review a little what the French were doing during these our dilatory, pompous proceedings.

The Marquis de Vandrueil, Governor and Lieutenant-General of New France, whilst he provided for the security of the frontiers of Canada, was principally attentive to the lakes. Being informed that we were making vast preparations at Oswego for attacking Niagara and Frontenac, he took and razed, in the month of March, the fort where we had formed our principal magazine, and in June following, destroyed on the river Chonenan, or Oswego, some of our vessels, and made some prisoners. The success of these two expeditions encouraged him to act offensively, and to attack us at Oswego. This settlement they pretended, and still insist on, to be an encroachment, or invasion, which we had made in time of profound peace, and against which, they said, they had continually remonstrated, during our blundering negotiating lawyer's residence at France. It was at first, say they, only a fortified magazine; but in order to avail themselves of its advantageous situation, in the centre almost of the French colonies, the English added, from time to time, several new works, and made it consist of three forts, as above described.

The troops designed for this expedition by the French amounted to near 5000 men, 1300 of which were regulars. To prevent his design being discovered, M. de Vandrueil pretended, in order the better to deceive us, who had so long before been blind, that he was providing only for the security of Niagara and Frontenac. The Marquis de Montcalm, who commanded on this occasion, arrived on the 29th of July at Fort Frontenac, and· having given the necessary directions for securing his retreat, in case it should have been rendered inevitable by a superior force, sent out two vessels, one of twelve, and the other of sixteen guns, to cruise off Oswego, and posted a chain of Canadians and Indians, on the road between Oswego and Albany, to intercept our couriers. All the forces, and the vessels, with the artillery and stores being arrived in the bay of Nixoure, the place of general rendezvous, the Marquis de Montcalm ordered his advanced guard to proceed to a creek called Anse aux Cabannes, three leagues from Oswego.

But, to carry on this account the more accurately and intelligibly to the reader, I shall recite the actions of the French and ourselves together, as a more clear and succinct manner of making those unacquainted with the art of war, more sensible of this important affair.

Colonel Mercer, who was then commanding officer of the garrison at Oswego, having, on the 6th of August, intelligence of a large encampment of French and Indians, about 12 miles off, despatched one of the schooners, with an account of it, to Captain Bradley, who was then on a cruise with the large brigantine and two sloops, at the same time desired him to cruise as far to the eastward as he could, and to endeavour to prevent the approach of the French on the lake; but meeting the next day with a small gale of wind, the large brigantine was drove on shore near Oswego, in attempting to get into the harbour—of which misfortune the Indians immediately gave M. de Montcalm, the French General, notice, who took that opportunity of transporting his heavy cannon to about a mile and a half off the fort, which he could not otherwise have done, had not there been some neglect on our side.

For on the 10th, the first division of the French being arrived at Anse aux Cabannes, at two o'clock in the morning, the vanguard proceeded, at four in the afternoon, by land, across woods, to another creek within half a league of Oswego, in order to favour the debarkation. At midnight their first division repaired to this creek, and there erected a battery on Lake Ontario.

Colonel Mercer, on the morning of the 10th, on some canoes being seen to the eastward, sent out the small schooner to make discovery of what they were. She was scarce half a mile from the fort, before she discovered a very large encampment, close under the opposite point, being the first division of the French troops above-mentioned. On this, the two sloops (the large brigantine being still on shore) were sent out with orders, if possible, to annoy the enemy—but this was to no purpose; the enemy's cannon being large and well pointed, hulled the vessels almost every shot, while theirs fell short of the shore.

This day and the next, the enemy were employed in making gabions, faucissons, and fascines, and in cutting a road across the woods, from the place of landing, to the place where the trenches were to be opened; and the second division of the enemy arriving on the 11th in the morning, with the artillery and provisions, the same immediately landed without any opposition. Though dispositions were made for opening the trenches on the 10th, at night, which was rather a parallel of about 100 toises* in front, and opened at the distance of about 60 toises from the fosse of Fort Ontario, in ground embarrassed with trunks of trees.

About five in the morning of the 11th, this parallel was finished, and the workmen began to erect the batteries. Thus was the place invested by about 5000 men, and 32 pieces of cannon, from 12 to 18 pounders, besides several large brass mortars and hoyets, among which artillery was part of General Braddock's. About noon they began the attack of Fort Ontario, with small arms, which was briskly returned. All this day, the garrison was employed on the west side of the river, in repairing the batteries on the south side of the Old Fort.

---

*A toise is a French measure, and contains about two fathoms or six feet in length.

The next morning (the 12th), at day-break, a large number of French batteaux were discovered on the lake, on their way to join the enemy's camp, on which, Colonel Mercer ordered the two sloops to be again sent out, with directions to get between the batteaux and the camp; but before our vessels came up, the batteaux had secured themselves under the fire of their cannon.

In the evening a detatchment was made of 100 men of the 50th (General Pepperell's) regiment, and 126 of the New Jersey provincials, under the command of Colonel Schuyler, to take possession of the fort on the hill, to the westward of the Old Fort, and under the direction of the engineer, Mr. M'Kneller, were to put it into the best state of defence they could—in which work they were employed all the following night.

The enemy on the east side continued their approaches to the Fort Ontario, but, with their utmost efforts, for a long time they could not bring their cannon to bear on it. However, drawing their cannon with great expedition, next morning (the 13th) about ten o'clock, to a battery erected within sixty yards from it, they played them very hotly on the garrisons, notwithstanding the constant fire kept on them, and the loss of their principal engineer, who was killed in the trenches. A council of war was immediately held by the officers of General Pepperell's regiment, who, observing the mortars were beginning to play, concluded it most advisable to quit Fort Ontario, and join Colonel Schuyler's regiment at Fort George or Fort Rascal; and an account of this latter battery being sent to Colonel Mercer, by the commandant of the enemy, ordering him to evacuate the fort, they accordingly did, about three in the afternoon, destroying the cannon, ammunition, and provisions therein, and managed their retreat so as to pass the river, and join the troops at the west side, without the loss of a man. These troops, being about 370, were immediately ordered to join Colonel Schuyler, and were employed all the following night in completing the works of that fort.

M. Montcalm immediately took possession of Fort Ontario, and ordered the communications of the parallel to be continued to the banks of the river, where, in the beginning of the night, they began a grand battery, placed in such a manner that it could not only batter Fort Oswego, and the way from thence to Fort George but also the intrenchment of Oswego.

On the morning of the 13th, the large brigantine being off the rocks and repaired, a detachment of eighty men of the garrison were put on board of her, and the two sloops, in order to go out immediately; but the wind continuing to blow directly into the harbour, rendered it impossible for them to get out before the place was surrendered. This night, as well as the night before, parties of the enemy's irregulars made several attempts to surprise our advance guards and sentinels on the west side of the river, but did not succeed in any of them.

The enemy were employed this night in bringing up their cannon and raising a battery. On our side we kept a constant fire of cannon and shells from the Old Fort, and works about it. The cannon which most annoyed the enemy were four pieces which we reversed on the platform of an earthen work, which surrounded the Old Fort, and which was entirely enfiladed by the enemy's battery on the opposite shore. In this situation, without the least cover, the train, assisted by a detachment of Shirley's regiment, behaved remarkably well.

At day-break, on the 14th, we renewed our fire on that part of the opposite shore, where we had the evening before observed the enemy at work in raising the battery.

The enemy, in three columns, consisted of 2500 Canadians and savages, crossed the river, some by swimming, and others by wading, with the water up to their middles, in order to invest and attack the Old Fort. This bold action, by which they entirely cut off the communication of the two forts; the celerity with which the works were carried on, in ground that we thought impracticable; a continual return of our fire from a battery of ten cannon, twelve pounders; and their preparing a battery of mortars and hoyets, made Colonel Mercer think it advisable (he not knowing their numbers) to order Colonel Schuyler, with 500 men, to oppose them; which would accordingly have been carried into execution, and consequently, every man of the 500 cut off, had not Colonel Mercer been killed by a cannon ball a few minutes after. The resolution of this valiant Colonel seemed to be determined to oppose the French to the last extremity, and to maintain his ground at Oswego, but his final doom came on so unexpectedly, that his loss was universally regretted.

About ten o'clock the enemy's battery was ready to play, at which time, all our places of defence were either enfiladed, or ruined by the constant fire of their cannon, Fort Rascal, or George, in particular, having at that time no guns, and scarce in a condition to defend itself against small arms—with 2500 irregulars on our backs, ready to storm us on that side, and 2000 of their regulars as ready to land in our front, under the fire of their cannon.

Fort Rascal might have been made a very defensible fortress. Lying on a hill, and the ascent to it so steep, that had an enemy been ever so numerous, they must have suffered greatly in an attempt to storm it. Why it was not in a better state, it becomes not me to say, but matters were so; and in this situation we were, when Colonel Littlehales, who succeeded Colonel Mercer in the command, called a council of war, who were, with the engineers, unanimously of opinion, that the works were no longer tenable, and that it was by no means prudent to risk a storm with such unequal numbers.

The chamade was accordingly ordered to be beat, and the fire ceased on both sides—yet the French were not idle, but improved this opportunity to bring up more cannon, and advanced the main body of their troops within musket-shot of the garrison, and prepared every thing for a storm. Two officers were sent to the French General, to know what terms he would give. The Marquis de Montcalm made answer, that they might expect whatever terms were consistent with the service of his Most Christian Majesty. He accordingly agreed to the following :—

ARTICLE I.

The garrison shall surrender prisoners of war, and shall be conducted from hence to Montreal, where they shall be treated with humanity, and every one shall have treatment agreeable to their respective ranks, according to the custom of war.

ARTICLE II.

Officers, soldiers, and individuals, shall have their baggage and clothes, and they shall be allowed to carry them along with them.

ARTICLE III.

They shall remain prisoners of war, until they are exchanged.

Given at the Camp before Oswego,
August 14th, 1756.

MONTCALM.

By virtue of this capitulation, the garrison surrendered prisoners of war, and the French immediately took possession of Oswego and Fort George, which they entirely destroyed, agreeable to their orders, after removing the artillery, warlike stores, and provisions.

But to describe the plunder, havoc, and devastation made by the French, as well as the savages, who rushed in by thousands, is impossible. For notwithstanding the Christian promise made by the General of his *Most Christian* Majesty, they all behaved more like infernal beings than creatures in human shapes. In short, not contented with surrendering upon the above terms, they scalped and killed all the sick and wounded in the hospitals; mangling, butchering, cutting, and chopping off their heads, arms, legs, &c., with spades, hatchets, and other such diabolical instruments, treating the whole with the utmost cruelty, notwithstanding the repeated intercessions of the defenceless sick and wounded for mercy, which were indeed piteous enough to have softened any heart possessed of the minutest particle of humanity!

Here I cannot help observing that, notwithstanding what has been said of the behavour of the officers of these (the 50th and 51st) regiments, I must, with the greatest truth, give them the characters of brave, but I wish I could say, experienced men—every one of them I had an opportunity of observing during the siege behaving with the utmost courage and intrepidity. Nor, in this place, can I omit particularly naming Col. James Campbell and Captain Archibald Hamilton, who assisted with the greatest spirit and alacrity the private men at the great guns. But for such an handful of men as our garrison then consisted of, and the works being of such a weak and defenceless nature, to have made a longer defence, or have caused the enemy to raise the siege, would have been such an instance as England for many years hath not experienced, and I am afraid will be many more before it will, for reasons that are too obvious.

The quantity of stores and ammunition we then had in the three forts is almost incredible. But of what avail are powder and balls if walls and ramparts are defenceless, and men insufficient to make use of them? In short, the French, by taking this place, make themselves masters of the following things, all which were immediately sent to Frontenac, viz., seven pieces of brass cannon, nineteen, fourteen, and twelve pounders; forty-eight iron cannon, of nine, six, five, three, and two pounders; a brass mortar of nine inches four-twelfths, and thirteen others of six and three inches; forty-seven swivel guns; 23,000lbs. of gunpowder; 8000lbs. of lead and musket ball; 2950 cannon balls; 150 bombs of nine inches, and 300 more of six inches diameter; 1426 grenadoes, 1070 muskets; a vessel pierced for eighteen guns; the brigantine of sixteen, a gœletta of ten, a batteau of ten (the sloops already mentioned), another of eight guns, a skiff of eighteen swivels, and another burnt upon the stocks; 704 barrels of biscuit, 1386 firkins of bacon and beef; 712 firkins of meal; thirty-two live oxen; fifteen hogs, and a large sum of money in the military chest, amounting, as the French said, to 18,594 livres.

On the 16th, they began to remove us. The officers were first sent in batteaux, and 200 soldiers a day afterwards, till the whole were gone, being carried first to Montreal, and from thence to Quebec. Our duty in the batteaux, till we reached the first place, was very hard and slavish; and during the time we were on the lake and river St. Lawrence, it appeared very easy and feasible for Commodore Bradley, had he thought proper, to have destroyed all the enemy's batteaux, and have prevented them from ever landing their cannon within forty miles of the fort. But he knew his own reasons for omitting this piece of service best.

Our party arrived at Montreal in Canada on the 28th. We were that night secured in the fort, as were the rest as they came in. The French used various means to win some of our troops over to their interests, or, at least, to do their work in the fields, which many refused, among whom was myself—who were then conducted on board a ship, and sent to Quebec, where, arriving on the 5th of September, we were lodged in a goal, and kept there for the space of one month.

During this our captivity, many of our men, rather than lie in a prison, went out to work and assist the French in getting in their harvest, they having then scarce any people left in that country but old men, women, and children, so that the corn was continually falling into the stubble for want of hands to reap it; but those who did go out, in two or three days, chose confinement again rather than liberty on such terms, being almost starved, having nothing in the country to live on but dry bread, whereas we in the prison were each of us allowed two lbs. of bread and half-a-pound of meat a day, and otherwise treated with a good deal of humanity.

Eighteen soldiers were all the guard they had to place over us, who, being greatly fatigued with hard duty, and dreading our rising on them, which, had we had any arms, we might easily have done, and ravaged the country round, as it was then entirely defenceless; and the town's people themselves fearing the consequences of having such a number of men in a place where provisions were at that time very scarce and dear, they thought of sending us away, the most eligible way of keeping themselves from famine, and accordingly put 1500 of us on board a vessel for England.

But before I continue the account of our voyage home to our native country, I shall just make a short retrospection on the consequences that attended the loss of Oswego, as appeared to us and the rest of the people at Quebec, who knew that part of America to which this important place was a safeguard.

As soon as Oswego was taken, our only communication from the Mohawk's river to the lake Oneida was stopped up, by filling the place at Wood's Creek with great logs and trees for many miles together. A few day afterwards, the forts at the great carrying place, and then our most advanced post into the country of the Six Nations, which I have before given a short account of (and where there were at that time above 3000 men, including 1200 batteaux-men, and which still gave the Six Nations some hopes that we would defend their country against the French), were abandoned and destroyed, and the troops which were under the command of General Webb retreated to Burnet's Field, and left the country and the Six Nations to the mercy of the enemy.

The French, immediately after the taking of Oswego, demolished, as it is said before, all the works there, and returned with their prisoners and booty to Ticonderago, to oppose our provincial army, under the command of General Winslow, who had shamefully been kept in expectation of the dilatory arrival of Lord Loudon, from attacking Crown Point, while the enemy were weak, and it was easily in our power to have beat them.

The consequences of the destruction of our forts at the great carrying place, and General Webb's retreating to Burnet's Field, is now, alas! too apparent to every one acquainted with American affairs. The Indians of the Six Nations undoubtedly looked upon it as abandoning them and their country to the French, for they plainly saw that we had no strong hold near them, and that (by the place at Wood's Creek being stopped) we could not, if we would, afford them any assistance at Onondago, Cayuga, and the Senekea's country, which were their chief castles—that the forts begun by us in those countries were left unfinished, and therefore could be of no use to them, and which, if we had kept the carrying place, we might have finished, and given them still hopes of our being able to defend them.

But despairing of our being further serviceable to them, those Iroquois, who were before our friends, and some of the others, have indeed deserted us, and the consequences of such their junctions with the French was soon after felt in the loss of Fort George on Lake Sacrament.

The fine country on the Mohawk's river, down to Albany, was by this step left open to the ravages of the enemy, and an easy passage opened to the French and their Indians into the provinces of Pennsylvania and New Jersey, by the way of Susquehana and Delaware rivers, which were before covered by our settlements on the Mohawk's river, and the Six Nations.

CUSTOMS, DRESS, &c., OF THE SAVAGES.

I SHALL here give the best description of the Indians, their way of living, &c., in my power.

It is difficult to guess what may be the number of the Indians scattered up and down our back settlements; but if their own account be true, they amount to many thousands. Be this, however, as it will, they are not to be feared merely on account of their numbers—other circumstances conspire to make them formidable. The English inhabitants, though numerous, are extended over a vast track of land, 500 leagues in length on the sea shore, and for the most part have fixed inhabitations, the easiest and shortest passages to which the Indians, by continually hunting in the woods, are perfectly well acquainted with; and as their way of making war is by sudden attacks upon exposed places, as soon as they have done the mischief at one place they retire, and either go home by some different route, or go to some distant place to renew their attacks. If they are pursued, it is a chance if they do not ensnare their pursuers, or if that be not the case, as soon as they have gained the rivers, so dexterous are they in the use of their canoes, that they presently get out of reach. It is to no purpose to follow them to their settlements, for they can, without much disadvantage, quit their old habitations and betake themselves to new ones—add to this, that they can be suddenly drawn together from any distance, as they can find their subsistence in travelling from their guns.

No people on earth have a higher sense of liberty or stronger affection for their relations. When offended, they are the most implacable vindictive enemies on earth, for no distance of place or space of time will abate their resentment, but they will watch every opportunity of revenge, and when such opportunity offers, they revenge themselves effectully.

They will sooner sacrifice their own lives for the sake of liberty than humble themselves to the arbitrary control of any person whatsoever. In battle they never submit, and will die rather than be taken prisoners.

Our late transactions in America testify that the friendship of the Indians is to be desired, and the only way to maintain a friendly correspondence with them is by making such propositions to them as will secure their liberties, and be agreeable to their expectations ; and not only by keeping these propositions inviolable as well as in time of peace as in time of war, but also renewing our treaties with them from time to time, for they are very jealous and tenacious of an affront or neglect. They are very proud, and love to be esteemed. In time of peace they live upon what they get from the white people, for which they barter skins, furs, &c. Their clothing, and every thing else they want, such as arms, they get in the same manner. In war time, they live upon what they can procure by their gun, and if that fails, upon roots, fruits, herbs, and other vegetables of the natural produce of the earth.

They have never the foresight to provide necessaries for themselves —they look only to the present moment, and leave to-morrow to provide for itself. They eat of every wild beast which they kill, without distinction. They always prefer game to vegetables ; but when they cannot get venison, they live on roots, fruits, and herbs. They destroy a great deal of meat at a time, when they have it in their power, and when they leave any, be it ever such a great quantity, it is rare if any of them will take the trouble to carry a pound of it, but will rather leave it behind them ; yet, notwithstanding this extravagance, such are their tempers, and they are so inured to hardships, that if they cannot conveniently get at food, they can and actually do fast sometimes for near a week together, and yet are as active as if they had lived regularly. All their spare time is taken up in contriving schemes to succeed in their intended expeditions. They can never be taken in a pursuit by any European. They will travel seventy miles a-day, and continue for months together, as I have reason to know from experience, and they are sure to bring their pursuers into a snare, if they are not wary, and have some Indians on their side to beat the bushes. When they are overtaken with sleep, they light a great fire, which prevents the wild beasts from falling upon them, for wild beasts have a natural aversion to fire—nor is it easy for an enemy to discover them in this condition —for the country is oue continued tract of thick wood, overgrown with brushwood, so that you cannot see the fire till you be within a few yards of it. They have nothing covering them from the inclemency of the weather but a blanket, something in the shape of a Highlander's plaid.

And further, to prevent their being long observed by their pursuers, or to be seen too soon when they have a mind to attack any plantation, they paint themselves of the same colour with the trees, among which they hide.

When they are to attack a plantation, they never come out till night, and then they rush instantly upon the farms, &c., and destroy everything, as well men, women, and children, as beasts—then they fall to plunder, and return to their lurking holes till another opportunity of plunder happens, when they renew their attack in the same manner—so that if some method is not taken to draw them into our interest, our colonies will be in continual alarm, and the country will soon become desolate, for nobody will venture their lives to settle on the back parts, unless the Indians are our friends.

The Indian manner of fighting is quite different from that of other nations. They industriously avoid all open engagements; and, besides ambuscades, their principal way is bush fighting, in the exercises of which they are very dexterous—for the back country being one continued wood, except some few spots cleared for the purpose of husbandry by our back settlers, the Indians squat themselves down behind the trees, and fire their muskets at the enemy. If the enemy advances, then they retreat behind other trees, and fire in the same manner, and as they are good marksmen, they never fire in vain, whereas their pursuers seldom hit.

Notwithstanding the political schemes of France are nearly brought to a period, yet if the Indians are not satisfied with the conclusion of a peace between us and the French as to America, I mean unless they are fairly dealt with, we shall gain but little by all our conquests—for it is the friendship of the Indians that will make Canada valuable to us. We have already more lands than we are able to manage ; but the advantage, nay, the necessity of keeping Canada I have already shewn, and therefore I shall go on with my account of the Indians.

When last in London, I remember to have heard some coffee-house politicians, chagrined at the devastations they made on our back settlements, say, that it would be an easy matter to root out the savages by clearing the ground. I answer, that the task may seem easy to them, but the execution of such a scheme on such a track of land would be so difficult, that I doubt whether there are people enough in Great Britain and Ireland to accomplish it in a hundred years' time, were they to meet with no opposition ; but where there is such a subtile enemy to deal with, I am afraid we should make but little progress in reducing the Indians, even allowing the country to be all cleared, as there are hills and other fastnesses to which the Indian can retire, and where they would greatly have the better of every attempt to dislodge them. The only way I would advise is, to keep friends with the Indians, and endeavour to prevail on them to settle in the same manner as the planters do, which they will be more easily brought to, if the French are excluded from Canada. For, notwithstanding their wandering way of life, I have the greatest reason to believe they have no dislike to an easy life. And as they have no temptations to murder, as they had when stirred up by the subjects of his Most Christian Majesty, they will soon become useful members of society.

When the English first arrived in the American colonies, they found the woods inhabited by a race of people uncultivated in their manners, but not quite devoid of humanity. They were strangers to literature, ignorant of the liberal arts, and destitute of almost every conveniency of life.

But if they were unpractised in the art of more civilized nations, they were also free from their vices.

They seemed perfect in two parts of the ancient Persian education, namely, shooting with the bow, and speaking truth. In their dealings, they commonly exchange one commodity for another. Strangers themselves to fraud, they had an entire confidence in others. According to their abilities they were generous and hospitable. Happy, thrice happy had they been, if, still preserving their native innocence and simplicity, they had only been instructed in the knowledge of God, and the doctrines of Christianity; and had they been taught some of the more useful parts of life, and to lay aside what was wild and savage in their manners!

They received the English upon their first arrival with open arms, treated them kindly, and shewed an earnest desire that they should settle and live with them. They freely parted with some of their lands to their new-come brethren, and cheerfully entered into a league of friendship with them. As the English were in immediate want of subsistance of the Indians, they, on their part, endeavoured to make their coming agreeable. Thus they lived for some years in the mutual exchange of friendly offices. Their houses were open to each other, they treated one another as brothers. But by their different way of living, the English soon acquired property, while the Indians continued in their former indigence—hence the former found they could easily live without the latter, and therefore became less anxious about preserving their friendship. This gave a check to that mutual hospitality that had hitherto subsisted between them; and this, together with the decrease of game for hunting, arising from the increase of the English settlements, induced the Indians to remove farther back into the woods.

From this time the natives began to be treated as a people of whom an advantage might be taken. As the trade with them was free and open, men of loose and abandoned characters engaged in it, and practised every fraud. Before the coming of the white people, the Indians never tasted spirituous liquors, and, like most barbarians, having once tasted, became immoderately fond thereof, and had no longer any government of themselves. The traders availed themselves of this weakness. Instead of carrying our clothes to cover the naked savages, they carried them rum, and thereby debauched their manners, weakened their constitutions, introduced disorders unknown to them before, and in short corrupted and ruined them.

The Indians, finding the ill effects of this trade, began to complain. Wherefore laws were made, prohibiting any from going to trade with them without a licence from the Governor, and it was also made lawful for the Indians to stave the casks, and spill what rum was brought among them—but this was to little purpose ; the Indians had to little command of themselves to do their duty, and were easily prevailed upon not to execute this law, and the design of the former was totally evaded, by men of some character taking out licences to trade, and then employing under them persons of no honour or principle, generally servants and convicts transported hither from Britain and Ireland, whom they sent with goods into the Indian country to trade on their account. These getting beyond the reach of the law, executed unheard-of villainies upon the natives, committing crimes which modesty forbids me to name, and behaving in a manner too shocking to be related.

At every treaty which the Indians held with the English they complained of the abuses they suffered from the traders, and trade as then carried on. They requested that the traders might be recalled, but all to no purpose. They begged in the strongest terms that no rum might be suffered to come among them ; but were only told they were at liberty to spill all rum brought into their country. At this time little or no pains were taken to civilize or instruct them in the Christian religion, till at length the conduct of traders, professing themselves of that religion, gave the Indians an almost invincible prejudice against it. Besides, as these traders travelled among distant nations of the Indians, and were in some sort the representatives of the English nation, from them the Indians formed a very unfavourable opinion of our whole nation, and easily believed every misrepresentation made of us by our enemies. There are instances in history where the virtues and disinterested behaviour of one man has prejudiced whole nations of barbarians in favour of the people to whom he belonged; and is it then to be wondered at if the Indians conceived a rooted prejudice against us, when not one, but a whole set of men, viz., all of our nation that they had an opportunity of seeing or conversing with, were persons of a loose and abandoned behavour, insincere and faithless, without religion, virtue, or morality? No one will think I exaggerate these matters who has either known the traders themselves, or who has read the public treaties.

If to this be added, what I find in the late treaties, that they have been wronged in some of their lands, what room will there be any longer to wonder that we have so little interest with them; that their conduct towards us is of late so much changed, that, instead of being a security and protection to us, as they have been hitherto during the several wars between us and the French, they are now turned against us and become our enemies, principally on account of the fraudulent dealings and immoral conduct of those heretofore employed in our trade with them, who have brought dishonour upon our religion, and disgrace on our nation? It nearly concerns us, if possible, to wipe off these reproaches, and to redeem our character, which can only be done by regulating the trade ; and this the Indians, with whom the government of Philadelphia lately treated, demanded and expected of us.

At present, a favourable opportunity presents for doing it effectually. All those who were engaged in this trade are, by the present troubles, removed from it ; and it is to be hoped that the legislature will fall upon measures to prevent any such from ever being concerned in it again. This is only the foundation upon which we can expect a lasting peace with the natives. It is evident that a great deal depends upon the persons who are to be sent into the Indian country--from these alone the Indians will form a judgment of us, our religion, and manners. If these then, who are to be our representatives among the Indians be men of virtue and integrity, sober in their conversation, honest in their dealings, and whose practice corresponds with their profession, the judgement formed of us will be favourable ; if, on the contrary, they be loose and profane persons, men of wicked lives and profligate morals, we must expect that among the Indians our religion will pass for a jest, and we, in general, for a people faithless and despicable.

DESCRIPTION OF THE BRITISH SETTLEMENTS, &c.

I SHALL now proceed to give a concise account of the climates, produce, trade, &c., of North America. And first,

NEW ENGLAND.

The province of New England appears to be vastly extensive, being about 400 miles in length, and near 300 in breadth, situated between 69 and 73 deg. W. long., and between 41 and 46 deg. N. lat. It was first settled by the Independents, a little before the commencement of the civil wars in England ; they transported themselves thither, rather than communicate with the church of England.

The lands next the sea in New England are generally low, and the soil sandy ; but further up the country it rises into hills, and on the north east it is rocky and mountainous. The winters are much severer here than in Old England, though it lies nine or ten degrees more south, but they have usually a clearer sky and more settled weather both in winter and summer, than in Old England ; and though their summers are shorter, the air is considerably hotter while it lasts. The winds are very boisterous in the winter season, and the north wind blowing over a long track of frozen and uncultivated countries, with several fresh water lakes, makes it excessively cold. The rivers are sometimes congealed in a night's time. The climate is generally healthful, and agreeable to English constitutions.

The fruits of Old England come to great perfection here, particularly peaches, which are planted trees, and we have commonly 1200 or 1400 fine peaches on such a tree at one time. Of the fruit of one single apple tree, in one season, nine barrels of cider have been made. English wheat I find does not thrive here, within 40 or 50 miles of Boston; but further up the country they have it in great plenty, and I think it comes to the same perfection as in Britain.. Now, why wheat should not grow near this city I confess I can assign no reason that will fully satisfy the reader's curiosity. The conjectures upon it are various ; some venture to say that it was occasioned by the unjust persecution of the Quakers, the Independents having vented their spleen against them in a way the most rigorous, and in flat contradiction to the laws of Christianity. All other grain but wheat thrives in this place with great success—in particular, Indian corn, one grain whereof frequently produces 200, and sometimes 2000 grains.

This corn is of three different colours, viz., blue, white, and yellow.

NEW YORK.

The situation of this province is between 72 and 76 W. long., and between 41 and 44 N. lat., about 200 miles in length, and 100 miles in breadth. The lands in the Jerseys and south part of New York are low and flat; but as you ascend twenty or thirty miles up Hudson's river, the country is rocky and mountainous. The air is much milder here in winter than in New England, and in summer it is pretty much the same. The produce and trade of New York and the Jerseys consist in cattle, and a good breed of horses. They have plenty of wheat and other grain, such as Indian corn, buck-wheat, oats, barley, and rye. It abounds also with stores of fish. They supply the Sugar Islands with flour, salt beef, pork, salt fish, and timber planks, in return for the produce raised there.

PENNSYLVANIA.

The extent of this colony is 200 miles in length, and 200 miles in breadth. The soil is much better than in Jersey, chiefly consisting of a black mould. The country rises gradually as in the adjacent provinces, having the Apalachian Mountains on the west, and is divided into six counties. The air, it lying in the 40 deg. of N. lat. is near the same as in New York, and very healthy to English constitutions. The produce and merchandise of Pennsylvania consists in horses, pipe staves, beef, pork, salt fish, skins, furs, and all sorts of grain, viz., wheat, rye, pease, oats, barley, buck-wheat, Indian corn, Indian pease, beans, potashes, wax, &c., and in return for these commodities, they import from the Carribbee Islands and other places, rum, sugar, molasses, silver, negroes, salt, and clothing of all sorts, hardware, &c. The nature of the soil in Pennsylvania, the Jerseys, and New York, is extremely proper to produce hemp, flax, &c.

If the government of Pennsylvania, since the death of its first proprietor, William Penn, had taken proper methods to oblige the traders to deal justly with the Indians, whose tempers, when exasperated with resentment, are more savage than the hungry lion, these disasters might have been in a good degree prevented.

I intend to conclude this argument in a few words, and shall endeavour to do justice on both sides by adhering strictly to truth. Know therefore, that within these late years, the Indians, being tolerably acquainted with the nature of our commerce, have detected the roguery of some of the traders, whereupon they lodged many and grievous complaints to Colonel Weiser, the interpreter between them and the English, of the injurious and fraudulent usage they had received for several years backwards from white people, who had cheated them out of their skins and furs, not giving them one quarter their value for them.

Likewise they remonstrated, that whereas hunting was the chief way or art they ever had to earn a livelihood by, game was now become very scarce, because the whites practiced it so much on their ground, destroying their prey. Colonel Weiser, their interpreter, advised them to bring down their skins and furs to Philadelphia themselves, promising that he would take proper care to see their goods vended to their advantage. Whereupon they did so, in pursuance of his instructions, and finding it their interest, resolved to continue in the way he had chalked out for them—for now they were supplied with every thing they wanted from the merchants' shops, at the cheapest rates. And thus it plainly appeared to the Indians that they had been long imposed on by the traders, and therefore they were determined to have no more dealings with them. This conduct and shyness of the Indians was very disagreeable to several gentlemen of the province, who were nearly interested in that species of commerce.

Accordingly, in the year 1753 and 1754, some of the traders had the assurance to renew their friendship with them, when, instead of remitting them clothes and other necessaries as had been usual and were most proper for them, they, with insidious purposes, carried them large quantities of rum in small casks, which they knew the natives were fond of, under the colour of giving it them gratis. In this manner were the savages inveigled into liquor by the whites, who took the opportunity, while they were intoxicated, of going off with their skins and furs; but the natives, recovering from the debauch, soon detected the villainy, and in revenge killed many of the traders, and went directly over to the French, who encouraged them to slay every English person they could meet with, and destroy their houses by fire, giving them orders to spare neither man, woman, nor child. Besides, as a further incitement to diligence in this bloody task, they promised the savages a reward of £15 sterling for every scalp they should take, on producing the same before any of his Most Christian Majesty's officers civil or military.

Thus our perfidious enemies instigated those unreasonable barbarians to commence acts of depredation, violence, and murder, on the several inhabitants of North America in 1754, and more especially in Pennsylvania, as knowing it to be the most defenceless province on the continent. This consideration promted the savage race to exhaust their malicious fury on it in particular.

MARYLAND.

This country extends about 150 miles in length and 137 miles in breadth. The lands are low and flat next the sea ; towards the heads of rivers they rise into hills, and beyond lie the Apalachian mountains, which are exceeding high. The air of this province is excessive hot some part of the summer, and equally cold in the winter, when the north-west wind blows ; but the winters are not of so long duration here as in some other colonies adjoining to it. In the spring of the year they are infested with thick heavy fogs that rise from the low lands, which render the air more unhealthy for English constitutions, and hence it is that, in the aforesaid season, the people are constantly afflicted with agues.

The produce of this country is chiefly tobacco, planted and cultivated here with much application, and nearly the same success as in Virginia, and their principal trade with England is in that article. It also affords them most sorts of the grain and fruits of Europe and America.

VIRGINIA.

The extent of this province is computed to be 260 miles in length, and 220 miles in breadth, being mostly flat land. For 100 miles up the country there is scarce a hill or a stone to be seen, The air and seasons (it lying between 36 and 39 of north lat.) depend very much on the wind, as to heat and cold, dryness and moisture, The north and north-west winds are very nitrous and piercing cold, or else boisterous and stormy, the south and south-east winds, hazy and sultry hot. In winter they have a fine clear air, which renders it very pleasant. The frosts are short, but sometimes so very sharp, that rivers are frozen over three miles broad. Snow often falls in large quantities, but seldom continues above two or three days at most.

The soil, though generally sandy and shallow, produces tobacco of the best quality, in great abundance. The people's usual food is Indian corn, made into hominy, boiled to a pulp, and comes the nearest to buttered wheat of any thing I can compare it to. They have horses, cows, sheep, and hogs, in prodigious plenty, many of the last running wild in the woods. The regulation kept here is much the same as in New England—every man, from sixteen to sixty years of age, is enlisted into the militia, and mustered once a year at a general review, and four times a year by troops and companies. Their military complement, by computation, amounts to about 30,000 effective men ; the collective number of the inhabitants, men, women, and children, to 100,500, and, including servants and slaves, to twice that number.

CAROLINA.

This colony is computed to extend 660 miles in length; but its breadth is unknown. The lands here are generally low and flat, and not a hill to be seen from St. Augustine to Virginia, and a great way beyond. It is mostly covered with woods, where the planters have not cleared it. About 100 miles west of the coast it shoots up into eminences, and continues to rise gradually all along to the Apalachian Mountains, which are about 160 miles distant from the ocean. The north parts of Carolina are very uneven, but the ground is extremely proper for producing wheat, and all other sorts of grain that grow in Europe will come to great perfection here. The south parts of Carolina, if properly cultivated, might be made to produce silk, wine, and oil. This country yields large quantities of rice, of which they yearly ship off to other colonies about 80,000 barrels, each barrel containing 4 cwt. ; besides, they make abundance of tar, pitch, and turpentine. They carry on also a great trade with deer skins and furs, to all places of Europe, which the English receive from the Indians in barter for guns, powder, knives, scissors, looking-glasses, beads, rum, tobacco, coarse cloth, &c.

The English chapmen carry their pack horses about 600 miles into the country, west of Charlestown ; but most of the commerce is confined within the limits of the Creek and Cherokee nations, which do not lie above 350 miles from the coast. The air is very temperate and agreeable both summer and winter. Carolina is divided into two distinct provinces, viz., North and South Carolina.

NOVA SCOTIA.

This colony extends about 600 miles in length, and 450 in breadth. The air is pretty much the same as in Old England, the soil is, for the most part, barren ; but where it is cleared and cultivated, it affords good corn and pasture. Here is fine timber, and fit for building, from whence pitch and tar may be extracted. Here also hemp and flax will grow, so that this country will be capable of furnishing all manner of naval stores. It abounds likewise with deer, wild fowl, and all sorts of game. On the coast is one of the finest cod-fisheries in the world. European cattle, viz., sheep, oxen, swine, horses, &c., they have in great abundance. The winters are very cold, their frosts being sharp, and of long duration—their summers moderately hot—so that the climate, in the main, seems to be agreeable to English constitutions.

CANADA.

I shall close the description of the American colonies with a short account of the soil and produce of French Canada. Its extent is, according to their map, 1800 miles in length, and 1260 in breadth. The soil in the low lands near the river St. Lawrence will indeed raise wheat ; but, withal, I found it so shallow, that it would not produce that grain above two years, unless it was properly manured. About twenty miles from the said river, so hilly and mountainous is the country, that nothing but Indians and wild ravenous beasts resort there. However, they have plenty of rye, Indian corn, buck-wheat, and oats, likewise of horses, cows, sheep, swine, &c. But I have observed that fruits of any kind do not come to such perfection here as in some of the English settlements, which is owing to the long duration and excessive cold of their winters. The summer is short and temperately hot. The climate, in general, is healthy and agreeable to European constitutions.

EMBARKATION AT QUEBEC FOR ENGLAND

It is now high time to return to the embarkation at Quebec. Five hundred of us, being to be sent to England, were put on board La Renomme, a French packet-boat, Captain Dennis Vitree, commander. We sailed under a flag of truce, and though the French behaved with a good deal of politeness, yet we were almost starved for want of provisions. One biscuit, and two ounces of pork a day being all our allowance, and half dead with cold, having but few clothes, and the vessel being so small that the major part of us were obliged to be upon deck in all weathers. After a passage of six weeks, we, at last, to our great joy, arrived at Plymouth, on the 6th of November, 1756. But these our troubles and hardships were not, as we expected, put an end to for some time—scruples arising to the Commissaries and Admiral there about taking us on shore, as there was no cartel agreed on between the French and English, we were confined on board until the determination of the Lords of the Admirality should be known. Lying there in a miserable condition seven or eight days, before we received orders to disembark,

which, when we were permitted to do, being ordered
from thence, in different parties, to Totness, Kingsburgh,
Newton Bushel, Newton Abbot, in Devonshire, I was
happy in being quartered at Kingsbridge, where I met
with such civility and entertainment as I had for a long
time been a stranger to.

In about four months we were again ordered to
Plymouth dock, to be drafted into other regiments,
where, on being inspected, I was, on account of the
wound I had received in my hand, discharged as incapable of further service, and was allowed the sum of six
shillings to carry me home to Aberdeen, near the place
of my nativity. But finding that sum insufficient to
subsist me half the way, I was obliged to make my
application to the honourable gentlemen of the city of
York, who, on considering my necessity, and reviewing
my manuscript on the transactions of the Indians herein
before mentioned, thought proper to have it printed for
my own benefit, which they cheerfully subscribed unto.
And after disposing of several of my books through the
shire, I took the first opportunity of going in quest of
my relations at Aberdeen.

After so long an absence, my personal appearance
must no doubt recall to the memory of my friends, the
manner of my being carried off in my infancy, and they
must receive me with wonder and amazement, whom
they had for many years deemed for lost. The satisfaction my presence gave them, of which they had been
so long deprived, it is not to be expressed ; and the
comfort I enjoyed in the prospect of seeing my nearest
relations, was in some degree a solace for the miseries
I had undergone.